Journeys with Jobey

Edward Giles

JOURNEYS WITH JOBEY

EDWARD GILES

The **Hallamshire** Press 2000

To my old pal Lionel Pickering,
the chairman of Derby County and
one of the club's greatest fans.

© 2000 Edward Giles

Published by The Hallamshire Press Limited
Broom Hall
Sheffield S10 2DR
England

Typeset by The Hallamshire Press Limited
Printed by The Cromwell Press, Wiltshire

British Library Cataloguing in Publication Data:
    A catalogue record for this book is available from the British Library.

ISBN 1 874718 48 2

Contents

By the same author:

Derby County Days
from Carter and Doherty
to Storer and Ryan, 1944–1956

Foreword

A football club is for life and despite his career taking him to Bristol, Manchester and Essex, Eddie Giles has never wavered in his support for Derby County. Now, with time to relax after his retirement from journalism, he has become one of the most accurate of football historians.

It is comparatively easy to churn out a book on football, as some of the offerings on the market prove. To write one that is precise and captures the flavour of a period is a far more demanding task. Eddie achieved that in *Derby County Days*, a book that covered the immediate post-war years.

Now he looks back further, to the days of George Jobey, who remains the longest-serving manager in the club's history. It is somehow typical of Derby County that his successful time in office ended not with a trophy but in trouble before the game's ruling body.

During his time with the *Derby Evening Telegraph*, Eddie shared several train journeys with Jobey. His eagerness to listen to Jobey gave the author an invaluable thread of first-hand knowledge. As one of his successors on the newspaper, I am greatly flattered that Eddie should ask me to contribute a foreword and can assure readers that they are in safe hands.

Gerald Mortimer
Derby Evening Telegraph

1924.

Derbyshire's hope came down with a crash in 1924 ; they finished at the bottom of the table and their record was little better than that of 1920. Out of 24 matches 13 were lost and the remainder were drawn, not a solitary win being recorded. W.W. Hill-Wood only played twice, and beside G.R. Jackson and Cadman, no batsman had a higher average than 20. Carter, who had done so well in 1923, was a complete failure, and Storer was even worse, his highest score in 26 innings being 18! Horsley, Bestwick, and Morton all bowled fairly well, but the team had no luck and on one occasion lost to Gloucestershire by nine runs.

Results: Played 24, won 0, lost 13, won first innings 4, lost on first innings 4, no result 3, points 15.23

DERBYSHIRE BATTING AVERAGES—COUNTY CHAMPIONSHIP MATCHES

	Inns.	Runs.	Highest inns.	Not outs.	Av.
Mr. J.L. Crommelin-Brown	6	202	74	0	33.66
Mr. W.W. Hill-Wood . . .	3	83	50	0	27.66
Mr. G.R. Jackson	38	855	103	3	24.42
S. Cadman	38	799	125*	3	23.82
Mr. C.J. Corbett	4	71	31	0	17.75
W. Horsley	35	494	66	7	17.64
Mr. L. Oliver	5	68	36	1	17.00
A. Morton	30	442	120*	3	16.37
L. Townsend	37	556	79	2	15.88
J.M. Hutchinson	38	583	143	1	15.75
J. Bowden	27	367	39	3	15.29
Mr. J.S. Heath	5	59	28	1	14.75
Mr. F.R. Heath	4	59	17	0	14.75
Mr. F.G. Peach	4	58	32	0	14.50
Mr. A.H.M. Jackson . . .	8	103	56	0	12.87
W. Carter	25	289	57	1	12.04
H. Elliot	37	283	32*	13	11.79
R. Pratt	6	51	17*	1	10.20
H. Storer	26	178	18	0	6.84
A. Ackroyd	6	38	15	0	6.33
W. Bestwick	29	80	18	7	3.63

The following also batted: Mr. E.H.R. Bedford, 3 and 0; J. Creswell, 0, 2*, and 0; S.T. McMillan, 24, 6*, and 0; A. Rose, 0; Mr. W.J.V. Tomlinson, 4 and 0*; and S. Worthington, 0 and 12.

Looking back to 1924—the year in which Harry Storer was described as being 'even worse than a complete failure' in the review of Derbyshire's cricket season. As recalled in chapter six, he buckled down to become one of the county's most dependable batsmen besides making a big success of his soccer career as both player and manager.

Preface

A S THE TITLE INDICATES, the central character in this book is Jobey, George Jobey, a steadfast Geordie who was the longest-serving manager in Derby County's history, with 14 Football League seasons in charge at their old Baseball Ground home.

Statistically, he is still second only to Brian Clough as their most successful manager, even though he failed to land either the top League title or the FA Cup. In his first season, 1925–26, he piloted them to promotion from the Second Division, then twice took them to runners-up position in Division One and once to the Cup's semi-finals as he kept them among the country's most prominent clubs throughout the 1930s.

The journeys of the title are both literal and figurative: the ones by train that I had the pleasure of making with him from Derby to Nottingham as we both attended Forest and Notts County matches during the early 1950s; and those down memory lane recalling incident-packed games featuring the many talented players he gathered around him. Some of those players were among the biggest bargains of the day, men such as Sammy Crooks, Jack Barker, Jack Bowers, Ike Keen, Jack Howe and Tim Ward, each costing only a few hundred pounds but rendering years of outstanding service and playing for England. Others rose to international standard with the Rams after commanding bigger, but not exorbitant, fees: Tommy Cooper, George Stephenson, 'Dally' Duncan and Ronnie Dix. This galaxy of stars was topped off by an envied parade of already-capped forwards: Harry Bedford, Hughie Gallacher, Charlie Napier, Dai Astley and Dave McCulloch.

To that impressive list can be added the Jobey signings who did not go on to play for their countries but were among the most valued players the club have ever possessed, notably Jack Nicholas, George Collin, Harry Wilkes, Peter Ramage, Jack Kirby, 'Chick' Musson and Jack Stamps. There was also Leon Leuty, who did not turn professional until after Jobey had left, but was taken on as an amateur under his management.

Leuty, a centre-half desperately unlucky to be denied a full cap, was one of six members of the team that won the FA Cup in 1946 who dated back to Jobey's days. There were three others who were kept out of that Wembley final by injury, and another who missed playing in it because of Army service. It was a most fitting legacy for this formidable North-Easterner to leave, though the manner of his leaving was, sadly, tarnished by the ban imposed upon him, and his directors, after the football authorities uncovered illegal payments made to players since his appointment.

It was while George Jobey was still in the soccer wilderness, even though his suspension had by then been lifted, that I made those journeys with him to and from Nottingham.

When he did eventually get back into the game, down among the strugglers in the Northern Section of the Third Division, he was beyond the normal retirement age of 65 and well past taking the firm grip that had made strong men quail during his domination of the Derby scene.

On the last occasion I met him at a match, after he had embarked upon that belated and ill-advised comeback, I was dismayed to see him kow-towing to officials who could never have had the privilege of employing him in his prime, and the way in which they discarded him soon afterwards, as detailed in the following pages, was an insult to a man who had devoted his life to the game and had done so with such distinction.

That connection with League football, going back to the middle of the first decade of the 20th century when he joined Newcastle United for just the £10 signing-on fee, is traced right through his playing days beyond the First World War, and then to his first coaching post at Wolverhampton from which he so unexpectedly quit the game, after a promotion-winning season, before Derby tempted him back for what were to be the peak years of his career that form the bulk of these reminiscences.

For most of his many years in football, both as player and manager, George Jobey was a contemporary of another formidable figure with a Derby County connection: Major Frank Buckley, who played at centre-half for the Rams (and once for England), and who was one of his successors at Molineux, cast in the same martinet mould. A close look is taken at the major's colourful and controversial managerial reign—and at the eventful one with Derby County of a contrastingly commonplace, but none the less dedicated, character named Cecil Potter, in setting the Baseball Ground scene on which Jobey so emphatically stamped his authority.

Memorable events recalled include an epic Cup battle that went to three replays; a last-minute equaliser in an eight-goal Cup thriller; a 4–0 win that was one goal short of clinching promotion; a missed penalty that cost a fifth equaliser; a record away win only a week after losing at home to the same club; a famous Scot's five-goal feat on an away ground; an impending 4–1 defeat that was transformed into a 5–4 victory—and so it goes on.

You can read, too, of the club promoted despite finishing only fifth in the Second Division; the cricketing soccer club chairman who scored ten runs for his county from one hit; the free-scoring forward who became a Lord Mayor; the family that had eight brothers with League clubs; the winger who dashed from a match in a judge's wig and gown to sing in light opera; and even of the player, one of the top names on Derby's roll of honour, who was once described as being even worse than a complete failure.

All this relates, of course, to the years long before the terms striker, sweeper, midfielder and referee's assistant came into general use. Positions on the field are those that applied to the 2-3-5 formation, with two full-backs, two wing-halves and a centre-half, and a forward line of outside-right, inside-right, centre-forward, inside-left and outside-left. They were also the days when there were no floodlights, no substitutes, no penalty shoot-outs, and when transfer fees rose to £14, 000, a figure that seemed so outrageous at the time, but turned out to be a minescule forerunner of the astronomical prices paid today.

Acknowledgements

In compiling this book, I have relied upon material collected while I was on the sports staff of the *Derby Evening Telegraph* during the first dozen or so of almost 50 years as a newspaper journalist, and this is augmented by facts and quotes I obtained in being fortunate enough to interview a good many of the former Derby County players who feature in the story. For the expansion of my account of George Jobey's days in charge at Wolverhampton I have been helped by the record of the Wanderers, *Wolves the Complete Record* published by Breedon Books, compiled by Tony Matthews with Les Smith.

I have also been grateful to be able to check, and expand, my Derby County facts in the appendix with another excellent Breedon product from the Complete Record series— the one on the Rams by Gerald Mortimer, the chief sports writer and former sports editor of the *Derby Evening Telegraph*, an old friend who has kindly consented to provide the foreword.

In several instances discrepancies have arisen, and in the clarification of these I am indebted to J.D. Dent, secretary of the Football League; David Barber, in the Football Association library; Jim Farry, former chief executive of the Scottish FA; Jim Norris, of Blackburn Rovers; Mervyn Baker, of Bristol; David Baggett, Derbyshire CCC's official statistician; Ken Smales, former secretary of Nottingham Forest who, as a Notts cricketer, took all ten wickets in a first-class innings; the sports editors of *The Sentinel* at Stoke and the *Evening News* at Bolton; and R. Taylor, secretary of Alfreton Town FC. I am also obliged to Steve Nicholson, sports editor of the *Derby Evening Telegraph*, for allowing me access to his newspaper's photographic files.

In obtaining other photographs, I am grateful for the assistance of Ian Hall, the former Derby County forward and Derbyshire cricketer who is secretary of the Rams' Former Players Association; John Bowers, son of the former Derby and England centre-forward and himself an ex-Rams player; Jean Parsons, whose father, George Stephenson, also has a prominent part in this story; Peter Morris and Chris Barwick, of the Hulton Getty Picture Library; Anton Rippon; and Joe Stack, of the Derby photographic firm W.W. Winter. In addition, Ernie Hallam, that doyen of Derby supporters, and David Halford, who now lays claim to being the oldest surviving former Rams player, have given invaluable help in the completion of some of the group captions. David has also been kind enough to loan me photographs taken during the club's tour of Germany in which he took part in 1934.

Two of the quotes that were not given to me direct by the players concerned have been taken from the books by Tom Whittaker, the former Arsenal manager (*Tom*

Whittaker's Arsenal Story; Sporting Handbooks) and Keith Farnsworth (*Sheffield Football—A History Volume I*; The Hallamshire Press).

As with my previous book *Derby County Days*, I have been fortunate to have the ready co-operation of Pauline Climpson, managing director, Pat Whitehead, Jenny Sayles, Andrew Fyfe and other members of The Hallamshire Press.

Finally, but definitely not least, I wish to acknowledge the tolerance my wife Joan has shown during the hours I have spent tapping away at my word processor. I trust you will find that at least some of those hours have proved worthwhile.

Eddie Giles *(second from left)* at Pride Park with Lionel Pickering, chairman of Derby County, Jim Smith, the club's manager, and *(right)* Milburn Shanks, who reported on the Rams for the *Derby Evening Telegraph* in the 1950s.

CHAPTER 1

Journeys with Jobey

Journeys with George Jobey from Derby to soccer matches at Nottingham – Reign as Derby County's manager ended by suspension – Big influence on the team that took the FA Cup back to Derby for the first time in the first post-war final – On the losing side with Newcastle United in 1911 Final – Reunited with Dave Willis at the Baseball Ground

I CAN SEE HIM NOW in my mind's eye, leaning forward from his seat opposite in the railway carriage, energetically wagging a finger to emphasise a point he was making in the vigorous, authoritative Geordie tones that had made many a Derby County player quail during his 14 years as the Rams' manager leading up to the outbreak of war in September, 1939.

George Jobey, now deprived of having footballers at his command, may not have been quite the martinet they remembered, but he remained a forceful, strong-minded character with a magnetic hold over his audience and views on soccer to be valued and respected. It has to be said though, that he was somewhat behind the times in his decided distaste of floodlit football which was then coming into vogue. He considered it unnatural to play soccer matches at night.

His reign at the Baseball Ground had ended under the stain of suspension from all football after a joint Football Association and Football League Commission had found that Derby County had paid illegal bonuses and inducements to players from the time he had joined them shortly before the start of the 1925–26 season. Five directors had been cast out with him, and the club fined £500.

The ban on George Jobey was lifted in November, 1945, but he was still on the outside looking in when we made those rail journeys together in the early 1950s. Although he continued to live in the Derby area, it was not back to the Baseball Ground that he went to do his looking. He preferred instead to make the short trip to Nottingham, and that was how he came to be a regular companion for Bob Parker and myself, on the return journey from Derby's Midland station, each Saturday during the soccer season.

I made the journey to report for the *Derby Evening Telegraph* on the home games of Nottingham Forest and Notts County. I did so under the most unimaginative *nom de plume* of R. Trent, though my prose was neither deathless nor as smoothly flowing as the river until I was finally allowed to use my own name. By-lines in those days were bestowed far less liberally than they are now.

Bob Parker did the much more admirable job of giving running commentaries on those same matches for patients in the Nottingham hospitals. He travelled all the way up from his home at Wombourne, near Wolverhampton, to do it, year after year, for hundreds of Saturdays, without ever letting his listeners down. No matter how difficult the journey in the depths of winter, or how drab the game he had to describe, this dedicated Welshman 'from Newport, Mon, [now Gwent] and proud of it' never lost his enthusiasm. Neither was he ever at a loss for words, not even after a particularly exciting match had exercised his vocal chords to the full.

Despite having no active part in Derby County's affairs during or after the 1939–45 war, George Jobey had an over-riding influence on the club's fortunes, not only while he was in charge for the decade and a half leading up to the war but also for several seasons afterwards. While he was manager, the Rams signed six of the players who shared in the defeat of Charlton Athletic that took the FA Cup to Derby for the first time in the first post-war final. Skipper Jack Nicholas, Jack Howe, Leon Leuty (who was an amateur while Jobey was in charge), 'Chick' Musson, Jack Stamps and 'Dally' Duncan were the six, plus three others, Frank Boulton, Jack Parr and Sammy Crooks, who were first choices along the road to Wembley until they were forced out by injury, and another, Tim Ward, who was demobilised from the Army too late to be considered.

Jobey master-minded no major honours during his Derby days, but he guided the Rams to promotion from the Second Division in his first season, twice to runners-up in the top flight, and once to the Cup semi-finals. For most of his years at the helm he

George Jobey, pictured soon after his appointment as manager of Derby County.
(Derby Evening Telegraph)

Skipper Jack Nicholas, one of George Jobey's most durable signings, carries off the FA Cup at Wembley in 1946 sitting on the shoulders of Jack Howe, another survivor from the Jobey era, alongside a third, Jack Bowers (holding football), the former England centre-forward who was then assistant trainer. Others in the picture, from the left, are Peter Doherty, manager Stuart McMillan, Jim Bullions, Leon Leuty, Sammy Crooks (in the background behind Bowers), trainer Dave Willis, 'Chick' Musson, holding the plinth, Vic Woodley, and Reg Harrison, who is oblivious to all as he examines his medal. Six of the players in Derby's team that day were signed while George Jobey was manager; three others missed their chance because of injury, another through Army service.

(Derby Evening Telegraph)

kept the club among the strongest and most pleasing to watch in the League—if literally at the cost of the unauthorised payments to star players that eventually led to his downfall.

In only three of his 14 seasons as manager did Derby finish in the bottom half of the First Division table, with a lowest position of 15th. In addition to being second twice, they were three times fourth and four times sixth. Statistically, he still stands a close second in the club's managerial ratings to Brian Clough, who, like George, hailed from the North-East's hot-bed of soccer—in Jobey's case from Newburn-on-Tyne, a coal-mining suburb just west of Newcastle.

Jobey started out in League football with Newcastle United. He was with them, but made only ten first-team appearances, when they won the First Division Championship in 1908–09 (for the third time in five seasons) and, although he missed the 1910 Cup Final in which they defeated Second Division Barnsley in a replay at Goodison Park, he was in the side when they again reached the final the following year. Once more a replay was needed, but Newcastle lost that one to Bradford City, who, in coming fifth, also ended three places above them in Division One. It was Newcastle's fourth failure in their fifth final in seven years, but, on this occasion, it was fitting that the trophy should go to a Bradford club, as a new cup was at stake for the first time and it had been made by the Bradford firm of Fattorini & Sons.

Neither before nor since has a Bradford team played in an FA Cup Final. It is also a curious fact that Newcastle were unable to win a final at Crystal Palace in five attempts, yet when Wembley became the venue they were the winners on each of the first five occasions they played there—three of them in five years in the 1950s. And, although Newcastle managed a scoreless draw with Bradford City on their last appearance at the dreaded Crystal Palace, the more superstitious of their supporters could point to a continuation of the jinx through injuries that deprived United of two of their best players, Peter McWilliam, a cultured Scottish international wing-half, and Albert Shepherd, the free-scoring England centre-forward who had cost the record fee of £1,650 from Bolton Wanderers.

Shepherd had the most inauspicious of starts on Tyneside in making his home debut in a staggering 9–1 defeat by Sunderland (he scored that lone goal from a penalty). Then, quickly reproducing the form which had brought him almost 100 goals for Bolton, he went on to help Newcastle to end that same season as champions, and he was their leading scorer for three consecutive seasons until he was put out of action only a week before they went back to Crystal Palace for the 1911 final.

A year earlier, he had obtained both goals—one from the first penalty ever to be awarded in an FA Cup Final—in the replay defeat of Barnsley at Everton's ground. Without him, against Bradford City, Newcastle missed their chances to retain the trophy at their unhappiest venue, then were beaten at Old Trafford by a simple 15th-minute goal from Jimmy Speirs, an inside-forward who had played once for Scotland while with Glasgow Rangers. The goal resulted from a mistake by Jimmy Lawrence, the experienced and long-serving goalkeeper who had gained what was to be his lone Scottish cap in a Goodison Park draw with England only a few weeks previously. Lawrence was normally most dependable, as his Newcastle record of nearly 500 League and Cup appearances testifies, but he was badly affected by the Palace hoodoo, making other costly errors in two of the five finals in which he played there.

Shepherd's injury kept him out of the game for almost two seasons; McWilliam's ended his playing career. However, the ligament damage the Scot suffered in winning his eighth cap, after collecting three title medals with Newcastle and taking part in four of their Cup finals, led him to an equally distinguished managerial career that he shared over the next 30 years between Tottenham (in two spells) and Middlesbrough.

Newcastle's inability to field their full-strength line-up against Bradford City was the cloud under which George Jobey found his silver lining—the place he would not otherwise have been given in both the original tie and the replay. Having played in only seven League games that season, all of them at wing-half, he was brought in to lead the attack in this team: Lawrence; McCracken, Whitson; Veitch, Low, Willis; Rutherford, Stewart, Jobey, Higgins, Wilson.

Dave Willis, the left-half, was to be reunited with Jobey as Derby County's trainer just over 20 years later. Signed by Newcastle from Sunderland in May, 1907, a year after Jobey's arrival at St James's Park from Morpeth Harriers, Willis spent six seasons with United before moving to Reading. He won a League Championship medal in 1909, but fate decreed that he would never be capped. The only time he was chosen for England, in 1912, a chill caused him to drop out on the eve of the match.

The outbreak of the Great War of 1914–18 brought Willis's playing career to an end. After serving throughout the war in the RASC he was appointed manager of Jarrow, the club with which he had first come into prominence as a player. From there, he began as a trainer with Raith Rovers, one of whose players became his son-in-law. This was Alex James, the skilful Scotland inside-forward who later excelled with Preston and Arsenal, and was among the 'Wembley Wizards' who humbled England with their famous 5–1 victory in 1928.

It was in 1933 that Willis rejoined Jobey. He had been Nottingham Forest's trainer for eight years when he resigned in order to fill the vacancy left at Derby by the departure of Laurie Edwards to Leicester City. Edwards was the former Powderhall sprinter who had held the job since Harry Curzon's move to Walsall in the 1921–22 season. Like Edwards and another of his predecessors, Arthur Latham, Willis was the England team's trainer on several occasions, but in that role he touched his peak with the 1946 win at Wembley that still stands alone on Derby County's FA Cup honours list.

Having reached his mid-sixties, Willis stepped down from the Rams' staff just over a year after that historic victory and, because of his age, he declined the offer of another

Dave Willis who was with George Jobey as a
player at Newcastle and trainer at Derby.
(Derby Evening Telegraph)

job as trainer from Notts County. Although he felt that he could no longer do himself justice in the demanding world of professional football, he did agree to enter the more sedate and less protracted sphere of county cricket, becoming Derbyshire's masseur and trainer. It was while he was on duty with Derbyshire that he died, suddenly, in London towards the end of May, 1949. He travelled there for a match with Surrey at the Oval, but had a fatal heart attack at Alex James's home at New Southgate. He was 67.

George Jobey and Dave Willis played together only a dozen times in Newcastle's first team during the six seasons they were both on United's books. Willis just managed to top a century of League and Cup appearances, but, with the competition for places so keen among the club's galaxy of talent, Jobey made only half as many before being transferred to Arsenal—or, to be exact, Woolwich Arsenal, as they were to be known for one more season before no longer being with the Woolwich.

After dropping the 'Woolwich' prefix, following their switch from Plumstead to Highbury, Arsenal were transformed into the main power in English soccer for most of the years during which Jobey later aspired to topple them while manager of Derby County, but when he joined the Gunners, at a fee of £500, they had just been relegated to the Second Division after going through almost a couple of dozen matches without a win.

Admirable as Arsenal's many achievements have been since then, the fact cannot be escaped that all those successes have been based on the flimsiest of foundations. They were promoted back to top status, which they have held ever since, from the unworthy *fifth* place in which they finished the 1914–15 season, the last before the League's activities were suspended because of the war.

This came about after it had been decided to add two clubs to each of the two divisions that then existed for the first post-war season of 1919–20, increasing the total membership to 44. When a similar expansion had been made in 1905, the clubs due for relegation to the Second Division, Bury and Notts County, had been reprieved to make up the new number in the senior section (then 20) with the pair who had earned promotion, Liverpool and Bolton Wanderers. It was therefore generally expected that the same procedure would be followed again, with the First Division's two bottom clubs of 1914–15, Chelsea and Tottenham Hotspur, staying up and being joined by the top two from the Second Division—champions Derby County, and Preston North End.

The League Management Committee did indeed, at first, indicate that such would be the case, but then had a change of mind. The Rams and Preston were to go up, as of right, but it was decided to invite applications from all the Second Division clubs to fill the other two vacancies in the enlarged Division One.

This was the point at which Henry (later Sir Henry) Norris saw his chance to indulge in some highly imaginative leap-frogging on Arsenal's behalf. Norris, a wealthy estate agent and property developer who was also Mayor of Fulham and Member of Parliament for Fulham East, had already overcome the objections of Tottenham Hotspur, Clapton (now Leyton) Orient, Islington Borough Council and local residents in uprooting Arsenal from the Manor Ground at Plumstead and relocating them in North London. His original plan to amalgamate Arsenal with the Fulham club, of which he was chairman, had been rejected by the League, and so had his alternative idea of having both sides share Fulham's Craven Cottage ground. But, in his ruthless determination to have control of the foremost club in the country, Norris had put the full weight of his power and influence behind his take-over of Arsenal, seeing that club as the best bet for the realisation of his ambitions—and now the League had given him the opportunity to take a short-cut.

With his pince-nez gleaming and his untidy walrus moustache twitching in his eagerness, he audaciously set about some intensive lobbying of the Management Committee and the delegates at the League's annual meeting. He also secured the significant support of the League president, John McKenna, and made a key ally of Chelsea. No wonder former Arsenal centre-half Bernard Joy, in his book *Forward, Arsenal!*, said Norris was 'nothing less than a dictator...one of the last soccer tzars'.

Chelsea could afford to be generous in promising to back Arsenal's domineering chairman, even though it was to be at the expense of the unfortunate Spurs, for their retention of First Division status was ensured at the outset. There had been some suggestion of their being the victims of a 'suspect' result in finishing only one point adrift of safety in 1915, and it was for what he called 'special reasons' that McKenna persuaded the delegates to allow the Stamford Bridge club to keep their place without being involved in the voting.

This left just the one vacancy, and the League's president, speaking for the Management Committee, condoned Norris's blatant manipulation of minds by urging Arsenal's election. He sought to justify such a transparently blemished recommendation by drawing attention to Arsenal's length of service to the League, spuriously ignoring the fact that it was almost a dozen years shorter than that of Wolverhampton Wanderers, who had occupied fourth place in the 1914–15 Second Division table, two points above the London club. Wolves, indeed, were one of the League's founder members.

This decision was also grossly unfair to Barnsley, who had finished immediately behind the promoted pair. Also, if a claim with official approval could be made for Arsenal, then what about Birmingham? They had ended level on points with Norris's club, and only just behind them on goal average, yet they, too, preceded Arsenal into the League when, as Small Heath, they had played in the Second Division's inaugural season.

It is inconceivable that such an injustice could even be contemplated today, and yet 18 of the delegates, as if mesmerised, duly yielded to all the pressures and voted Arsenal, or more accurately, vaulted Arsenal, into the First Division. Next in the poll, 10 votes behind, came the hapless Spurs, cynically shanghaied into Division Two. They were followed by Barnsley, with five votes, Wolves (4), Nottingham Forest (3), Birmingham (2) and Hull City (1).

Hull, in seventh place in 1915 on the same number of points as Arsenal and Birmingham, had some excuse for being optimistic enough to go to the vote, but Forest were certainly pushing their luck from third off the foot of the Second Division.

Justice was belatedly done when Tottenham, under the astute guidance of Peter McWilliam, romped away with the Division Two title at the first attempt in 1919–20, but it was not long before that swift elevation emphasised the ill-feeling that had been aroused between themselves and Arsenal. With these North London rivals now back together in the First Division, their meeting at White Hart Lane in September, 1922 was so rough that there were disturbances on the terraces and a player on each side was sent off (Arsenal won 2–1, but lost 2–0 in the return game at Highbury a week later). The FA ordered a Commission of Inquiry, the outcome of which was a month's suspension for an England international in the Spurs team, the censuring of two Arsenal men, and a warning that Tottenham's ground would be closed if there was any more crowd trouble.

By then, George Jobey was just starting out in management with Wolverhampton Wanderers, having followed his one season with Arsenal, 1913–14, by briefly assisting Bradford, guesting for Hamilton Academicals during the war, and spending 1919–20 with Leicester City before winding up his playing career at Northampton.

Jobey's first match for Arsenal was also their first at Highbury. It was played on September 6th, 1913, and he netted the first of the goals that got them off to a 2–1 winning start at their new ground against Leicester Fosse—City's forerunners. It was not an entirely happy debut for him, however. He ricked an ankle in scoring, and was trundled back to his lodgings on a milk cart belonging to a dairyman, a keen Arsenal supporter, whose depot was close by in Gillespie Road. Quite a humble contrast to the affluence Arsenal eventually achieved.

It was not, however, with Sir Henry Norris still lording it over Highbury that the Gunners fired themselves up to the days of glory for which that controversial knight had schemed and thirsted. Nemesis caught up with him at the beginning of the 1927–28 season, when he and William Hall, who had been a fellow director at Fulham before rejoining him on the Arsenal board, were suspended by the FA and League for breaking the rules. An appeal to the High Court failed, bringing the end to Sir Henry's dreams of soccer grandeur.

Norris was succeeded as Arsenal's chairman by Sir Samuel Hill-Wood, a man with strong Derbyshire connections, who had built up his home club, Glossop North End, to reach the First Division at a personal cost of some £30,000—big money in those days when most of their players were amateurs.

Glossop's first season in the League, 1898–99, was the one in which the system of promotion and relegation was introduced in place of the 'test match' play-offs and the Derbyshire club rose instantly from the Second Division as runners-up to Manchester City. Unfortunately, they went straight back, finishing last with only four wins and 18 points from their 34 games, but they soldiered on through 15 more Second Division seasons before resigning from the League after the First World War. Their fortunes had declined from being as high as fifth in 1901, and sixth in 1910, to ending the final pre-war season at the bottom of the table again.

Like Sir Henry Norris, Sir Samuel Hill-Wood was an MP, representing the High Peak division of Derbyshire from 1910 to 1929. Although soccer was his first love, as an administrator, he also enjoyed cricket and played for Derbyshire, captaining them as plain S.H. Wood around the turn into the 20th century. His four sons, three of them cricketing Blues, all followed him to Eton, and then into the Derbyshire team. Worcestershire had seven Foster brothers who made them known as 'Fostershire,' but the Hill-Woods provided the only instance of a father and his four sons all playing first-class cricket for the same county. One of those sons, Denis, also followed his father as chairman at Highbury, taking over after Sir Samuel's death at the age of 77, early in 1949.

Samuel Wood was no great shakes as a cricketer, but he got himself into the record books by scoring 10 runs off one hit during Derbyshire's match against the MCC at Lord's in May, 1900. In the same innings there were two sevens in William Storer's unbeaten 175 in the total of 383 that set up a Derbyshire victory by 107 runs.

Those freaks of scoring arose from the experimental 'net system' which the MCC tried in their club games in the early part of that season. The ground was enclosed on the normal boundary by a net of two to three feet in height. It was first decided that when the ball went over the netting the batsmen should score three runs, and that when it was stopped by the net two runs should be added to those run. This proved too clumsy to be practical however, and the whole idea was abandoned after modifications had brought no better result.

Wisden, the Cricketers' Bible, considered that:

> There was something to be said for the plan of having all the hits run out, and perhaps the experiment would have had a better chance if there had been no allowance of two runs when the ball was stopped by the netting. The plan, as adopted, placed brilliant hitting at a discount, and it put such a premium on hits that just reached the ring that it deserved to fail.

The Derbyshire man's ten-in-one began with a cut for an all-run four and he gained the two-run bonus because the ball reached the net. Then the ball was overthrown to the opposite net, giving a further bonus of two, and the batsmen crossed for another couple while it was on its way. The suffering bowler was C.J. Burnup, later captain of Kent, who played for Cambridge University at both cricket and soccer and, as a Corinthian, was selected at the winter game for England against Scotland.

There was also a footballing connection with the only other batsman to have scored 10 runs from one stroke in first-class cricket, but, where Albert Hornby was concerned, the football was of the Rugby, not Association, variety. Hornby, irreverently known as 'Monkey' owing to his slight, but nimble, physique, was nine times an England Rugby Union international. He captained Lancashire at cricket for nearly 20 seasons, and it was for his county that he made half of his 20 runs, in a total of 100, off one delivery from Surrey's James Street at the Oval in 1873.

CHAPTER 2

Bleak Start – and Finish

Jobey begins management with relegation at Wolverhampton then resigns after immediate promotion – Controversial dismissal after wilderness years end at Mansfield – Varied career of colourful Major Buckley

FLOURISHING AS WERE MOST OF HIS SEASONS at Derby County, managership for George Jobey began with relegation at Wolverhampton and ended on another depressingly low note when he was dismissed for alleged 'neglect of duty' by lowly Mansfield Town.

After leaving Leicester in 1920, Jobey turned down an offer to join the Welsh club Ebbw Vale as player-manager, preferring to go into the newly-formed Third Division with Northampton Town, where he became player-coach. He increased his total of League and Cup appearances beyond 200, spread over five clubs, before finally retiring as a player to join Wolves as manager-coach in September, 1922.

He and Albert Hoskins, who was appointed secretary, filled the gap left by Jack Addenbrooke, who had first signed for the Wanderers as a reserve defender way back in 1883, and had been their secretary-manager since 1885. Wolves battled through to five FA Cup finals, winning two, during Addenbrooke's 37 years as their first holder of that dual role. Latterly, however, they had fallen on troubled times, slipping into the lower regions of the Second Division, and in his final season they again went uncomfortably close to further relegation in gaining only three victories from their last 20 matches.

The years of struggle took such toll of Addenbrooke's health that in the summer of 1922 he was sent on six months' sick leave. This, though, did not have the desired effect, and his death that autumn led to George Jobey's appointment, in harness with Hoskins. In also bringing in George Holley, the former Sunderland and England forward, as trainer, Wolves appeared to have put their future in safe hands, but the rot had set in so thoroughly that the first season under the new management team was one of the worst in the club's history, culminating in their descent into the Northern Section of the Third Division.

Things went wrong from the very first game, in which they were beaten at home by Derby County, and only nine wins were gained as they plunged to the foot of the table with a mere 27 points, eight behind the other relegated club, Rotherham County, who two years later merged with Rotherham Town to form the Rotherham United of today.

Deficiencies were glaring in both defence and attack. Jobey sought to make some improvement by signing a couple of tall, quality players from Everton—George Brewster, a former Aberdeen centre-half who had recently helped Scotland to defeat England at Hampden, and Stan Fazackerley, an inside-forward who had toured South Africa with the FA—but consistency remained sadly lacking as poor results undermined the team's confidence.

Brewster did not last out that miserable season with Wolves. He drifted off to Wales with Lovell's Athletic, then soon afterwards he became one of the first British players to try their luck in North American soccer before returning to his homeland as player-manager of Inverness in the Highland League. Fazackerley, who had also played in the United States, and had scored for Sheffield United in their defeat of Chelsea in the 1915 FA Cup Final before Everton paid the then top fee of £4,000 for him, produced a fair 1922–23 dividend for Wolves with a dozen goals in that number of League games. Too often, however, he lacked support in an attack that wasted too many chances.

To add to Wolves' problems, their ground was closed for a week because of their fans' misbehaviour during a home defeat by Leicester, and when they went to Filbert Street the following Saturday they conceded seven goals in a match for the second time in a matter of months. Dwindling crowds and a balance sheet which sank several thousand pounds into the red set the seal on the setbacks of this first season under Jobey's management that could scarcely have been more depressing.

It was at this low point that this determined, no-nonsense son of the gritty North-East showed himself in his true light, and a year later Wolverhampton Wanderers were back in the Second Division, champions of the Third North by one point from Rochdale.

They lost only three of their 42 games, were leading scorers in the section with 76 goals, and tightened up their defence so competently that they gave away just 27—second only in the whole League to the miserly 26 conceded by the Lancashire club which pressed them so strongly for the one promotion place.

Harry Shaw, snapped up from Hednesford Town, formed a dependable full-back partnership with the reinstated Ted Watson, a hard-tackling Tynesider, and Bill Caddick, a former Grenadier Guardsman from Wellington Town, seized the opportunity to establish himself in the central defensive position vacated by Brewster. But the Jobey deal that had the biggest bearing on the transformation was the £1, 000 outlay on another fellow Tynesider, Tom Phillipson, a centre-forward from Swindon Town who, like his new manager, had entered the League with Newcastle United. Phillipson, a future Lord Mayor of Wolverhampton, did not make his debut with Wolves until Christmas Day, 1923, but within a fortnight he got off the mark with a hat-trick in a 7–1 win at Ashington. The potent strike force he formed with Fazackerley and Harry Lees, a former Notts County amateur, tipped the scales towards the immediate escape from Division Three. Between them, they scored almost two-thirds of the 80-plus goals the club claimed in League and Cup that season.

By the time Phillipson left Molineux early in 1928, for a short stay with Sheffield United, he had chalked up 111 goals in 159 games for Wolves. At that time Harry Wood was the only player to have scored more for the club. He had set out towards his tally of 126 by scoring once on his debut, and making two others, in a 7–0 FA Cup defeat of Derby St Luke's back in October, 1885. The record has since been raised to 170 by 'Artillery Billy' Hartill, then to 194 by John Richards, the England forward who was briefly on loan to Derby County in the early 1980s, and to well beyond 200 by Steve Bull.

Phillipson's 36 Second Division goals in 1925–26 failed to clinch another promotion, as fourth-placed Wolves finished eight points behind the runners-up Rams, who went up with Sheffield Wednesday, but they set the Wanderers' individual record for a League season which stood until Dennis Westcott netted 38 in the First Division in 1946–47. Even Bull, with 34 in the Fourth Division championship side, could not surpass Phillipson's League total during the 1987–88 season in which he amassed 52 in all matches, though he inched one ahead of it with 37 as the Division Three title was won a year later.

Phillipson's high ratio of goals to games made him one of George Jobey's most astute signings, but it was under new management that he enjoyed his seasons of greatest prosperity. The cheers for the prompt promotion Jobey supervised had barely died down when, to general astonishment, the manager-coach sprang the big surprise of the 1924 close season by suddenly announcing that he was deserting soccer to go into the hotel business.

Albert Hoskins, who, like Jack Addenbrooke, had been a Wolves reserve player before joining the backroom staff—originally as assistant secretary—stepped into the breach by combining his secretarial duties with those of manager for a couple of years. He then took up a similar post with Gillingham, afterwards reverting to secretary only with Torquay United. He was succeeded at Wolverhampton by Fred Scotchbrook, another who had been unable to make the top grade as a player, with the other Wanderers of Bolton, before going behind the scenes, first as coach, then assistant secretary at Burnden Park. Scotchbrook first went into management with Stockport County a few months after George Jobey had temporarily departed from Molineux, but before the next season was out so was he. The Cheshire club dismissed him as they headed for the relegation from the Second Division they had only narrowly avoided the previous year.

Scotchbrook's appointment by Wolves the next month, March, 1926, was destined to be of even shorter duration, for he left in a huff soon after criticising the club's policy at the 1927 annual meeting. In common with others before him, he had fallen foul of interference by the directors. Decisions had been taken out of his hands and financial constraints had seriously curbed his efforts to strengthen the team.

Fortunately for Wolves, a contrastingly free rein was conceded to his successor, Major Frank Buckley, a commanding figure who, like Jobey, was accustomed to issuing orders, not receiving them. Buckley, a former Derby County half-back, was to lead Wolves to the brink of the first League and Cup double of the 20th century, about which more will be recalled later in this chapter. It was also fortunate for Derby County that they were able to persuade George Jobey back into football only just over a year after he had begun his self-imposed retirement, but, here again, a closer look at the eventful seasons through which he piloted them will have to wait a little longer.

Major Frank Buckley, a man of many clubs as player and manager. He won his one England cap while with Derby County.

George Jobey. It was not often that he was photographed without his hat.
(Derby Evening Telegraph)

For the moment, we move well ahead, to the gloomier period in which Jobey was left feeling baffled and bitter when offers from prominent clubs were conspicuously absent after the ban on him had been lifted in 1945. He once admitted to me that the biggest mistake he ever made in his private life was not to follow up a suggestion that he could become a freemason.

Ironically, when some interest did start to be shown in him, if only from unfashionable quarters of the League, he was prevented from taking advantage at that particular time by the illness of his wife. Mansfield Town, for one, invited him to be manager in the summer of 1949. They were seeking a replacement for Roy Goodall, the former England full-back and captain who had resigned to join the training staff of Huddersfield Town, the club in whose defence he had gained League medals in five successive seasons during the 1920s—the first three as champions, the two others as runners-up.

Having found Jobey unavailable, Mansfield paid a transfer fee of £750 to take Freddie Steele, a pre-war England centre-forward, from Stoke City as player-manager. When Steele, who had scored five goals out of eight in one of Derby County's heaviest defeats, left late in 1951 to continue in that capacity with Port Vale, Mansfield reverted to having a non-playing manager in once more turning to Jobey—this time successfully, even though he was by then of pensionable age. There were some 30 applicants for the job, but Jobey was asked to add his name to the list and duly came out at the top.

Sadly, all too soon it was to prove a most unhappy alliance. The old warhorse was given a two-year contract, with the option of a further year that would have taken him up to the age of 70, only to find that the odds were stacked against him almost from the day he took over. After only one full season he was out in the cold again—and there he was to remain.

He was still definite enough in his ideas, still had the physical strength to cope with the special difficulties of managing a little Northern Section club, but times, regrettably, had passed him by and left him too far behind to catch up after his long absence from a position of authority.

The call had come at least five years too late. Attitudes were changing from those pre-war days when he had ruled the Derby roost with an iron resolve that had put him, along with Frank Buckley, among the keenest disciplinarians soccer had known, yet also one who had earned respect and loyalty. So-called player power had still to erupt, but the age gap between Jobey and his new charges was an obvious handicap, too wide to bridge.

In his years at Derby, he was held in awe by even the more experienced of the many star players he had on his books. One of them, Ronnie Dix, the former 'Boy Wonder' who, at the age of 15 while with Bristol Rovers, was the youngest League scorer, recalled that 'when he walked into the dressing room you wouldn't hear a word, even with all those famous players, and he had a caustic tongue which he used often'.

Jobey did not regularly attend training, but Sammy Crooks, the England right-winger who was Derby's most-capped player in those days, retained a vivid memory of his match rehearsals. He recalled:

> Believe me, they were a revelation. He used to stand on the touchline, and his commentary was just like a quick-fire radio commentary—but in reverse. He didn't give an eye-witness account of what we were doing right. Instead, he made a very forthright statement on what we were *not* doing right.

At Mansfield, however, Jobey was past taking such a strong line, and he could no longer rely on his word going unquestioned. Furthermore, the club's parlous financial situation put a great strain on his reputation as one of the best judges of young players as he was given instructions only to recruit those who were either amateurs or on a free transfer.

When I last met him, at a third-round FA Cup-tie which packed a record crowd of nearly 25,000 into Field Mill, his cut-price team did well to lose to emerging Nottingham Forest by just the one goal, hit home by a scoring machine named Wally Ardron. On that same day, Derby County threw away a 4–1 home lead against Chelsea to be taken to a replay which they lost in extra time.

Two years earlier, Mansfield had been runners-up to promoted Rotherham in Division Three North. They ended the season in which Jobey joined them in a respectable sixth place, and although there was then a marked decline, their veteran manager had good reason to feel some satisfaction given the difficult circumstances forced upon him, when they finished his first complete season with them comfortably clear of having to apply for re-election. It therefore came as a crushing blow when he was abruptly dismissed just a few months later for 'neglect of duty' because he had missed a sub-committee meeting.

His sense of injustice was heightened by the fact that the letter informing him of that high-handed action reached his Derby home while he was away on a scouting expedition which he was combining with a holiday back in the North-East area that had proved such a rich hunting ground for him in his managerial hey-day. He explained:

> I spent the first week up there searching for players at Sunderland, Newcastle and Darlington, and I was on holiday the second week. The letter I found waiting for me when I got back was dated July 8, and since that date I had signed an inside-forward named Murray from Darlington. I was interested in certain other players in the North-East, but as soon as the clubs concerned told me that they would require a fee I had to call off negotiations.

The allegation that he was not fully committed to Mansfield's cause also made very strange reading in view of his decision, soon after his appointment, to give away his two tickets for the 1952 FA Cup Final in which his first two clubs were in opposition. He put business before pleasure as two young players in the Darlington district had been recommended to him, and on the Saturday of the Wembley match—which Newcastle won with a late goal from Chilean George Robledo against a plucky Arsenal side reduced to ten men by a first-half injury to Walley Barnes, their Welsh international full-back—presented him with his last chance to see them in action that season. So he went north instead of south, but turned both players down.

Jobey, who had not been happy at Field Mill for some time before his sacking, also had to contend with two attempts to undermine his position, quite apart from the restrictions on his signings. He successfully resisted one of them, a suggestion that he should take a cut in his £1,000-a-year salary, and although he could not alter the other— the directors' decision, reached without consulting him first, to make all their players available for transfer—he did refuse to part with the only three who attracted offers because he regarded them as the key members of the team.

Those three, acquired at a total cost of only £3,500 before the bar on spending, were winger Charlie Adam and centre-half Norman Plummer, signed together from Leicester City, and Chris Marron, a centre-forward from Chesterfield. Adam and Plummer had been in the Leicester team beaten by Wolves in the 1949 FA Cup Final.

Of the proposed pruning of his wage packet, Jobey said 'I objected to this, but it is possible that if I had been previously approached on the matter I might have considered taking a reduction, especially in regard to the club's circumstances'.

The sub-committee, formed to discuss the playing side of the club, had only one meeting before the one Jobey unknowingly failed to attend. That was the meeting at which, again without prior consultation, he was informed that no more money could be provided for new players.

As at Derby, he left a club whose affairs were under investigation, though this time he was not involved. The FA–League Commission's inquiry arose from allegations by a former Mansfield secretary, W.J. Warner, about breaches of the rules during the years from 1947 to 1951. The Commission announced their findings in December, 1953, five months after Jobey's departure. They were satisfied that irregular payments had been made to player-manager Steele, two former Leicester City players, half-back Grogan, and Welsh international full-back Dai Jones, and to George Antonio, the ex-Stoke and

Derby forward who had been signed from Doncaster Rovers and by then was player-manager at Oswestry. Mansfield Town were fined £500, and also had to meet the costs of the inquiry. Chairman W.M. Hornby was suspended along with two other directors, one of whom had since left the board. Jones, Steele (£250 each) and Antonio (£50) were also fined, and Grogan severely censured.

Four other directors and one former director were cautioned for failing to exercise proper supervision of the club's affairs, and at the League's next annual meeting Arthur Oakley, the chairman, created quite a stir by revealing that the Management Committee had 'seriously discussed Mansfield's expulsion from the League'.

James Jenkins, soon to be Mansfield's mayor, took over as chairman of the Town's reconstituted board, and Stan Mercer, a former Blackpool, Leicester, and Accrington forward who had become the club's secretary and assistant manager since having to give up playing through injury, succeeded George Jobey as manager.

The 33-year-old Mercer, who was said to be paid 'nothing like as much' as Jobey, replaced Tim Ward as the youngest manager then in the League. Ward had narrowly taken that distinction from Fred Stansfield, player-manager at Newport (who, at 35, was just two months Ward's senior) on being appointed to the Barnsley post earlier that year—after an eight-day false start as manager at Exeter before his recall to the Yorkshire club he originally joined as a player from Derby County.

George Jobey went on his way still hoping to find a new job. 'I have been in football all my life' he said, overlooking his year out of it after leaving Wolves, 'and I am prepared to consider any offer that comes along.' But, as was only to be expected at his age, no further opening was forthcoming.

At 68, after nearly half a century in football and more than 30 years since embarking upon his managerial career, he was less than two years younger than Frank Buckley, then the doyen of soccer managers, who had just moved to what was to be his final club, Walsall. For Buckley, too, the old magic had waned. Walsall finished his first full season at Fellows Park exactly where he had found them—seeking re-election at the foot of Division Three South—and a year later they were next to last. After that, nearing his 72nd birthday, he had no alternative but to follow Jobey into honourable retirement.

Buckley's connection with League football stretched back three years beyond Jobey's to 1903, when he turned professional with Aston Villa after serving in the Army during the Boer War, and it lasted just over two years longer. From Villa he travelled via Brighton and Hove Albion, both Manchester clubs, and Birmingham, to Derby County, where he spent the three most successful seasons of his playing career as a hard-working, adventurous centre-half, before moving on to Bradford City for a short spell during which Jobey was a neighbour at Park Avenue.

Almost a century of League and Cup appearances by Buckley for the Rams began with their promotion back to the First Division, but ended in their return to the Second—from which their swift escape without him in 1914–15 lasted for only the first two post-war seasons. It was while he was a Derby player that he gained his only England cap, albeit in a 3–0 defeat by Ireland at Middlesbrough.

The leadership qualities that were to serve Buckley in such good stead during his many years in football management came right to the fore in the First World War. In December, 1914, more than ten years after having been a sergeant instructor in the 2nd

Battalion King's (Liverpool) Regiment, he enlisted in the 17th Battalion of the Middlesex Regiment, the famous Footballers' Battalion, and rose to become its commanding officer on his promotion to major, a rank he proudly used for the rest of his life. Neither a drinker nor a smoker, he positively demanded the respect he automatically received with his strong sense of discipline and his upright military bearing. Some six feet tall, well spoken and well dressed, and with a predilection for plus-fours, he cut a most imposing figure.

Buckley, one of whose five brothers, Chris, was also a centre-half with Aston Villa (and later their chairman) before joining Arsenal at about the time George Jobey left the Gunners, added to his seven clubs as a player with seven more as a manager, beginning in March, 1919, at Norwich. He was rejoined at the East Anglian club by Arthur Latham, the former Derby full-back who moved there as trainer after being replaced in that role at the Baseball Ground when manager Jimmy Methven was asked to combine the two jobs as part of economies the Rams made because of dwindling receipts. Buckley went to Norwich, then members of the Southern League, as a player-manager, but, rising 36 and still feeling the effects of a war wound, he turned out only once for their first team.

Buckley was forced to sell a forward, Sam Jennings, to Middlesbrough for £2,500—the first of the big sales for which he became noted. Shortly after this, a crisis at the club led to the resignation of six of the directors and Buckley himself. This denied him the distinction of being Norwich's first manager in the League when, in 1920, they were elected original members of the Third Division.

He was out of football for the next three years, working as a commercial traveller, before Blackpool brought him back with a salary that made him one of the best-paid managers in the game. His four years at Bloomfield Road were typical of all his others in the managerial chair, colourful and controversial. His flamboyant style provoked such objections from one group of fans that they inaugurated a Supporters' Club in an attempt to strengthen their hand against him.

From leading the Second Division, Blackpool blundered into a battle to avoid relegation, and even when they recovered, to some extent, as Buckley concentrated on a youth policy, dissatisfaction was fuelled by his sale of two of the club's most effective and experienced players—full-back Herbert Jones, to Blackburn Rovers for £3,850, and centre-forward Harry Bedford, to Derby County for £3,250.

Criticism was like water off a duck's back to the major, but even he could not conceal his disappointment at the failure to sustain a promotion challenge, and he did not need much nudging when Wolverhampton Wanderers approached him early in the 1927 close season. His switch back to the Midlands was, eventually, a sound career move with a greater potential for progress, but it certainly did not seem so when Wolves trailed nearly 20 points behind Blackpool's Division Two champions of 1930. Although Buckley's Molineux men went up as table-toppers two years later, they went dangerously close to sharing the relegation that befell Blackpool the following season.

Unrest among his club's supporters surfaced once more when some disgruntled fans stormed onto the pitch and damaged the goal posts after one particularly frustrating home defeat. Also, in August, 1938, there was another strong wave of protest over an outgoing transfer when Bryn Jones, the Welsh international inside-forward, was sold to Arsenal even though the fee boosted Wolves' finances and pushed the record up to what many saw as the ultimately ridiculous heights of £14,000. Little did they know!

Behind that sensational deal, however, lay the success story Buckley was at last unfolding on the back of his emphasis on youth. The lengths to which he went in that direction were extreme, even allowing for his customary scorning of the conventional. Centre-half Stan Cullis captained Wolves at the age of 19 (and England at 22); wingers Jimmy Mullen and Alan Steen made their First Division debuts at 16; and, during the 1939–45 war, Cameron Buchanan, a Scottish schoolboy, appeared in a few regional first-team games at the tender age of 14.

Such was the abundance of talent Buckley's scouting system unearthed that in the second half of the 1930s more than £130,000 from sales flowed into the Wanderers' coffers. When offset against the money they themselves spent in the transfer market during that period, this produced a credit balance of around £90,000, enough to wipe out the bank overdraft and mortage on the ground and make Wolves one of the most affluent clubs in the country.

To those mathematics—exceptional for those days, if chicken feed by the current standards—could be added the turn-around of the team from relegation candidates to genuine title contenders. This was achieved amid a whirl of publicity the resourceful Major cultivated by sending his players to a psychologist, and also subjecting them to 'monkey gland' treatment that he omitted to unmask as simply innoculations against the common cold.

Success soared to the stage where Wolves were First Division runners-up in both the last two pre-war seasons—only one point behind Arsenal on the first occasion, and in 1939 with a side, whose average age was in the early twenties, that raised hopes of the double in also reaching the FA Cup Final. Having scored five goals against both Leicester and Grimsby on their way to Wembley, and seven in the League against Everton, shortly before knocking out the Goodison club (that year's champions) in a quarter-final, they were among the hottest of favourites against a Portsmouth team from the lower half of the First Division. Their 4–1 defeat was, therefore, one of the biggest upsets in the history of the competition, but Buckley had built so shrewdly that Wolves retained a firm basis for continued success when they resumed Football League and FA Cup combat after the war had cut them off in their prime. The only surprise was that he was not still there to direct it.

It was under the management of Ted Vizard, the former Bolton and Wales winger, that Wolves were third in the First Division's first post-war season. Then, from 1949 to 1961, under Stan Cullis they were three times champions (twice in successive years), three times runners-up, and third on three other occasions. On top of all that, they were twice FA Cup winners and once losing semi-finalists after a replay.

Shortly before the war Wolves had put Buckley on a life contract and given him a substantial rise besides a big endowment insurance. In the last complete pre-war season of 1938–39 he was the highest-paid manager in the game, with total earnings of £4,800 made up of a £2,000 salary, a £1,000 bonus for taking the club to the Cup Final, plus half of one per cent of the gate receipts. But, as he put it, 'some of the unsettling effect which the war was having on everybody crept into my life' and there were also what he called 'petty differences' as he and the directors prepared for the return to peacetime football. Consequently, he was in the mood for another move, even when the offer that came from Notts County meant he would be dropping into the Third Division, but at Meadow Lane he ran into more friction with his board before League soccer had been resumed. His early departure became inevitable after the death of his main backer, R.A. Shipstone, the wealthy brewer.

Having just sold Jesse Pye, who ranked high with Jackie Sewell among his best signings for Notts, to his old club Wolves for a clear profit of £10,000, Buckley took only a couple of weeks to find another berth—still in Division Three, but this time in the Northern section instead of the Southern.

Hull City, after their closure for the transitional season of 1945–46, were about to start up again at their new Boothferry Park ground, but their chairman, Harold Needler, had asked Buckley, at a chance meeting, if he could recommend a manager capable of coping with the big rebuilding job that was necessary. The challenge was too tempting for Buckley himself to resist, but it was not long before another rift arose when his wholesale team changes and experiments jeopardised the quest for promotion. Then came the transfer of Raich Carter from Derby County, to be his assistant in addition to carrying on playing, and only a few days afterwards Buckley resigned because of 'policy disputes.'

Again, another door was quick to open. Over at Leeds, the man who wanted Buckley as manager, Sam Bolton, had just taken over as chairman from Ernest Pullan, who had

Jesse Pye *(left)*, a notable Buckley signing for Notts County, in Wolves clothing at the Baseball Ground, where he later played for the Rams. Derby's Leon Leuty and *(right)* Bert Mozley can only look on with him as goalkeeper Terry Webster makes a great, but unavailing, effort to prevent Johnny Hancocks putting the visitors on their way to a 2–1 victory early in the 1949–50 season.

resigned after walking out of a board meeting on being outvoted over the major's proposed appointment.

This time Buckley stayed for five seasons. He smartly wiped out a five-figure overdraft mainly by selling two internationals: Irishman Con Martin, to Aston Villa, and Welshman Aubrey Powell, to Everton. He also discovered, in the versatile Welsh giant John Charles, the player he rated as the greatest of his many 'finds'—and there was a very wide choice. At one time it was estimated there were at least 350 players still in the game who had either been signed by him or taken on trial, though many of them had readily been discarded as he had continually tinkered with his team's formation.

For all his skill as a wheeler dealer, Buckley found the task of leading Leeds up from the Second Division beyond him. As at Hull, their promotion was to be gained under the man who again replaced him, Raich Carter. Buckley left Elland Road by what was announced as a 'mutual and friendly agreement', but his forthright manner put him at odds yet again with his directors when, just over two years later, he lost his last post at Walsall on which his hold was being weakened in any case by his age and lack of success.

Buckley lived on for nine more years, celebrating his 81st birthday the month before his death at Walsall in Christmas week, 1964. For George Jobey, who, sadly, spent his final years in straitened circumstances at his home in the Chaddesden suburb of his adopted town, the end came at a Derby hospital on May 9th, 1962, at the age of 76— just a few weeks before one of his old boys, Tim Ward, followed an older one, Harry Storer, into the managerial hot seat at the Baseball Ground which he had occupied with such a high degree of competence over so many seasons.

Raich Carter, a former Derby County
captain, who twice followed Frank Buckley,
another ex-Rams player, as manager, and on
both occasions won promotion.
(Derby Evening Telegraph)

CHAPTER 3

Potter the Nearly Man

*Cecil Potter twice guides Derby to brink of
promotion, and one step from Wembley's first FA Cup
Final – Crilly and Thoms follow him from
Hartlepools United – 'Gentleman Jim' Moore scores
five; Storer twice nets four – Cup Marathon with
Newcastle – Eight Keetley brothers with League clubs*

C ECIL BERTRAM POTTER, George Jobey's immediate predecessor as Derby County's manager, was the Nearly Man. Nearly, but not quite, in both the Football League, where he piloted the club to the brink of promotion back to the First Division in each of the last two of his three seasons in charge, and the FA Cup, in which his men were just one step away from the first final to be staged at Wembley.

In moving to the Baseball Ground, Potter saddled himself with the intimidating task of following Jimmy Methven, whose service to the Rams dated back more than 30 years to 1891. A resolute full-back in more than 500 games during the first 15 of his seasons with Derby, latterly as captain, Methven earned further widespread respect in a dozen League seasons as manager. Twice he piloted the club to promotion, but failing eyesight made the end of his long reign inevitable in the wake of a third relegation. In those difficult and demanding circumstances, the arrival of the bespectacled Potter, in his early thirties and little known, was something of a let-down for Rams supporters who had been expecting the charismatic Colin Veitch[1] from Newcastle, but Potter built wisely and well on the strong nucleus of talent Methven had left him, and he handed

---

1. Colin Campbell McKechnie Veitch, one of the most versatile of footballers, captain of both his club and his country, and chairman of the PFA, played for Newcastle in five FA Cup finals (only one of which they won), and helped them to win three League titles, during a playing career that lasted from 1899 to 1914. His name suggests he was a Scot, but he was born at Newcastle-upon-Tyne and played six times for England from 1906 to 1909. After retiring as a player during the First World War, he coached Newcastle's junior teams until his controversial dismissal in 1926 ended his 27 years with United. He then spent two years as Bradford City's secretary-manager before becoming a sports reporter with the *Newcastle Chronicle*. He died in 1938 from pneumonia while convalescing in Switzerland.

on nine of the players Jobey mainly relied upon to clinch that elusive promotion in the season after his departure.

Potter, the son of a church minister, hailed from West Hoathly, a village between East Grinstead and Haywards Heath in Sussex, but he moved to Suffolk at an early age and in the summer of 1910 joined Ipswich Town, then of the Southern Amateur League, from the neighbouring club Melton. A year later he turned professional as an adaptable forward with Norwich City, for whom he was joint top scorer in the last Southern League season before the normal soccer competitions were suspended because of the 1914–18 war, but he did not stay on to accompany them as founder members of the Football League's Third Division in 1920.

Instead, he signed in 1919 for Hull City, having just spent a season with them as a guest player after also assisting Tottenham. Again, however, he soon moved on, making only ten Second Division appearances for the Humberside club—half of them at wing-half—before being appointed player-manager of Hartlepools United in the 1920 close season. This was at about the same time as George Jobey's transfer from Leicester to Northampton.

With the expansion of the new Third Division into North and South sections for 1921–22, Hartlepools were among those admitted to the Third North. Potter did well to steer them to a final fourth place, even though they were 14 points behind Stockport the promoted champions, but that first season of League football was a bad one financially for his new club. As prospects of an improvement in that direction were not exactly encouraging, he had no hesitation in accepting the offer, in July, 1922 that, promised greater scope and made him the first of Derby County's managers with a North-East connection. Jobey, of course, was the second, Brian Clough the third, Peter Taylor the fourth, Arthur Cox the fifth, and Jimmy Smith the sixth—Clough as a player with both Middlesbrough and Sunderland, and also as manager of Hartlepools United; Taylor as a Boro goalkeeper and Hartlepools assistant manager; the last two as former Newcastle managers.

Potter's first near-miss with Derby came on March 24th, 1923, at Chelsea's ground. That year's first FA Cup Final at Wembley seemed destined to feature the Rams as they progressed to their ninth semi-final (their 12th including replays) with the youngest team that had ever represented them—and without conceding a goal to any of the four clubs they overcame en route. At Stamford Bridge, however, they never recovered from the shock of having their defence breached twice in the first nine minutes by West Ham, and their hopes crumbled in the ruins of a 5–2 defeat.

The Rams slipped to 14th in the Second Division that season, the lowest final position they had occupied in the League up to that time. The Hammers, on the other hand, offset their disappointment of losing to Bolton Wanderers at the brand new Empire Stadium by scrambling into the second promotion place behind Notts County. They just pipped Leicester City on goal average despite being beaten at home by the champions in their last match. Even so, there were still pointers from League form in favour of a semi-final success for Derby, albeit distant ones, from the beginning of the season because they had followed a scoreless draw at Upton Park with a 2–1 win in the return game at the Baseball Ground.

Cecil Potter fielded the same team in all five of Derby's games in their Cup run, and in 16 matches that season in all. The team was:

Ben Olney; Bert Chandler, Tommy Crilly; Johnny McIntyre, Harry Thoms, Syd Plackett; George Thornewell, Jimmy Lyons, Randolph Galloway, Jim Moore, Lionel Murphy.

The Rams' new manager went back to Hartlepools United to make two of his former players, Crilly and Thoms, his first signings for the Rams on the eve of that 1922–23 season. Both these Stockton-born defenders went on to give the club excellent service before again moving on together in the 1928 close season to Crystal Palace with inside-forward Jimmy Gill, who, as will be recalled later, had himself joined the Rams with a clubmate.

After war-time Army service in France and Salonika, Tommy Crilly joined Hartlepools United when they were in the North-Eastern League. He was a member of the side that gained a 2–0 win at Wrexham when they played their first Football League match in the new Third Division North in 1921. He stepped straight into Derby's team as replacement for the injured Archie Ritchie, and was an automatic choice for five seasons, exceeding 200 appearances before spending five years with Palace. From there he moved to Northampton Town, with whom, as captain, he shared in another memorable 2–0 victory when they defeated Huddersfield Town, then leaders of the First Division, in a fourth-round FA Cup tie at Leeds Road. Further Cup glory followed while he was player-manager of Scunthorpe United, then members of the Midland League. Late in 1935, during his first season with that club, they knocked out Coventry City, who were

Tommy Crilly, pictured during the 1950s while he was licensee of the Hilton Arms in Osmaston Road, Derby. He and Harry Thoms joined the Rams from Hartlepools United in 1922 and left together for Crystal Palace in 1928.
(Derby Evening Telegraph)

managed by his former Derby clubmate Harry Storer. They won a replay after forcing a draw at the Highfield Road ground where they had been trounced by seven goals in the competition a year earlier.

On ending his playing days with Scunthorpe in 1937, Crilly returned to spend the rest of his life, up to his 65th year in January, 1960, at Derby, where he became licensee of the Hilton Arms in Osmaston Road. He revived his keen interest in the Rams ('my best club') by looking after the Reserves and Colts during the Second World War, and later by taking organised parties to the first team's away matches in addition to being a regular spectator at the Baseball Ground. His son Dennis played for the County's Colts as an amateur, and was afterwards with Atherstone in the Birmingham Combination.

Harry Thoms, who was twice wounded while serving in France during the 1914–18 war, trained as an electrical engineer before joining Hartlepools United. For about half of the £1,000 combined fee with Crilly, Derby County acquired a commanding, stopper-type centre-half who was noted for the strength of his shoulder charging. His near-200 games for the club included all but two of those in the 1925–26 promotion side, which he captained. After retiring from playing, he went back to the North-East, to Newcastle, where he died towards the end of 1970, aged 72.

Of the other members of the 1923 side that took Derby to their first FA Cup semi-final for 14 years, the third newcomer since Jimmy Methven had handed over the managerial reins was another North-Easterner, the splendidly named Septimus Randolph Galloway. A former boy musician in the Army, he was signed from a tramways team in his native Sunderland on the recommendation of 'Spud' Murphy, with whom he had been associated in Army football during the war. As Murphy had solved a pressing left-wing problem caused by the departure of Alf Quantrill to Preston (seven players were tried there in some five months before Murphy settled in), so Randolph Galloway, a former full-back, ended a quest that had pushed Potter into having five different players at centre-forward in successive games.

On the first Saturday of December, 1922, less than a month after signing professional forms, Galloway made his debut in a home match with Southampton, the club he was also to face when he last played for the Rams at the Baseball Ground nearly two years later. Neither he nor his new team-mates scored in a defeat on the former occasion, but he got one of the three goals, his 30th in 75 appearances, when the Saints were beaten on his home farewell. His last game for Derby was at Chelsea a week later, when Murphy was the visitors' successful marksman in a 1–1 draw.

Murphy, who had been playing for the Melton Mowbray club in Leicestershire, turned professional with the Rams in February, 1922, only a few days before playing his first League match in a comfortable home win over Clapton Orient, and he was soon being hailed by one enthusiastic local journalist as 'a genius'. Though that may be regarded as something of an exaggeration, he does hold a high place on the list of the club's outstanding left-wingers. He fell only one short of a half-century of goals in playing more than 200 games over some six years before leaving for Bolton, from where he went on to complete his career with Mansfield Town, Norwich City and Luton Town. He was back in Derby when he died, at the age of 73, in 1968, four years after Galloway.

Derby players and officials of the 1922–23 season. *Back row (left to right):* Johnny McIntyre, Steve Bloomer (then on the coaching staff), Bert Chandler, Harry Thoms, Cecil Potter (manager), Ben Olney, Tom Crilly, Harold Wightman, Syd Plackett, Laurie Edwards (trainer). *Front row:* Frank Keetley, George Thornewell, Jimmy Lyons, Randolph Galloway, Jim Moore, Lionel ('Spud') Murphy. Of these players, only Chandler, Lyons and Galloway were not with the Rams when they won promotion back to the First Division in 1925–26, George Jobey's first season as Derby's manager.
(Hulton Getty)

Galloway, whose fine form at full-back in schoolboy football had earned him selection for the North against the South, made his switch to centre-forward while with the Yorkshire Regiment in the last year of the war, after returning from service in India. His progress in his first season with Derby was checked by a broken nose, but he really came into his own in 1923–24, when he and inside-forwards Jackie Whitehouse and Harry Storer between them scored more goals (65) than any other League club's middle trio except Bolton's. Galloway's share was 21.

For clearing the first of the four Cup hurdles on their way to their Chelsea date with West Ham in 1923, Derby were indebted to some superb saves by Ben Olney, a Londoner brought up in the Birmingham area who was then in the first of his five seasons as a Rams regular. Their Blackpool visitors, who included two future Derby forwards, Harry Bedford and Georgie Mee, gave the County a real roasting for much of the first half, but the Seasiders ended up the unfortunate victims of an unconvincing home display, losing to goals scored by Moore and Lyons.

In the next round, on the other hand, Derby coped capably with a tricky task on being drawn away to Bristol City, who had a formidable record at Ashton Gate and were that season's Third South champions. The Rams progressed with something to spare as skipper Moore netted two in the first half, then, after being brought down, sportingly declined the chance of a hat-trick by leaving it to Lyons to convert a penalty with the last kick of the match.

Moore was again on the mark as the Wednesday (like Blackpool then with Derby in the Second Division) were defeated by the only goal in the heavy going at the Baseball Ground in the next round. It was an exhilarating game despite the conditions, and was decided by the captain's header only five minutes from the end. There was also just the one goal, scored by Galloway in the opening half, when Moore and his men confounded the pundits by knocking out First Division Tottenham in the quarter-final at White Hart Lane, but a win by a bigger margin would not have flattered Derby.

So to Stamford Bridge, a venue that was viewed inappreciatively by the Rams and their supporters because it was almost as good as a home tie for West Ham. The Upton Park club were certainly made to feel at home as they surged into an early two-goal lead, but wingers Thornewell and Murphy missed reasonable chances before two more West Ham goals in the first 15 minutes of the second half put the issue beyond all doubt. As the Hammers naturally eased up, Derby replied through Moore and an own goal by full-back Billy Henderson, only for their perplexed defence to be pierced for a fifth time. But for the brilliance of Olney, the margin could have been still wider.

Billy Brown and Billy Moore both scored twice for West Ham, whose other goal came from Jimmy Ruffell. This was their team, the same line-up that lost 2–0 to Bolton Wanderers at Wembley: Hufton; Henderson, Young; Bishop, Kay, Tresadern; Richards, Brown, Watson, Moore, Ruffell. George Kay, the captain, who had started his career with Bolton, was manager of Liverpool when they won the First Division championship in 1946–47 and were losing Cup finalists in 1950.

Jimmy Moore's five goals in five Cup games in 1923 were almost half as many as he scored in 35 League matches that season and five of his 11 in the Second Division came on Christmas Day, the first five in a 6–0 home win against Crystal Palace. 'The ball just came to me at the right time' he modestly said. These were almost the exact words that Irishman Peter Doherty repeated after he had scored his five in a defeat of Aston Villa by the same margin, also at the Baseball Ground, more than 20 years later.

Handsworth-born Moore, known as 'Gentleman Jim' was a centre-forward when Derby paid Glossop North End £1, 500 for him in May, 1911, but he soon showed that his remarkable dribbling powers made him more suited to either of the inside-forward positions. The promotion season of 1914–15 was his most successful as a scorer, with 22 goals in his ever-present 38 League games, but, with the war intervening and the Rams declining, he had to wait for his lone England cap until shortly after the semi-final exit against West Ham. He then formed an all-Derby right wing with George Thornewell and was a scorer in a 4–2 win over Sweden in Stockholm, in this team:

Williamson (Arsenal); **Ashurst** (Notts County), **Harrow** (Chelsea); **Patchitt** (Corinthians), **Seddon** (Bolton Wanderers), **Tresadern** (West Ham United); **Thornewell** (Derby County), **Moore** (Derby County), **Bedford** (Blackpool), **Walker** (Aston Villa), **Unwin** (Middlesbrough).

That was the first of four caps for Thornewell, who also scored. Billy Walker obtained England's other two goals. Derby's nippy little right-winger, who had come to Jimmy

'Gentleman Jim' Moore, scorer of
five goals in one match. He twice
helped the Rams to promotion.
(Derby Evening Telegraph)

George Thornewell—he and Sammy
Crooks were Derby's only regular
right-wingers between the wars.
(Derby Evening Telegraph)

Methven's attention while he and the then Rams manager had been working at the Rolls-Royce factory during the 1914–18 war, retained his place when England again won in Stockholm, by 3–1, a few days later. The Moore who scored twice on that occasion was, however, West Ham's not Derby's.

Thornewell's two other caps were also gained in winning sides abroad, in Paris in successive years. In the first of those games, in 1924, one of the scorers was England debutant Harry Storer, who by then he had moved forward into Jimmy Moore's place at inside-left in the Derby County team after making most of his early appearances at wing-half since his transfer from Grimsby Town.

Although born at Romiley, near Stockport in Cheshire, George Thornewell, the youngest of eight children, was only a few years old when his mother moved the family to Derby after his father's death, and he played for St James's Road School and Derby Boys before impressing Methven in the Rolls-Royce side. He left his apprentice training at the factory to train as a pilot in the Royal Air Force, as the Royal Flying Corps had recently been renamed, but the war ended before he could go into action, and he completed his apprenticeship on his return to civilian life.

Methven, again taking up his duties with Derby County, promptly made sure of securing Thornewell's registration for the Rams, and when they resumed their activities early in 1919 the new winger turned out for them in a Midlands Victory League that involved only three other clubs—West Bromwich, to whom Derby were runners-up, Aston Villa and Wolves. An automatic choice when League football was started up again later that year, Thornewell went on to make almost 300 appearances, stretching into the ninth post-war season.

In 1922–23, Derby County won only one of their ten remaining League matches after their hopes of a fourth Cup Final appearance had been dashed so decisively by West Ham. They were in some danger of joining Jobey's Wolves down into the Third Division as they lost each of their last five games, finishing only four points clear of the relegation zone. Yet in both the two other seasons of Cecil Potter's reign as manager, with largely the same set of players, Derby went desperately close to getting back into the First Division.

The most agonising of those two near-misses occurred in 1923–24. The Rams were deprived of promotion by a fraction of a goal, ending the season level on points with Bury who went up with Leeds United. With only two weeks to go, the odds favoured Derby, for they were second on goal average and had two more games to play, home and away against mid-table Leicester City, whereas third-placed Bury, who were also on 49 points, had only one match remaining. That was at home against a struggling Coventry City who, it transpired, were postponing their relegation for just one more season. The Lancashire club swung the odds back in their favour with an emphatic 5–0 victory, while Derby unexpectedly slipped up 3–0 at Filbert Street, leaving the Rams needing to triumph also by 5–0 in their final fixture to snatch the second promotion spot.

Three Bury directors in the Baseball Ground crowd of some 20, 000 on the following Saturday were dismayed to see Derby showing a relentless determination that earned them three goals without reply before the interval, and the hopes of the visitors from Gigg Lane seemed almost certain to be dashed when a fourth goal was added with the second half barely 20 minutes old. That, though, was where the scoring stopped. Try as they might, Derby just could not grab that vital fifth goal, Leicester surviving luckily when Moore and Galloway both struck an upright. The 4–0 win stranded Derby 0.015 of a goal short of going up. Bury's average was 1.800, Derby's 1.785. The final top placings were:

	P	W	D	L	F	A	Pts
Leeds United	42	21	12	9	61	35	54
Bury	42	21	9	12	63	35	51
Derby County	42	21	9	12	75	42	51
Blackpool	42	18	13	11	72	47	49

Jim Moore, recalled for only his fifth first-team game that season (and his first for three months) scored two of Derby's goals in that dramatic finale against Leicester. The others came from Storer and Galloway.

Such a shattering stumble at the final hurdle left the Rams rueing their missed chances despite being the highest-scoring club in the top two divisions. In just over three months, from the beginning of December until early March, they failed with four penalties—

wastefulness that was especially expensive in a 1–0 defeat at Hillsborough. There was, however, one very good reason why Bury could be considered well worthy of regaining First Division status at Derby's expense, for although they lost 2–1 at the Baseball Ground in the first round of the Cup, they were the only club to do the double over the Rams that season, beating them by 1–0 at Gigg Lane and 2–0 at Derby.

In those days, home and away matches between clubs were played on successive Saturdays, and late in the September of that 1923–24 season there was one of the most extraordinary quick changes of fortune in County's clashes with Bristol City, who were then newly out of Division Three South but destined for an immediate return. First, City won 3–2 at Derby, the decisive goal coming when Tom Crilly put the ball into his own net in attempting to pass back to goalkeeper Ben Olney. Then, a week later, the Rams turned the tables in the most amazing manner by running up eight goals without response at Ashton Gate for the biggest away win in their history. The hero of the hour was Harry Storer, who scored four in a row. Galloway netted twice, the other goals coming from Thornewell and Syd Plackett, a centre-forward turned wing-half from Sawley who had embarked upon a League career after recovering from wounds suffered during the fighting on the Somme in 1916. Plackett's was the first of only three goals he was to score for the club in more than 150 games before moving to Notts County.

Harry Storer also scored four in a 6–0 win in that season's Boxing Day home game with Nelson, the Lancashire club destined to go down with Bristol City, but in the final reckoning Derby were to regret the 2–1 defeat at Nelson that had spoiled their Christmas the previous day. A disputed penalty and an own goal cost precious points after Galloway had given the Rams an interval lead with an early breakthrough. Olney parried the spot kick, awarded when a shot cannoned off an upright onto one of Crilly's arms, but Newnes, the taker, followed up to score at the second attempt.

Derby's two other goals in the crushing of Nelson at the Baseball Ground were netted by Jackie Whitehouse, a schemer-scorer whose total of 17 that season—his first with the club following his signing from Birmingham—admirably complemented the 27 by Storer and the 21 by Galloway. All but one of those goals by Whitehouse, who had guested for Derby during the war, came in the League, the exception being the last-minute Cup winner against Bury. This led the Rams to an epic second-round clash with Newcastle United that extended to four meetings before the First Division club continued their advance towards victory over Aston Villa in the Wembley final.

That marathon lasted for seven hours, produced 20 goals, and was watched by an aggregate of 128, 391 spectators who paid £9, 113. Its duration equalled a record for the competition proper [2] that was also matched, curiously enough, in the same second round, by the tie in which Crystal Palace defeated Notts County by the odd goal of three after three scoreless draws.

---

2. In 1911–12, Barnsley beat Bradford City at the fourth attempt, by 3–2 after three scoreless draws in the fourth round. In 1922–23, Sheffield United twice drew 0–0 with Nottingham Forest in the first round, then by 1–1, before winning 1–0. That was the season in which the Blades, like Derby County, missed the chance to play in the first Wembley final. They lost 1–0 to Bolton in the other semi-final.

Harry Storer—one of whose four-goal feats came in a record away win at Bristol.
(Derby Evening Telegraph)

Jackie Whitehouse, a key signing from Birmingham after guesting for Derby during the First World War.
(Derby Evening Telegraph)

In the qualifying rounds of the following season, two ties (Barrow v Gillingham and Leyton v Ilford) went to five meetings, as had one between Woolwich Arsenal and New Brompton during the preliminary stages in 1899. It was not until 1955 that the nine hours Barrow had taken to overcome Gillingham took second place to a third-round serial in which Stoke City finally put paid to a Bury side that included two former Derby County players, Norman Nielson and Cecil Law. Including a first replay at Stoke which had to be abandoned after 22 minutes of extra time because of a snowstorm, that epic extended over five meetings to nine hours, 22 minutes, before Stoke snatched the decider at Old Trafford just one minute from the end of another extra period.[3]

The first three games between Derby County and Newcastle in February, 1924, all ended at 2–2. In each of them the Rams fielded a team that showed just two changes from the side that reached the previous season's last four, at inside-forward: Whitehouse

---

3. After all that, Stoke lost 3–1 at Swansea in the fourth round on the following Saturday. Their final replay with Bury, played on January 24th, was the seventh match between the clubs since Christmas Day, for the Cup marathon was preceded by League games over the holiday period in which Stoke won 3–2 at home and drew 1–1 at Bury.

and Storer for Lyons and Moore. Derby very nearly went out in the original tie at the Baseball Ground, but Storer saved them with his second goal only two minutes from time. Yet it was a match they might well have won, for Harry Thoms shot wide from the penalty spot after full-back Russell handled when the ball already appeared to be over the line; then Tom McDonald was made a gift of Newcastle's first goal, and the same player scored their second while Crilly was off the field injured.

Derby were the better side that day, but again it was not until the closing minutes that they survived in the first replay on Tyneside. Newcastle fully deserved the interval lead they gained through Scottish internationals Neil Harris and Willie Cowan, and it took an own goal to raise Rams hopes which Galloway salvaged with an equaliser from a late corner by Murphy, their outstanding player.

The venue for the second replay caused quite a problem. Derby wanted to play it at Sheffield, but Newcastle preferred Leeds. Manchester was agreed upon as a compromise, but that had to be ruled out when it was realised that Manchester City were to meet Halifax Town at Old Trafford in their second replay. Burnden Park, Bolton, was the eventual choice, and this time it was Newcastle's turn to feel fortunate to stay on the Cup path. Offsetting goals by Galloway and Thornewell, one in each half, they scored first from a controversial penalty, then following a disputed free kick in the last minute of extra time.

Bolton neutrals in the crowd were particularly vociferous in their disapproval of the penalty which was awarded while left-winger Stan Seymour (later a powerful figure at Newcastle in an administrative capacity) was appealing for a corner kick after Chandler had appeared to tackle him legitimately. Thoms also made what many considered a fair tackle when he conceded the free kick that led to the last-gasp equaliser and although he then headed the ball away as it was put into the goalmouth, it fell at the feet of the unmarked Seymour who promptly put it back into the net.

As a result of those dubious decisions the referee was changed for the third replay at the request of both clubs, J.T. Howcroft, of Bolton, taking over from E.E. Rothwell, of St Anne's-on-Sea. Again there was difficulty deciding on a neutral venue—so much so that it was agreed not to have one, the matter being settled by the toss of a coin. This was won by Newcastle, giving them the considerable advantage of playing once more on their own ground.

Derby had to make their first team change in four matches, the injured Thornewell giving way to Frank Keetley, a member of the remarkable Derby footballing family that produced eight brothers who were all professionals with League clubs. This was the list, as given to me by Frank:

> Albert–Burton United (for whom he played in the Second Division at 17).
> Arthur–Tottenham Hotspur.
> Charlie–Leeds United, Bradford City and Reading. (The youngest of the brothers. He scored 110 goals in 169 League and Cup games for Leeds, whom he helped to promotion to the First Division in 1927–28. In one Central League game he scored seven goals for their reserve side against Bolton.)
> Frank–Derby County, Doncaster Rovers, Bradford City, Lincoln City, Hull City.

Harold–Doncaster Rovers, Mansfield Town, Blackburn Rovers.
Jack–Hull City.
Joe–Bolton Wanderers, Accrington Stanley, Liverpool, Wolves, Wrexham,
    Doncaster Rovers.
Tom–Bradford, Doncaster Rovers, Notts County.

In all there were 11 brothers and a sister. The other brothers, Bill (the eldest), Laurence and Sydney, did not play football professionally. Frank, the only one of them to turn out for Derby County, joined the Rams in 1921 from the Victoria Ironworks team in the town which also supplied most of his brothers to League football. He made just over 80 League and Cup appearances before moving to Doncaster in the summer of 1926. While with the Rovers, he played on the right wing in an attack that contained three of his brothers: Harold at inside-right, Tom at centre-forward, and Joe at inside-left. The odd man out was named Hargreaves, a left-winger who was later with Sunderland.

When I met Frank Keetley, some 15 years before his death a couple of months short of his 67th birthday at the start of 1968, he was the licensee of the Red Lion Inn at

Frank Keetley, the only member of the Derby
family of footballing brothers to play for the Rams.
(Derby Evening Telegraph)

Sidbury, a village near Bridgnorth. He had moved there almost 20 years earlier, on beginning a two-year spell as Worcester City's player-manager in the mid-1930s. In that role he followed Jackie Whitehouse, who moved to the Southern League club after post-Derby service with Sheffield Wednesday, Bournemouth and Folkestone Town. When Frank Keetley also left Worcester City he joined Whitehouse as a southern area scout for Derby County—a role in which he got off to a flying start by putting forward the recommendation that led to the Rams' signing from Cheltenham Town of Tim Ward, a wing-half who went on to play for England and to include Derby County among the clubs he managed.

Frank Keetley had only limited first-team opportunities during the 1925–26 season in which Derby County at last regained First Division status, but after leaving Doncaster he helped both Bradford City (1928–29) and Lincoln City (1931–32) to promotion from the Third North. Early in 1932, he also completed the only case of two brothers each registering a double hat-trick in a League game. Some three years earlier, Tom had scored his six for Doncaster against Ashington. Frank emulated him for Lincoln against Halifax Town, claiming all his goals in the second half.

The Derby County team in which Frank Keetley took over on the right wing for the fourth and deciding clash with Newcastle at St James's Park on February 13th, 1924 was:

Olney; Chandler, Crilly; McIntyre, Thoms, Plackett; Keetley, Whitehouse, Galloway, Storer, Murphy.

Newcastle, who called upon 15 players during the serial, fielded:

Mutch; Hampson, Hudspeth; Mooney, Spencer, Gibson; Low, Cowan, Harris, McDonald, Seymour.

In each of the three previous games Newcastle had been the first to score. On this occasion it was Derby who set the pace, Galloway giving them a 15th-minute lead. Five minutes later, however, Harris equalised, and on the half-hour he put United ahead. Galloway brought the scores level again shortly before half-time, only for Harris to round off a splendid hat-trick almost immediately. The second half was only eight minutes old when Seymour made it 4–2 and, although Storer reduced the deficit with half-an-hour left, Cowan sealed a well-deserved victory with the home side's fifth goal. This has remained Derby County's longest ever Cup-tie, but not Newcastle's. In 1989, in the third round, their fourth meeting with Watford went to extra time before they were beaten by an only goal.

On now to Cecil Potter's third and final season as Derby County's manager in 1924–25—and to another so-near promotion. Without a Cup run to distract them (they fell to Bradford City at the first fence) the Rams again came third in the Second Division, and although they this time ended two points behind the runners-up, it was not until the last fortnight that they slipped out of the top two in losing narrowly to Stoke at the Baseball Ground. Their remaining two games, away to Coventry and at home to Blackpool, were both drawn, and the promotion places stayed firmly in the possession of Leicester City and Manchester United. This was how they finished:

	P	W	D	L	F	A	Pts
Leicester City	42	24	11	7	90	32	59
Manchester United	42	23	11	8	57	23	57
Derby County	42	22	11	9	71	36	55
Portsmouth	42	15	18	9	58	50	48

Some Derby fans even began to wonder if the club really wanted to go up, an odd notion that was soon to be nailed on the head under the George Jobey regime. In fact, the Rams had done well to sustain their challenge for so long under the handicap of injuries to such key men as Storer, Thornewell, Thoms and Plackett. Having been out from shortly before Christmas until near the end of March, Storer was injured again scoring the only goal of a tetchy home match with Chelsea, and the faithful Jim Moore continued to deputise manfully in his further absences. The other gaps were plugged by Frank Keetley, Harold Wightman, who took over in central defence, and Bernard McLaverty, a former Durham City captain whose half-back versatility stood Derby in good stead over more than seven seasons, but chiefly as a stand-in, before his departure to Norwich City.

The main change Cecil Potter made that season was brought about by the illness that caused Randolph Galloway to drop out of the side after the first two games. The man brought in at centre-forward, Albert Fairclough, proved so successful that Galloway could not re-establish himself on his return to fitness, and, priced at £ 2,500, was soon on his way to Nottingham Forest. After sharing the rest of his playing career between Luton, Coventry and Tottenham, Galloway was trainer-coach of Sporting Lisbon, who won the Portuguese championship in each of the three seasons he spent with them, and then of the Penarol club that had eight players in Uruguay's World Cup-winning team of 1950. On returning to England, Galloway took up a similar post with Gillingham but resigned after only six weeks. He died ten years later, in 1964.

The bustling Bert Fairclough scored nearly 40 goals for Eccles Borough in one Lancashire Combination season before entering League football in 1913 with Manchester City, who signed him, along with a couple of his clubmates—his younger brother and a player named Abbott—at a combined fee of £300. All three found few opportunities with City, playing only just over a dozen first-team games between them. Bert also had a lean time at Preston, against whom he had scored five goals in a reserve match, before blossoming with Southend United.

His consistent scoring for the Essex club, including two hat-tricks, soon caught the attention of Bristol City with whom, in successive seasons, he had the roller-coaster experience of going close to reaching the First Division, being relegated from Division Two, climbing back as Third South champions, and then going down again immediately before his transfer to Derby County in the 1924 close season.

Despite missing several matches through injury, Fairclough was the Ashton Gate club's top scorer in their 1922–23 promotion season, his 21 goals including eight in four games and a hat-trick on his reappearance at Southend. With Derby he soon revealed the good form he had shown in getting one of City's goals in their win at Derby the week before the Rams' eight-goal romp in the West Country, scoring four times in a 5–1 home win against Fulham in only his third match for the County. Among his 22 in 32 games in his first season with Derby there was also a hat-trick in a 6–1 defeat of Portsmouth.

Fairclough, however, blotted his copybook when he incurred a 14-day suspension after being ordered off, and in a crucial match at Leicester the week before the costly failure against Stoke the Rams dropped another vital point in a scoreless draw when he had a penalty saved in the last minute. At the beginning of April, a Wightman goal earned an important home victory over the other promoted club, Manchester United, but Derby went without a further success in their remaining six matches. Four of them were drawn, three without a goal, as the prize of promotion once more drifted just out of reach.

Cecil Potter intended to leave football to take over a dairy business in Sussex when he parted company with Derby County in the summer of 1925, but within a few days he was approached by Huddersfield Town, who were looking to fill the daunting gap caused by Herbert Chapman's move to manage Arsenal.

In accepting the post, Potter had to contend not only with the comparisons that were inevitably made with his illustrious predecessor—who had piloted the Yorkshire club to the First Division championship in each of the last two seasons—but also with attempting to maintain that momentum while adapting his new team's style to the demands of the recent change in the off-side law.

In June, 1925, the month before Potter took over at Huddersfield, the International Board decided, at a meeting in Paris, to adopt the Scottish FA's proposal that a player should not be off-side if two defenders, instead of three, were nearer their own goal-line. Huddersfield had an early experience, in a 5–5 draw at Tottenham, of the freak, high-scoring games that the uncertainties of this alteration produced before defences got to grips with it, but Potter had inherited a playing staff of such strength, freshly augmented by the signing of the brilliant Scottish winger Alex Jackson from Aberdeen, that his new charges duly pulled off the title hat-trick with five points to spare despite losing their last two matches. It was an achievement to which Herbert Chapman was to point Arsenal, who were runners-up that year, but one that, due to his untimely death, he was unable to see through to its conclusion.

For Huddersfield, who had prefaced their League triumphs with victory in the 1922 FA Cup Final (two years after being losing finalists), the transformation was astounding since the financial crisis of late 1919 that had almost driven them out of existence. What was more, they were runners-up in both the next two seasons after their title treble, but by that time Cecil Potter was no longer their manager. He had just the one year in charge, resigning only a few days before the 1926–27 campaign opened because the stress of keeping Town at the top had taken toll of his health.

He again planned to leave the game, yet before the end of the year he was tempted back to manage Norwich City, one of his former clubs as a player, who were then struggling in the Southern Section of Division Three. Early in the following season Norwich went to the head of the table for the first time, but they tailed away to finish in the lower half, and they were down at the bottom when, in January, 1929, Potter resigned in the wake of a 5–0 third-round home Cup defeat by the amateurs of the Corinthians.

An application for re-election was avoided as Norwich improved after his exit to finish 17th for the second successive season, five points above wooden spoonists Gillingham. There was no way back for Potter, this time no change of mind. He stayed out of soccer and lived to enjoy a long retirement that lasted until October, 1975, when he died at the age of 86.

CHAPTER 4

Jobey Finds Blackpool So Bracing

*Fazackerley and Davison rejoin Jobey from Wolves –
Plackett only ever-present in 1925–26 promotion side
– Big deal brings goalscoring Bedford back to
Derbyshire – Late slip-ups lost title chance –
'Shortie' the Singing Winger – Cooper and Collin
in full-back partnership*

A ND SO BACK WE COME TO GEORGE JOBEY, an inspired choice as manager of
Derby County. Brought back into the game in 1925 from his year's absence in
the hotel business, he readily succeeded where Cecil Potter had so narrowly failed,
restoring the club to the top flight in his first season.

The regulars, from Jimmy Methven's reign, who still remained for the Rams' belated
rise as runners-up to the Wednesday were goalkeeper Olney, wing-halves McIntyre
and Plackett, wingers Thornewell and Murphy, inside-forward Storer and the versatile
defender Wightman, with Keetley, McLaverty, Moore and Ritchie in reserve. Added
to these were Potter signings Crilly and Thoms in defence, Fairclough and Whitehouse
in attack. The consistent Bert Chandler had just left for Newcastle, having gone close
to 200 League and Cup appearances, and Jimmy Lyons, the former Hednesford forward
whose high point had been to score all four goals in a defeat of Rotherham, had joined
Wrexham after being kept in the background for the past couple of seasons.

The basic changes made initially by George Jobey were at right-back and centre-
forward. For his first match—goalless at Hull after a kick-off delayed by a missed train
connection on the way—his only alteration from Potter's first-choice line-up was the
temporary inclusion of Jim Tootle in Chandler's place as Tom Crilly's partner. Tootle,
signed as defensive cover from Southport the previous Christmas Day, was to have
only two further opportunities before giving way to Harold Wightman.

Injury put Bert Fairclough out of the reckoning after the opening day, and to fill that
vacancy at the head of the attack Jobey first turned to one of the two players who, as
in Potter's case with Crilly and Thoms, rejoined him from the last of his previous clubs.
This was Preston-born Stan Fazackerley, who having fallen out of favour at Wolverhampton after being a key member of the team Jobey had guided out of the Third
North in 1924, had been on loan to Kidderminster Harriers while on the Wanderers'
transfer list. Fazackerley, signed by Derby a few days before Jobey's appointment,

scored two goals on his debut in a 3–1 home win over Clapton Orient, but those were his only goals for the Rams' first team in which he made just two further appearances. Then nearing his 35th birthday, he was well past his best and shortly before the end of that 1925–26 season he retired on medical advice.

The other player reunited with George Jobey at the Baseball Ground was centre-half Tommy Davison. He became a Derby player on the same August day of 1925 that his old boss accepted the County's offer. Jobey had signed him for Wolves from Durham City, to whom he had graduated from Tanfield Lea Juniors shortly before their move up from the North-Eastern League to the Football League's new Third Division North. Although his first-team chances had been restricted at Molineux by the consistent form of Bill Caddick, he had received one of the inscribed gold watches presented to Wolves' players by a group of the club's admirers to commemorate their promotion as the Third North champions in 1924. The watch was one of his most treasured possessions.

Davison, a most popular mine host at the Nottingham Arms in Derby's London Road when I met him, also found it difficult at first to break into Derby County's League side—so consistent remained his fellow North-Easterner, Harry Thoms. The Rams' captain was the kingpin of one of the most efficient half-back lines of the time, flanked by Johnny McIntyre and Syd Plackett for the best part of the three seasons, culminating in the eventual clinching of the return to the First Division.

Indeed, Davison played only once in the promotion side, making his debut in a narrow defeat at Southampton in Thoms' rare absence through injury. In the following season he did not get into the team at all as Thoms achieved the ever-present record Plackett alone maintained in the escape from Division Two. It was not until December, 1927, more than two years after his move to Derby, that Davison gained an extended opportunity as Thoms finally faded from the scene. Having survived war wounds in France, Thoms proved a real bargain for Derby at £500, playing in nearly 200 games. Davison, after getting close to a century of appearances, was himself ousted by Jack Barker, a centre-half who was to become one of George Jobey's soundest signings and rank among the most resolute of defenders ever to represent the Rams. He features prominently later.

Another Jobey jewel solved the problem at centre-forward which caused the greatest concern in the early months of the new manager's reign. The emergency arose when Bert Fairclough again dropped out through injury, after returning in place of Fazackerley for only one match—or 80 minutes of a match to be exact. Recalled at Blackpool on September 12th, 1925, Fairclough scored both goals by which Derby gained a rare away win over the Seasiders after falling behind in the third minute. Unfortunately, ten minutes from time he was carried off with a torn thigh muscle, and the man who replaced him as County's first choice after his recovery was his opposite number in that game.

Altogether, George Jobey tried four leaders of the Rams' attack in their first six games of the season (the other two were Whitehouse and Keetley) before going into the transfer market for the player who produced the attacking punch that at last broke through the promotion barrier. For a fee of £3,250, he pulled off one of the most publicised deals of the season by bringing back to Derbyshire from Blackpool the free-scoring Harry Bedford, forerunner in the succession of top-grade centre-forwards for whom Derby County were to be renowned throughout the remaining inter-war years.

Tommy Davison, who played for George Jobey with both Wolves and Rams.
(Derby Evening Telegraph)

Harry Bedford, first of the free-scoring centre-forwards during George Jobey's Derby reign.
(Derby Evening Telegraph)

Born at Calow, near Chesterfield, Bedford played for Grassmoor Ivanhoe in the Chesterfield and District League before joining Nottingham Forest near the end of the 1914–18 war. His colleagues at the City Ground included his elder brother Walter (better known as 'Nutty') and in the last season before League football was resumed he made a few appearances in teams that also included Noah Burton and Harold Wightman as guests.

Basford-born Burton, who had signed for Derby as an amateur at the end of 1915, rejoined the Rams fresh from scoring the goal which gave Forest the Victory Shield at Everton in 1919. He ended the first post-war League season as the County's leading scorer, if with a modest tally of 12 in the League and one in the Cup, but, with relegation inescapable, he was then caught up in the team's goal drought that also engulfed his fellow inside-forward, 'Tiddler' Murray, who had won an England amateur cap before leaving Bishop Auckland to turn professional at Derby.

After just that one depressing season of 1920–21, Murray moved to Middlesbrough, then went into Scottish football with Hearts and Dunfermline. Burton's departure, at about the same time, took him back to Forest. There he enjoyed the most successful period of his career in helping them to win the Second Division title in 1922 and becoming one of their most popular players before retiring ten years later.

Harold Wightman, who came from Sutton-in-Ashfield, also found his way back to Forest—but not until 17 years after being taken onto the Baseball Ground playing staff in May 1919. He made almost 200 appearances for the Rams, eventually becoming George Jobey's assistant, before returning to the Chesterfield club he had first joined as a teenager. From there, in 1930, he became manager-coach of Notts County, then was briefly back with Derby as chief scout between spells as manager at Luton and Mansfield.

He went back to the City Ground, in the summer of 1936, as the first team manager to be appointed by Forest. By that time, however, the Reds had been down in the Second Division again for more than ten years, and he was unable to lift them from its lower reaches before being replaced by Billy Walker, the former Aston Villa and England forward, towards the end of the last pre-war season of 1938–39.

Harry Bedford scored twice on his Second Division debut for Forest in a 4–1 home win over Rotherham in September, 1919. It was another two-goal display, in which he gave Blackpool's defence a real run-around, that persuaded the Seasiders to make a successful bid of about £1,500 for him in March, 1921. Then aged 21, he was on the threshold of a career that was about to take off in a big way.

Harold Wightman, an adaptable defender who became
George Jobey's assistant.
(Derby Evening Telegraph)

Almost exactly a year earlier, Blackpool had upset their supporters, and also their chances of promotion, by accepting a badly-needed £3,000 fee from Birmingham for Joe Lane, another centre-forward with a keen eye for goal. This doubly detrimental effect was to be repeated when continued financial difficulties at Bloomfield Road forced Bedford's sale to Derby, but in the meantime the problem Lane had left behind him was admirably solved as the ex-Forester fired up the Lancashire's club's attack with 118 goals in 180 games—even though promotion remained elusive. Bedford was twice the country's top scorer, with 32 goals in 1922–23, and 33 in 1923–24, and to two England caps he added an appearance for the Football League in which he netted four times against the Irish League.

Bedford was to keep up the good work with Derby, scoring 152 goals in 218 matches, averaging nearly 30 a season in just over five years, before moving on to Newcastle. At that point, his total of 270 made him the most prolific scorer in English first-class soccer since the First World War. He was such an immediate success at the Baseball Ground, with early hat-tricks against Swansea and Stoke (he had the ball in the net a fourth time in the 7–3 defeat of the Potters, but just after the final whistle) that Bert Fairclough had to drop into the Third Division with Gillingham to find a first-team place.

Coincidentally, Harry Bedford's first match for Derby County was at the ground of his first League club, and although he did not make a scoring debut he provided the pass from which 'Spud' Murphy completed a 2–1 win. The Rams' first goal was a rare one by Harry Thoms, the second of four for Derby; Noah Burton netted against his old club for Forest.

It was in Derby's next fixture that Bedford got off the mark, with three of their five goals against Swansea on his first home appearance. After scoring a dozen in his first eight games he went on to total 28 in 35 League and Cup matches, putting him well clear of the club's next highest scorers, Murphy (13) and Storer (9). He was also to be the Rams' top marksman in each of the next four seasons. Five of his goals in 1925–26 came as the double was landed with two 4–1 victories over the Wednesday—the champions with whom they went up. He scored two at Hillsborough, and did the hat-trick in the return game. Another goal was the one that fittingly clinched the climb in the final home match, against an Oldham Athletic side that included the former Derby favourite Horace Barnes.

Whether or not it was simply a case of relaxing when the pressure was off, defeats in their last two games cost County the title. Perhaps it was not altogether surprising that, with Bedford again their scorer, they lost 2–1 away to Chelsea, their closest rivals for the second promotion place. There was quite an anti-climax, however, when they completed their programme with a 3–0 defeat away to the bottom club, Stockport County—especially as the new centre-forward hero failed with a twice-taken penalty and Jimmy Gill had a goal disallowed when, according to one account, 'to everybody but the referee it was obvious that the ball was over the line'. As a rare low point in a season that otherwise had so much to savour, that setback at Stockport compared only with the shock 4–1 reverse at Third Division Southend which knocked the Rams off the Cup trail after they had battled through two replays to account for Portsmouth.

Bedford, usually a reliable penalty-taker, admitted to me that his worst experience was missing the chance of a winner from the spot near the end of a home game against

Huddersfield, who had gone three up inside the opening half-hour but had been pulled back to 4–4.

In another home match, this time against West Ham, and with the Rams five goals ahead, skipper Harry Storer decided that a penalty kick conceded in the final minute should be taken not by Bedford, who had already scored four times, but by Tommy Davison. Davison made such a success of the job, tucking the ball away into one corner of the net while the long-serving Ted Hufton, an England goalkeeper who earned something of a 'penalty king' reputation for his saves from the spot, threw himself full length in the opposite direction, that he was again called upon when Derby were next awarded a penalty in front of a Sunderland crowd which included many of his friends and relations.

Telling me the story against himself, Tommy recalled that the home goalkeeper, a young man named Robinson, puzzled him by standing close to his right-hand post as he prepared to shoot. Nevertheless, he decided to try 'selling the dummy' that had worked with Hufton and hit the ball straight at where the goalkeeper was standing after shaping to send it into the opposite corner. But Robinson did not move—except to bend down calmly and save. The Rams lost 3–1 and, as Davison cheerfully confessed, that spot of embarrassment caused them to hand the responsibility for taking penalties back to Bedford.

In the 1925–26 promotion season, Jackie Whitehouse took over the penalty-taking from Fairclough before Bedford came into the side, converting one in a draw with Southampton at the Baseball Ground. Bedford then made a successful start to the job when he obtained from the spot one of his two goals that sent Wolves home pointless a few weeks afterwards, but he was out injured on the day the next penalty was awarded to Derby—against Blackpool of all teams. In his absence, the kick was planted past goalkeeper Best, who was making his debut for Bedford's former club by another newcomer, Jack Hart, a 19-year-old centre-forward George Jobey signed from Mansfield Town less than 48 hours after Bedford had been put out of action during the second replay of the third-round Cup-tie against Portsmouth at Leicester.

Hart, a Bolsover-born six-footer, had scored 45 goals in 16 matches for Mansfield, then a Midland League club, whom he joined from Firth Park, a Sheffield junior team, after assisting Bolsover Colliery in the Derbyshire Senior League. That impressive haul had included eight hat-tricks, bags of five and six in reserve games against Whitwell among them, but with Derby his first-team chances were limited to just four as Bedford's deputy.

In those few matches he scored three times, and the penalty that got him off the mark on his debut towards the end of January in 1926 set the Rams on their way to a 5–2 home victory against the club then managed by their former centre-half Frank Buckley. Derby's other men on the mark were Enos Bromage, Frank Keetley, Harry Storer and George Thornewell.[1] It was the first time all five forwards had scored for the club in one game since November 1895, when John Miller, John Paul (a former Hibernian winger standing

---

1. In the interim there were four other matches, each of them at home, in which five different Derby players scored, but not all of them were forwards. Those games, with the non-forwards shown in italics, were: November 1896, Derby 5 (J. Goodall, *Cox*, *Stevenson*, Miller, *J. Turner*), Stoke City 1; January 1897, Derby 8 (Bloomer 3. Fisher 2, J. Goodall,

The Placketts

Sydney Plackett, the only player to take part in all Derby County's 42 matches when they won promotion back to the First Division in 1925–26, was a descendant of the well-known Breaston family who could field complete football and cricket teams. His father helped Long Eaton Rangers to win the Birmingham Cup, and was captain of Loughborough at the time Syd was born at Sawley in September, 1897.

After starting out at centre-forward with the Sawley United Church team, Syd, just turned 17, joined the Army early in the 1914–18 war and was wounded during the heavy fighting on the Somme in 1916. Following his demobilisation in March, 1919, he spent a season as captain of the Sawley Discharged Soldiers Federation club, still as a centre-forward. Having fully regained his fitness, he showed such impressive form, scoring regularly in the Long Eaton and District League, that Derby County snapped him up for just the £10 signing-on fee in January, 1921, after he had been given two trials by Doncaster Rovers and also attracted the attention of Notts County and the Wednesday.

Soon afterwards, he was switched so successfully to left-half that he made all of his 156 League and Cup appearances for the Rams in that position, forming a most effective middle line with Johnny McIntyre and Harry Thoms, and causing Harry Storer to be switched from there to inside-forward after recovering from injury.

Notts County, for whom he played approaching 100 League games, eventually signed Plackett in February, 1927, but they had to pay the Rams what was described as a 'respectable' price. He was 52 when he died at the White Horse Inn, Whitwick, in Leicestershire, in May, 1949.

Laurence (Lol) Plackett was the first Derby County player with an ever-present record in a Football League season—in the inaugural campaign of 1888–89 during most of which he formed the Rams left wing with his brother Henry. Both played at Long Eaton before joining the Rams, and both moved to Nottingham Forest.

A. Goodall, McQueen), Barnsley St Peter's 1; February 1899, Derby 6 (Boag 2, Oakden, MacDonald, *A. Goodall*, Bloomer), Wolves 2; November 1902, Derby 5 (*A. Goodall*, A. Turner, Bloomer, *Warren*, Richards), Sunderland 2. The game with Barnsley St Peter's was in the first round of the FA Cup; the others were in the League.

in for John Goodall), Jimmy Stevenson, each with two apiece, Hugh McQueen and Steve Bloomer had shared the goals in the 8–0 defeat of Small Heath.

Enos Bromage was a member of another prominent Derby footballing family which, though smaller in number, outdid even the Keetleys in supplying three of its members to the Rams. He was making his only senior appearance of that promotion season—as left-wing deputy for Murphy—and one of only six he was allowed in the four years between his arrival from Sheffield United and his departure to Gillingham. He was subsequently with Nottingham Forest, Chester and Wellington Town.

Blackpool's defeat at Derby on Jack Hart's debut day was the first of three successive heavy reverses they suffered on their travels, with five goals also conceded against Port Vale in the Potteries and six at Swansea, but they lost only twice more in their last dozen matches to finish sixth in the Second Division table. Derby County also ended on a strong note, with five straight wins before their late fade-out after clinching the runners-up promotion place, and, with Chelsea losing at Portsmouth in their last match, the Rams had five points to spare over the Stamford Bridge club in these final leading positions:

	P	W	D	L	F	A	Pts
Sheffield Wednesday	42	27	6	9	88	48	60
Derby County	42	25	7	10	77	42	57
Chelsea	42	19	14	9	76	49	52
Wolverhampton W	42	21	7	14	84	60	49
Swansea Town	42	19	11	12	77	57	49
Blackpool	42	17	11	14	76	69	45

After so successfully settling the centre-forward question, George Jobey had other difficulties to deal with that season which arose on the run-in to promotion. He was deprived of Jackie Whitehouse from the turn of the year because of an operation for appendicitis, and an injury caused Harry Storer to miss the last two months of the season. In finding the answers soon after the veteran Jim Moore,[2] in responding to a couple of emergency calls, had become the only member of the 1914–15 title team to aid this further regaining of top status, Jobey made Harry Bedford feel even more at home by going back to Blackpool to snap up inside-forward Jimmy Gill and left-winger Georgie Mee at a joint fee of £3,750.

---

2. Moore's first-team chances had been restricted, first by the switching of Harry Storer from wing-half to inside-forward, and then by a knee injury that required an operation after he had regained his place. He was brought back in February, 1926, at centre-forward at Southampton, scoring in a 2–1 defeat, then three days later played at inside-right at Swansea, where Derby lost 2–0. Those games took his League appearances for the Rams to 203, in which he totalled 75 goals. He also scored seven times in 15 Cup-ties. One of eight players placed on the transfer list in March, 1926, he moved to Chesterfield, for whom he had guested during the 1914–18 war. In November the following year he left there for Mansfield Town, and in March, 1929, he joined Worcester City.

The deal was completed the day before Sheffield-born Gill's first League club, the Wednesday, were the visitors to the Baseball Ground, so, although the newcomers had been signed too late to be considered for selection, they were invited to travel down to Derby to watch the match which the Rams won comfortably with one of Bedford's hat-tricks. When I met Georgie Mee on one of his return visits to Derby in the 1950s, he still remembered very clearly having to sit out that defeat of the Wednesday. He told me:

> Jimmy and I sat on the touchline and saw Derby gain a clear-cut victory. We were most impressed, but Jimmy remarked as the game ended 'I can see one weakness—the inside-right position'. Turning to him, I retorted 'What? You can see a weakness after they've won so easily? It looks to me as if there are 11 weaknesses. We'll be in the reserves next week!'

That jocular prediction proved only half right. Mee did have to wait a little longer for his Derby debut, but on the following Saturday Gill was brought into the side—not at inside-right but at inside-left, where he filled the injured Storer's place. What was more, he scored the goal that earned another victory, away to a Stoke City team heading for relegation to the Northern Section of the Third Division. Soon after that, Gill was switched to partner George Thornewell in his usual position on the attack's right flank, and Murphy was moved to the other inside-forward berth to accommodate Mee on the left wing for the rest of that season.

Jimmy Gill, who followed Harry Bedford from
Blackpool to Derby with Georgie Mee.

The Invisible Reporter

Harry Bedford suffered from one of Georgie Mee's japes one Christmas while the Rams were staying at a hotel for an away match. After a late breakfast, Mee, disguising his voice, phoned Bedford and told him that he was a news-paperman who would like an interview with him later in the day. Harry agreed, and at the appointed time he waited in the lounge for the 'reporter'.

Several of the other players, who were in on the secret, tried to persuade Bedford to go with them for a walk, but he refused because he was 'waiting for a friend'. The Rams' centre-forward waited there in vain for more than an hour, and it was not until the players were returning home on the train that he discovered that he had been the victim of one of 'Shortie' Mee's leg-pulls. What he had to say bears no repetition here.

Mee, whose younger brother Bertie[3] managed Arsenal's double-winning team of 1970–71, had been Blackpool's established outside-left throughout Bedford's stay at Bloomfield Road, but Gill, a former schoolboy international, had not joined the staff there until the month after the centre-forward's move to Derby. In fact, Gill, who had gained a reputation as one of the fastest forwards in the game while with the Wednesday, played only a few times in the same Blackpool front line as Mee, and he made little more than a dozen appearances for the Seasiders before George Jobey signed him. The most fruitful period of his career up to that time had been spent with Cardiff City, for, after leaving Sheffield in time for the Welsh club's admission to the Second Division in 1920, he not only helped towards immediate promotion, as runners-up to Birmingham, but also went very close to being a member of the first team from outside England to win both the First Division title and FA Cup.

As the last day of the 1923–24 season dawned, Cardiff were at the top of the table, one point ahead of Huddersfield Town. The week before, Cardiff had won 2–0 at home

---

3. Bertie Mee, who, like his brother, was born at Bulwell, near Nottingham, was a winger on Derby County's books shortly before the 1939–45 war, but did not play in their first team before moving to Mansfield, where his playing career was ended by injury. After Army service he qualified as a physiotherapist and in 1960 joined Arsenal as trainer and physio. Then, from 1966 until his retirement in 1976, he became their manager. He returned to the game with Watford as general manager until 1986, after which he continued for a few more years as a director.

against Birmingham, but their concluding return game at St Andrew's was goalless. Thereby hung the distressing tale of the Birmingham fist that cost them the League title. In the last minute, a shot from Welsh international Len Davies was bound for the net when Percy Barton, a defender capped by England, fisted the ball out. Davies himself took the penalty kick, but Dan Tremelling, who later kept goal for England, brought off a brilliant save. Huddersfield, meanwhile, were completing a 3–0 home victory over Nottingham Forest that put them level on points with Cardiff, and the Yorkshire club edged to the start of their title hat-trick by a fractionally superior goal average (0.024) with figures of 60 33 to 61 34. Forest had a similarly close escape from relegation, at Chelsea's expense.

In the following season, although Cardiff slipped back to mid-table, they reached Wembley. Gill was at inside-right in the team that lost there to Sheffield United—by a single goal scored by left-winger, Fred Tunstall, just after the half-hour—but he had left for Blackpool by the time the Welsh club again won through to the final two years later and made history by becoming the first club to take the trophy out of England.

The story has been told many times, but bears repetition here, of how the ball trickled into Arsenal's net for the late decider, when another goalkeeping Dan, named Lewis, (who soon afterwards was capped by Wales) fumbled a speculative low shot from Scottish centre-forward Hugh Ferguson. The sheen on the goalkeeper's brand new jersey was partly blamed for his failure to prevent the ball slipping under his right arm, and for their subsequent finals the London club made a special point of having their keeper's new jersey washed before the game in an attempt to avert a similar mishap.

Successful though Jimmy Gill was with Cardiff City, heading their scorers' list in two of his five seasons at Ninian Park besides scheming to consistently good effect, the reason given for his short stay at Blackpool was that he did not blend satisfactorily with his new colleagues. He did not show up too well in the heavy defeat at Derby the month before his move there, but neither that below-par display nor Gill's age—he had turned 32 the previous November—deterred George Jobey. In banking on the player's experience, Derby's manager was rewarded with a return of 35 goals from 66 matches before Gill departed to Crystal Palace in the 1928 close season, in company with Tommy Crilly and Harry Thoms.

Gill's best season with the Rams was their first back in the First Division, 1926–27, during which he missed only two games and became joint leading marksman with Bedford in the League on 22 goals. One of his most memorable matches was at the Baseball Ground that Easter, when he scored twice, and also hit a post, as the Rams rallied from being three down in 28 minutes to draw 4–4 with Huddersfield. The Town, fading to runners-up behind Newcastle in their unsuccessful quest for a fourth consecutive championship, ended the game thankful for the point, as Murphy was also denied by the framework twice, and Bedford failed with a penalty kick.

Arsenal, the club soon to emulate Huddersfield's hat-trick of League titles, fell the following season to a hat-trick of goals Gill so narrowly missed against the men from Leeds Road. Recalled in the wake of a dismal Cup replay defeat by Forest at Nottingham as Derby languished 16th in the League, he outshone his famous opposite number, Charlie Buchan, by outgunning the Gunners at Highbury in a victory that completed

This Derby team won at Villa Park with a goal by McIntyre on December 27, 1927. *Back row (left to right):* Johnny McIntyre, Mick O'Brien, George Collin, Harry Wilkes, Billy Carr, Bill Bromage (assistant trainer). *Front row:* Arthur Bacon, Jackie Whitehouse, Harry Storer, Harry Bedford, George Stephenson, Georgie Mee.
(A Wilkes & Son)

the double over the Londoners and was more emphatic than the 4–3 margin suggested. Arsenal's centre-forward, Jimmy Brain, also scored three goals, but Gill and his colleagues were convinced that two of them should not have counted. They unsuccessfully protested that the ball was over the by-line before Joe Hulme centred for the first one, and that Brain fisted it into the net for his third.

A week later, despite two more Gill goals, the Rams lost by the same score in making the mistake of playing a short-passing game against Burnley on a Baseball Ground mudheap. They were also beaten in their next two matches, but relegation worries were then swept aside by an undefeated run of ten games, including home victories of 5–0 against Manchester United and 7–1 against Cardiff City on successive Saturdays, which boosted them to a final fourth place.

Harry Bedford, who enjoyed one of his four-goal sprees in that win over the Welshmen, was by then well into the rich vein of scoring form that led him to equal 'Snobby' Bentley's club record for a League season with 30 goals in 1929–30. His haul in the 1926–27 season, during which he shared the club's scoring lead with Jimmy Gill in the

First Division, was, in fact, his smallest while with Derby County, though he increased it to 26 with another four in a 6–2 away Cup win over Bradford City (one of his shots burst the net) before a shock 2–0 home defeat by Third Division Millwall in the fourth round. That was a case of third time lucky for Millwall, who had conceded eight goals without reply as their previous Cup meetings with Derby County had resulted in defeats in a 1903 semi-final, and in the first round seven years later. The opening goal in their revenge victory was put into his own net by Plackett; the other one was a late penalty.

By coincidence, Jimmy Gill's last game for Derby, during Easter 1928, was back at Hillsborough against his former club who had so nearly been the opponents in his first. Again, it was an eventful encounter. The Wednesday, staging a successful battle against relegation in the season before they won two successive titles, scored twice in the first ten minutes through Jimmy Seed and Jimmy Trotter, who were to forge another profitable partnership at Charlton Athletic, as manager and trainer respectively. Twenty minutes from time, Wednesday still led by those two goals, and would have doubled that lead but for two penalty failures, one in each half, by Mark Hooper, rated by many as the finest uncapped winger of his day, who was usually so reliable from the spot. The Rams took advantage of those lapses by recovering to salvage a point with goals by Johnny McIntyre and George Stephenson, both of whom figure prominently in the next chapter.

That match was also notable for the rare appearance, the fifth and last on Derby's right wing, of Dan Kelly, an understudy from Hamilton Academicals who was added to that summer's exodus from the Baseball Ground. He joined Torquay United as a prelude to further League service with York City and Doncaster Rovers. Also that day, the goalkeeper was Jack Hampton, a reserve who had only rare opportunties of promotion to the first team. He had been with George Jobey at Wolverhampton and, like Harry Wilkes, for whom he deputised, had previously played for Wellington Town.

Back now to Georgie ('Shortie') Mee, Jimmy Gill's companion in the move from Blackpool to Derby, who was one of the most colourful characters the Rams have ever possessed. He was a miner at Bestwood during the First World War when Jimmy Cantrell, the Tottenham centre-forward who was then guesting for Notts County (from whom he had joined Spurs) recommended him to the Meadow Lane club's manager, Albert Fisher. Mee recalled:

> Jimmy took me under his wing, becoming such a guide and friend to me that I have felt indebted to him ever since. It was he who put me on the right road at the outset of my career.

Notts, however, failed to appreciate his true worth, releasing him to Blackpool in 1920 after only one season. Manager Fisher was no doubt influenced by his first sight of the 16-year-old, who, as his 'Shortie' nickname implied, then stood at only 5ft. Georgie, who grew to be 5ft 4in at his tallest, invoked the wondering comment: 'He's a bit of a small 'un, isn't he?'

Blackpool, on the other hand, had no doubts. Indeed, he became such a valued member of their team, with his exceptional pace and the accurate centres from which Harry Bedford prospered, that he did not miss a match for four consecutive seasons and set up the club's record of 209 successive appearances—195 in the League and 14 in the Cup. That run began on Christmas Day, 1920, in a narrow home win over Barnsley, and ended on September 12th, 1925, when Blackpool lost 2–1 to Derby County, also at Bloomfield Road. The Supporters' Club gave him a gold watch and chain to commemorate the achievement.

In all, Mee played in 230 League and Cup games for the Seasiders, and although not noted as a scorer, with just 21 goals, he did have his moments. The most memorable came on the first Saturday of March, 1922, when one of his two goals in the 2–1 defeat of Nottingham Forest was among the most spectacular ever seen at the Blackpool ground, a real scorcher from some 40 yards out. With Derby, too, he remained a creator rather than a scorer, totalling only 15 in 155 games.

Having finally lost his place at Blackpool to Percy Downes, a lively winger from Gainsborough Trinity, 'Shortie' was a couple of months into his second full season with Derby County before he at last managed to oust 'Spud' Murphy, who had reclaimed his outside-left spot for most of the Rams' first season back in Division One. Not long after having to give way to Mee, Murphy moved to Bolton Wanderers in part exchange for Albert Picken, a former Wellington Town and Wolves winger who never broke into Derby's first team.

A run of just over 40 games for Mee was then broken by an attack of typhoid fever that kept him out for five months in the winter of 1928–29, but back he came to miss only four matches when the Rams were First Division runners-up the following season. He remained first choice until just under a year before his departure to Burnley in September, 1932. In the next summer he moved to Mansfield, then, after a diversion

Georgie Mee in his playing days…and pictured on a return visit to Derby in the 1950s.
(Derby Evening Telegraph)

out of the League to Great Harwood, he had two spells with Accrington Stanley either side of a few months at Rochdale.

That took him up to the 1939–45 war, after which he was in charge of Blackpool's reserve side in the Central League for four seasons before stepping down to concentrate on his running of the Shakespeare Hotel in the town. For relaxation, he joined the Magicians' Circle, a company of conjurors, and until shortly before his death at Poulton-le-Fylde in 1978 he continued to attend matches regularly at Bloomfield Road, where he was 'very appreciative of the free facilities Blackpool extend to me as one of their old players'. He also followed the progress of Derby County with undiminished interest, and at his hotel he had what was known as the 'Derby Room' in which were hung photographs of Rams players and team groups—most particularly one of Steve Bloomer that was given to him by a Derby supporter, and one of the team that won the FA Cup in 1946.

In later life he put on some weight, but it was not until he was nearing his 51st birthday that he played his last match. He was on the left wing in a Blackpool Past and Present team against Charlie Chester's Comics XI in a charity match which attracted a crowd of about 15,000 to Bloomfield Road in September, 1950. The personalities from Blackpool shows who took part included Jimmy Edwards, as goalkeeper, and Charlie Chester and Nat Jackley, in the forward line. The referee was Stanley Matthews, England's 'Wizard of Dribble' winger, who had his Blackpool team-mates Stan Mortensen and Harry Johnston as his linesmen.

Of his many years in football, Georgie Mee looked back most fondly on those he spent with Derby County. He told me:

> I truly enjoyed every minute I spent at Derby. They were the best club I ever had, the grandest lot of players one could wish to be with, and there was a wonderful team spirit throughout. I was always regarded as a bit of a comedian, and no doubt I helped to keep up the good spirits with my joking, which, however, did sometimes get me into trouble! There are times when every player gets the 'bird' from the crowd, and I had my share of such bad patches. But I always tried to see the funny side of it, and generally I found that by smiling back at my critics I softened their anger and would have them cheering a few minutes later.

A sense of humour, in addition to his footballing ability, was not Mee's only strong point. He was also an accomplished singer, and, apart from being a Blackpool pierrot, he was a member of the Derby Amateur Operatic Society while with the Rams. He was the man, clad in a judge's wig and gown, seen dashing down a Derby station platform one Saturday night, hurrying to sing with the Society in The Gondoliers after changing aboard the train on the way back from a match at Chelsea.

One of Georgie's singing highlights occurred at a Sunderland theatre one evening before Derby County played at Roker Park. The leading lady sang a song that was all the rage at that time, 'Let Me Call You Sweetheart', and, as Georgie had been plugging it at Blackpool during the previous summer, he joined in the chorus. Encouraged by this, two of his clubmates, the Tommies Cooper and Davison, pushed him onto the stage, where he completed a harmonious duet. Next day, though, he and his comrades had nothing to sing about as Sunderland were 4–0 winners.

Snowy-haired Tommy Cooper was George Jobey's other big signing in the promotion season of 1925–26. He came from Port Vale at a fee of £2,500 only a few weeks after the arrival of Gill and Mee. Here was a full-back, stylish and speedy, whose tackling, strong positional sense and accurate distribution made him fit to rank among the finest defenders ever to play for England—if open to some criticism in that he was not a particularly good header of the ball. He would surely have won more than his 15 caps but for cartilage operations on both knees that also restricted his appearances for the Rams in two of the eight complete seasons in which he was otherwise an automatic choice. As it was, he totted up 266 League and Cup games, taking over the captaincy three years before moving to Liverpool for £8,000 late in 1934—then a record fee for both clubs.

Tommy Cooper leads out the Rams, followed by Jack Barker and Jack Kirby.
(Derby Evening Telegraph)

Cooper, who hailed from Fenton, one of the Potteries five towns that make up Stoke-on-Trent, began his career with Trentham in the Cheshire League, from where he joined Port Vale on the eve of the 1924–25 season. He made his Vale debut, as the deputy for an injured player, in a team that included another future England international, Alf Strange, later of Sheffield Wednesday, on the December day they defeated Alfreton Town 8–2 in an FA Cup qualifying tie. Cooper established himself so quickly that George Jobey was on his trail for Derby less than 18 months later.

The Rams lost 2–0 at home to Portsmouth when Cooper first played for them on March 13th, 1926, the Saturday after his signing, but he was the best defender on the field and promptly made the right-back position his own—first alongside Tom Crilly, then with Crilly's successor, George Collin. When he first stepped onto the international stage, against Ireland in Belfast on October 22nd, 1927, England were beaten by the same score as on his Derby debut. Then, early the following month, he was put out of the running for a second cap (until a year later, when he helped to beat the Irish at Liverpool) by an injury that caused him to miss the rest of Derby's season.

It was Cooper's injury that gave Collin his first chance in the Rams' League side, a chance he enthusiastically grabbed to become a member of the team in 333 more matches over nine seasons before going back to his native North-East to join Sunderland. And what an eventful entry it was by George! For it came in a 4–4 draw at Cardiff at the beginning of a sequence of six matches that produced 40 goals. These were the details:

1927			Opponents	Derby scorers
Nov 19	A	4–4	Cardiff City	Stephenson 2, Crooks, Bedford
Nov 26	H	4–6	Wednesday	Whitehouse 2, Mee, Stephenson
Dec 10	H	6–0	Blackburn R	Bedford 2 (1 pen), Stephenson 2, Crooks, Whitehouse
Dec 17	A	3–3	Middlesbrough	Stephenson, Crooks, Whitehouse
Dec 24	H	4–1	Birmingham	Stephenson, Mee, Crooks, Bedford
Dec 26	H	5–0	Aston Villa	Bedford 2, Whitehouse 2, Stephenson

Despite being in a defence that let in four goals, Collin made a creditable start, his performance earning him this praise from the *Derby Evening Telegraph* critic:

> Collin's play indicates that Mr Jobey has found in him a class young back. This nicely-made defender was very cool, and in manoeuvre and in kicking was very discriminate.

Yet Collin almost certainly would never have found his way to Derby County but for an injury he suffered at an early stage of his career. While still a teenager, he left the North-Eastern League club West Stanley for Arsenal, with whom he spent some 18 months on the reserve strength before failing to agree new terms. As a result, he became one of the first signings made for Bournemouth by Leslie Knighton, the former Manchester City manager who had moved to the South Coast from Arsenal after displeasing Sir Henry Norris by challenging the authority of the Highbury club's chairman with his demands to buy costly new players. Collin's form for Bournemouth soon attracted attention, but one First Division club who were intent on securing his transfer broke off their negotiations when he had the misfortune to break a leg.

So, instead of signing for a rival of the Rams, Collin went back home to County Durham, and on his recovery he re-entered the ranks of West Stanley. There he was spotted by George Jobey, who had to agree terms with both West Stanley and Bournemouth—where he was still on the retained list at £1,000—in taking him to the Baseball Ground just a couple of weeks before that goalful game at Ninian Park in which he at last made it into the First Division.

Safe but unspectacular, Collin was remarkably consistent, missing only four games out of 136 at his peak, and he was most unlucky not to follow Tommy Cooper into the England team. Cooper, one of the most modest of men, was only too ready to recognise

George Collin, who might never have played for Derby but for breaking a leg.
(Derby Evening Telegraph)

that he owed much to the solid play of his partner, and that it was not his ability alone that made him the more noticeable on the field. He once told a Derby pressman:

> You fellows don't give nearly enough credit to George Collin. I could not play well if George was not a fine player, but you pick on me more because of my fair hair.

Cooper had to contend for his England caps with strong competition from such accomplished defenders as Huddersfield's Roy Goodall, Warney Cresswell, of Everton, and Tommy Smart from Aston Villa. He skippered the side in what proved to be the last of his internationals, a 4–0 win over Wales in Cardiff, on September 29th, 1934. He was a late withdrawal through injury for the next game, against Italy, the month before George Jobey, putting sentiment aside, decided that the time had come to part with a player who, though still a force to be reckoned with, had reached the age of 30.

Cooper's replacement for the match with Italy was George Male, who was brought in for an all-Arsenal full-back partnership with Eddie Hapgood, the new captain, that was to represent England on ten consecutive occasions over two years, and 13 times in all. There will be more about that 'Battle of Highbury', which England won 3–2, in the chapter dealing with Jack Barker, another renowned Derby defender to captain club and country.

Although he had now entered the footballing veteran age, and come to the end of his international career, and although, as at Derby, he was sometimes criticised for a lack of strength in the air, Cooper remained Liverpool's first-choice right-back to the finish of the last full pre-war season of 1938–39, totalling 150 League appearances and ten more in the Cup. As one of the most respected and experienced men in the game, he was also a natural inheriter of the Anfield club's captaincy, and, just as he had struck up such a fine understanding with George Collin at Derby, so he settled comfortably into another formidable partnership with Ernest Blenkinsop,[4] with whom he had first played for England, before the former Sheffield Wednesday full-back left for Cardiff.

On the outbreak of war, Cooper joined the Military Police, and while with them, serving as a sergeant, he met a tragic end on June 25th, 1940. He was killed in a road accident near Aldeburgh, in Suffolk, when the motor-cycle he was riding was in a head-on collision with a double-decker bus. Soccer had lost one of its greatest personalities. He was buried at Nottingham Road cemetery, in Derby, the following Saturday, when the bearers were Sammy Crooks, Harry Bedford, George Collin, 'Dally' Duncan, Tommy Davison and George Stephenson.

---

4. Blenkinsop, who cost Liverpool £6,500 earlier in the year in which Cooper moved to Anfield, was a key player for Wednesday, whom he joined from Hull City, when they rose from the Second Division with Derby County in 1926 and then won the First Division championship in two successive seasons from 1928–30. In August, 1939, nearly two years after his transfer from Liverpool to Cardiff, he moved to Buxton, and during the Second World War he guested for Halifax Town and Bradford before becoming a publican.

George Collin spent two years at Sunderland, the scene of a blot on his career when he was ordered-off[5] (though there was talk of his being the victim of a mistake by the referee) towards the end of his Derby County days. From Roker, he dropped into the Third Division with Port Vale, then had time for only a few games with Burton Town before war broke out. After that he lost interest in football, even as a spectator, though he did go to Wembley for the first post-war FA Cup Final in which the Rams at long last carried off the trophy.

Search for the 'Loth' Teeth

George Jobey was so delighted with the 3–2 victory over Blackburn Rovers in the fourth round of the FA Cup in January, 1932, that he treated his team to a lavish dinner after the match. Full-back George Collin had a special, if embarrassing, reason to remember that celebration party.

As he was being driven away from the hotel by Sammy Crooks, he leaned out of the car window to exchange a few parting words with some of his colleagues. Suddenly, he turned round to Sammy with a horror-stricken look on his face and said 'Thtop, for goodneth thake. I've loth my teeth!'

'Out we piled' recalled Crooks, 'and I must have struck a whole box of matches before George pounced on his treasured false teeth, which were lying in the middle of the road.'

He continued to play enthusiastically at cricket however, and when I met him he was still good enough, in his late forties, for a few runs as an opening, or No 3, batsman with his local Spondon club, or, in midweek, in the Long Eaton Spinners side that also included Tommy Davison. In his younger days, he was a member of the South Moor Colliery cricket team in his native County Durham, and before the war he played for Heanor Town in the Notts and Derbyshire Border League.

---

5. Only two other Derby County players were ordered off in first-team games during the period between the two world wars: Bill Paterson and Bert Fairclough. Paterson, like Fairclough, a centre-forward, was signed from Cowdenbeath early in 1921, and returned there in the summer of 1924 after scoring two dozen goals in 68 League and Cup games. A year later he re-entered the Football League with Coventry City, then moved to Springfield in the United States.

On returning to the Derby area to make his home at Spondon, Collin 'teamed up' again with two other former Rams players, Arthur Groves and Jack Kirby, as employees of British Celanese. A year or two later he joined the Rolls-Royce Fire Service, where, Harry Bedford another ex-County favourite, was among his fellow workers. In retirement, George lived until 1989, to the age of 83.

George Collin and his wife at their Spondon home in the 1950s.
(Derby Evening Telegraph)

CHAPTER 5

Dividends from Soccer Scandal

Leeds City banished from League – Two of their auctioned-off players, Lamph and Stephenson, find their way to Derby – Last-minute penalty save prevents a fifth equaliser – Goalkeeper Olney capped by England after leaving Rams for Aston Villa – Stand-in scores four – McIntyre the £10 bargain

ONE OF FOOTBALL'S BIGGEST SCANDALS broke in 1919, when Leeds City were put out of business after a joint Football Association and Football League inquiry into their affairs. In due course, Derby County indirectly acquired two members of their staff of 22 professionals who were auctioned off along with all the equipment.

Allegations that the Yorkshire club had paid guest players over the odds in expenses during the recently-ended First World War were brought to the attention of the authorities by a disgruntled City full-back named Charlie Copeland who had been in dispute over a pay rise. The practice of over-paying had not been limited to Leeds, but they were the only ones at whom the finger was specifically pointed, and the full weight of officialdom crashed down upon them when they failed to offer any kind of defence.

Not even the intervention of the Lord Mayor of Leeds, who volunteered to take over the club, could cause the Commission to be lenient. Out Leeds City had to go, after having collected ten points from the eight Second Division fixtures they had fulfilled up to the first week of October in the 1919–20 season. Their record was inherited by Port Vale.[1] In addition, five of the City's officials were banned for life: four directors headed by chairman Joseph Connor and, not so understandably, Herbert Chapman, who was then only just beginning to build his reputation as one of the game's greatest managers.

The fact that Chapman's head was on the block was surprising because he was away on war work at a munitions factory when the illegal payments were claimed to have

---

1. In March, 1968, Port Vale were themselves expelled from the League, to take effect at the end of that season, and fined £2,000 by the Management Committee, for allegedly making illegal payments to players, but they were readmitted before the expulsion came into force. They had already been fined £2,000 by the FA for the same offence.

been made. He was therefore reprieved when evidence to that effect was belatedly given, and he strode majestically on to his great deeds with Huddersfield Town and Arsenal.

Rising quickly from the ashes of Leeds City came the new club, Leeds United. Within hours of the headline-hogging player-auction, a meeting attended by more than a thousand of the banned club's shocked supporters unanimously agreed to the formation of a new one, and Yorkshire Amateurs sportingly made way for the fledgling United at Elland Road. To begin with, the newcomers replaced Leeds City Reserves in the Midland League; for the ensuing season they were elected to the Second Division of the Football League. Their first opponents in that higher sphere, to whom they lost 2–0 away, were Port Vale, who had completed Leeds City's fixtures with a mid-table total of 40 points.

The two players whose paths led to Derby County after they had been among those put up for auction at the Metropole Hotel in Leeds on that humiliating day of October 17th, 1919, were Tom Lamph, a Gateshead-born wing-half, and George Stephenson, a former Northumberland Boys inside-forward from New Delaval Villa. With fees set

George Stephenson, signed from Aston Villa after
being among the players sold by auction when Leeds
City were expelled from the League.
(loaned by Mrs Jean Parsons, his daughter)

from £100 to £1, 250, Stephenson went to Aston Villa for £250, and Lamph to Manchester City for £800. Lamph moved on to the Rams inside six months, but more than eight years went by before Stephenson left Villa for the Baseball Ground.

At Villa Park, George Stephenson joined his two elder brothers, Clem and Jimmy. Clem, also an inside-forward, had been transferred to the Aston club from Durham City back in 1910 after spells with West Stanley, Blyth Spartans and New Delaval Villa. The lesser-known Jimmy was a winger who had been signed straight from Seaton Delaval in 1914. Jimmy and Clem played several times in the same Aston Villa forward line, sometimes as partners on the right flank, but all three were never together in the League side. As had happened to Clem soon after joining Aston Villa, George was loaned out to Stourbridge for a few months to enable him to gain regular playing experience, and shortly before his return Clem was taken to Huddersfield Town by Herbert Chapman at about the same time that Jimmy moved to Sunderland. Jimmy also played for Watford, Queen's Park Rangers, Boston United and Ashington.

There were two other Stephenson brothers—Ned, who was a wing-half in local football but enjoyed greater success as a bowls player with the New Delaval Welfare Club, and Bob, the youngest, who shared his soccer between New Delaval Villa, Manchester City (but not in their first team), North Shields and Pegswood United.

Clem Stephenson, who was one of Leeds City's war-time guests, picked up two Cup-winner's medals with Villa—the second of them against Huddersfield, with whom he promptly collected another before skippering them to their First Division title treble in his famous left-wing partnership with Billy Smith. In his last full season of 1927–28 he took part in his fourth Cup Final, but on that occasion he was on the losing side against the Blackburn team which included George Thornewell.

George Stephenson played in all five forward positions then commonly employed in the 2-3-5 formation and was used only sparingly in Villa's first team until the mid-1920s. In the meantime the club's inside-forward positions were firmly in the grip of Billy Walker, one of the most accomplished players in the club's history, and Billy Kirton, a £500 bargain at the Leeds City auction, who scored the extra-time winning goal against Huddersfield in the 1920 Cup Final. George Stephenson was given his overdue chance to establish himself at Villa when Kirton eventually faded into the background, and he took his opportunity so well that he had matured into just the type of forward Derby County needed, with nearly 100 League games under his belt, by the time George Jobey persuaded Villa to part with him on Remembrance Day in 1927.

The Rams, then wallowing in the bottom half of the table and struggling to stabilise themselves in the First Division after having finished their first season back there in 12th place, conceded three goals to Everton without reply when Stephenson made his debut for them at Goodison Park the next day, but he went on to score 12 times in the next ten League games—plus one in a Cup win at Millwall—in sparking a revival that was sustained for a final fourth place. That spurt came during the high-scoring sequence which, as recalled in the previous chapter, began in a 4–4 draw with Cardiff. The Welsh club were involved in another eight-goal spree, but as 7–1 losers (four for Bedford), when they played the return game at the Baseball Ground a week after Manchester United had been beaten there 5–0 (two each for Bedford and Stephenson).

In his third season with Derby, Stephenson himself scored four goals in the match that stuck most in his memory from among the 120 he played for the club before his sudden and unexpected transfer to Sheffield Wednesday in February, 1931. It was at home to Grimsby Town and this is how he recalled it to me:

> Every time we scored, Grimsby would equalise, and I remember turning to Harry Bedford, after they had done so for the fourth time, and saying 'How many goals have we to score to beat this lot?' Eventually, however, we won by 5–4, but Grimsby missed a penalty in the last minute of the match.

The Rams' goalkeeper that day was Harry Wilkes, who laughed when I spoke to him about that fluffed spot kick by the Town's centre-forward, Joe Robson. 'It wouldn't be right to say I saved his shot' he said. 'It hit me!'

Stephenson's sharp form in one of Derby County's most impressive forward lines of the inter-war period (Crooks, Whitehouse, Bedford, Stephenson, Mee) earned him a place on England's Continental tour after the 1927–28 season, and he scored twice on his international debut in a 5–1 defeat of France in Paris. He also played, without scoring, in a 3–1 win over Belgium at Antwerp two days later, but had to wait for a third cap, his last, until he was with the Wednesday. He then partnered his former Derby clubmate Sammy Crooks on the right wing in a side which also included Tommy Cooper. Again the match was in Paris, but this time the French gained revenge in a 5–2 victory.

Saved from the Danish Police Cells

In 1926, Derby County's tour at the end of the season was to Denmark and Sweden—and George Jobey had to do a lot of explaining to stop his players ending up in the Copenhagen police cells.

After one game, the whole Rams party were invited to a night club. Midway through an enjoyable evening, the club was raided by the police and all but one of the Derby players were bundled into the Danish equivalent of a Black Maria. The one overlooked was 'Spud' Murphy, who, shouting 'Hey, wait for me', jumped onto the step of the police vehicle and was driven off to the lock-up with his clubmates.

Not one of them spoke a word of Danish, but they were released after George Jobey had turned up and sorted things out with some typically brisk negotiating. It turned out that the police had rounded up the Rams because they were not members of the club. All ended happily, and they were feted as if they were royalty after winning all but one of their six tour matches—three of them in Copenhagen.

But even George Jobey was left powerless after another social function while the Rams were again on tour in Denmark two years later. One of the Derby players pinched his taxi, and he had to walk three miles to the County's hotel in the early hours of the morning.

Another interesting point about Stephenson's first two games for England is that they were also the first two for goalkeeper Ben Olney, who only a few months earlier he had left Derby County for Aston Villa. He had asked for a transfer after failing to regain the place he had lost through injury to Harry Wilkes, who, ironically, had been turned down by Villa because they had considered him too small. Olney was languishing in the Rams' reserve side when negotiations were opened by Villa. It was on their ground, while with Stourbridge, that he had given the outstanding display, for England against Scotland in a junior international match, that had led him to Derby. Villa completed the deal, which made Olney their fifth keeper of 1927–28,[2] shortly after Derby had landed a League double over them for the first time by winning 1–0 at Villa Park the day after gaining a 5–0 home victory on Boxing Day.

Olney, who had missed only three matches in four successive seasons and set a record of 240 League and Cup appearances by a Derby goalkeeper,[3] was one of the Rams' most popular players. Indeed, when he first came up against his former club, just under a year later, he was greeted by cries of 'Good old Ben' from County fans in the crowd. Villa were again beaten, by 3–2, but he gave a superb display that helped to keep him in the England reckoning for two games against South Africa. In the words of one onlooker:

> The barrier was Olney. The ex-Ram stood between his old colleagues and goals on numerous occasions. He appeared to have set himself out to prove to the County that he was still a fine goalkeeper, and he succeeded in such a way that his former clubmates must almost have despaired of ever beating him.

Only one former clubmate, Bedford, did beat him. Derby's other scorers were Jack Robson, a former Hull winger who did not join the Rams from Reading until after Olney had left, and Villa full-back Teddy Bowen, who put the ball into his own net.

Jack Robson, who helped Reading to the Third Division South championship in 1925–26, spent most of his time with Derby as deputy to Georgie Mee before sharing the rest of his League career between Southend, Chester, Rochdale and Oldham. I met him while he was licensee of the Crown Hotel in the Allenton district of Derby, where he described his years with the Rams as 'my happiest in football'. Another product of the North-East, he had no connection with Derby until he joined the Rams, but he was among many of the club's former players who returned to settle in the town after retiring from soccer. He was first a publican at Hull, his wife's birthplace, and he and his family had a very lucky escape there during the blitz in the Second World War. He told me:

> There were half-a-dozen pubs in that particular area in the centre of Hull, and all of them were flattened to the ground except ours, the Paragon. But

---

2. Villa's goalkeepers that season before Olney were Tommy Jackson, who had been on their losing side in the 1924 FA Cup Final against Newcastle, Johnson, a signing from Buxton, Goddard and Hickman.
3. Olney's record was beaten by Reg Matthews (246), and then by Colin Boulton (301). Including other competitions, Boulton had a full total of 344.

Ben Olney in
typically alert
action.

Jack Robson who
was blitzed out of
his Hull pub.
(Derby Evening Telegraph

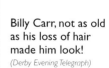

Billy Carr, not as old
as his loss of hair
made him look!
(Derby Evening Telegraph)

although its walls were left standing, the Paragon was completely gutted and all our possessions went up in the blaze. We had a really tough time, believe me.

Two other Robsons, unrelated, were on Derby's books at the same time as Jack—full-back Billy, from Wearside, and inside-forward Norman, from Tyneside, both of whom also had mainly a reserve role. Several years earlier the club also had a Jim Robson, who came from the same Seaton Delaval area as the Stephensons, but he played only a few first-team games as Harold Wightman's deputy. Many years later, while Brian Clough was the manager, there was John Robson, an England Under-23 full-back who was a regular in the sides that won the titles of Second Division (1969) and First Division (1972) but cruelly had his career cut short by multiple sclerosis after a move to Aston Villa which brought the Rams their then record transfer fee of £90,000. With Villa, he gained two League Cup winner's medals and another promotion from Division Two.

Like Jack Robson, Ben Olney returned to Derby as a publican after finishing with football. He played nearly 100 games for Villa but failed to be on the winning side in three further games against Derby County before going via Bilston United (latterly as player-manager) to Walsall and then Shrewsbury Town. He revisited the Baseball Ground as Moor Green's goalkeeper when he was first a licensee in Birmingham. Then, his playing days over, he moved to the Normanton Hotel for a while before taking a job at the Rolls-Royce factory where he was working at the time of the illness which led to his death in 1943 at the early age of 44.

It was one of the big disappointments of George Stephenson's career that, in common with Olney, he was unable to play for England against another of the home countries. He was selected for a match against Ireland, in Belfast, soon after being chosen for the Football League against the Irish League, but on both occasions he had to cry off through injury.

Stephenson's transfer to Sheffield Wednesday, in company with Tommy Davison, surprised him almost as much as it did Rams' supporters, for he agreed to join the Hillsborough club only an hour after first hearing that they wanted him. He scored the last of his 56 goals for Derby in a 4–1 home win over Huddersfield Town—the club he would later manage. His last match for the County was another high-scoring encounter with Grimsby Town, at Blundell Park. Jack Bowers scored a hat-trick, but the Mariners won 5–3.

The move to Sheffield also came as quite a shock to Davison, for although he had lost his first-team place to Jack Barker he had recently reclaimed it, if temporarily, in Barker's absence through injury after four other players—Billy Carr, Archie Scott, Freddie Jessop, and even Harry Bedford—had been centre-half stand-ins.

Carr, another Seaton Delaval and Northumberland Boys product, was one of Cecil Potter's last signings for the Rams. He was used by George Jobey mainly as reliable full-back cover in making just over 100 League appearances before bowing out with Queen's Park Rangers. After one match, at home to West Bromwich, in which he gave probably his best display for the first team as George Collin's partner against the then Cup holders, Jobey told him 'If you had a few more hairs on your head, you'd be worth another £5,000 on that performance!' In laughingly telling me of that, Billy remarked that his hair began to thin while he was comparatively young and caused a good many folk to suppose that he was well into the veteran stage.

In almost a dozen years on the Baseball Ground staff, Carr demonstrated his value as a versatile reserve by playing in every position except goal. He continued to live and train in Derby after QPR had paid £350 for him, and, on ending about three seasons with the London club, he worked for many years at Derby Power Station. When I met him, not long after he had turned 50, he was also an enthusiastic and energetic leader of the Firs Estate Youth Club. He had a particular interest in basketball, which he was still playing along with leaders of other youth clubs in the Derby area.

Archie Scott was signed from Airdrieonians as a possible successor to Johnny McIntyre at right-half. However, with Jack Nicholas coming in to make that position his own throughout the rest of the pre-war years after McIntyre's move to Chesterfield, he played in little more than 30 first-team games in seven seasons before joining Brentford. Half-a-dozen of those appearances were made in the Rams' First Division runners-up season of 1929–30. With Brentford, he turned out just twice when they won the 1934–35 Second Division championship, and from Griffin Park he went to Reading as trainer.

Freddie Jessop, who was born at Barrow Hill, a Derbyshire village not far from Chesterfield, was spotted for Derby County by Arthur Latham, the Rams' former full-back and trainer, while playing for a Staveley works side in the Chesterfield Junior Hospital Cup Final. He turned professional at the age of 18, shortly before Derby's promotion back to the First Division was secured. Then a left-back, he weighed only about nine stones, not very heavy for a defender, but the Rams built him up on egg flip, malt and full-time training, and over the next decade he served them nobly, if chiefly as a reserve (nearly 100 senior games) as one of the most adaptable players on the books.

Freddie Jessop, a keen golfer as well as a versatile footballer.
(Derby Evening Telegraph)

Jessop played in all three half-back positions, and also at inside-forward in addition to full-back, with a cheerful willingness that he summed up admirably with this answer to one of my questions:

> Outstanding matches? I think I can say they all were, for I truly enjoyed every one in either the first, second or third team. Still, there is one particular game I would like to mention.
>
> I always fancied playing in the forward line, and it was there that I had the chance to show my paces during the match I have in mind. It happened early in my career, about 1932. We played over in Belfast against a team of past and present Irish internationals. Derby had promised to take the full League side, and, as Harry Bedford was selected to play but was not sure that he would stand up to it, I stripped and sat with the trainer.
>
> In the first few minutes Tommy Ruddy,[4] our inside-left, got a nasty cut over the eye, so, of course, yours truly took his place. Well, to cut a long story short, I collected four of the best, thanks mainly to Sammy Crooks sending over some centres which just asked to be rattled home, and we won 7–3. All three of the Irish side's goals were scored by Joe Bambrick, Linfield's international centre-forward, who later played for Chelsea. After that match I had quite a few offers to stay and play in Ireland, but I preferred to keep going with the Rams.

Having already battled back from breaking a leg in a fifth-round FA Cup defeat by Manchester City at Maine Road, keep going with the Rams he did, until December, 1937, when he moved to Sheffield United. The Blades' manager, Teddy Davison, the former Wednesday and England goalkeeper who later managed Chesterfield, sign-ed him to play in, and coach, the reserve team in the Central League, but because of injuries he was soon needed in the Second Division side and, again appearing in sever-al positions, he stayed in for most of a season they ended desperately close to promo-tion. Sheffield United had the same number of points as Manchester United, who went up with Aston Villa on goal average. A year later, however, the Blades did get back into the First Division, pipping their Wednesday neighbours by one point for second place behind Blackburn, and Freddie Jessop helped them in almost a dozen of their games.

Then came the war, and soon after its start he was loaned out as a guest to Lincoln City. He was captaining their successful side in the League North when his playing days were abruptly halted by an accident at work, smashing a heel in a 30-foot fall from a ladder. Back he went to his old trade as a boot and shoe repairer, running his own business at Dronfield.

---

4. Tom Ruddy, who played for Stockton Shamrocks in his junior days along with Tom Crilly, was a £500 signing by the Rams from Darlington. That was in May, 1928, the month in which Crilly left Derby for Crystal Palace in company with Harry Thoms, who was also born at Stockton-on-Tees, and Jimmy Gill. Ruddy played in only 22 League games, scoring nine goals, before moving to Chesterfield with Johnny McIntyre on December 8th, 1931. He later assisted Linfield in the Irish League.

George Stephenson and Tommy Davison both left Sheffield several years before Jessop turned up in that city at Bramall Lane. Davison was the first to make a move, having spent only one full season at Hillsborough and made just 18 first-team appearances. He was taken to Coventry by former Derby clubmate Harry Storer, then the manager at Highfield Road. Immediately a regular first-team choice, Davison played in just over 100 Third Division South games as Coventry twice went close to promotion in successive seasons and he scored his most unforgettable goal by equalising in the last minute of a Cup replay against Reading.[5]

Midway through the 1934–35 season, however, he was ousted in regrettable circumstances by George Mason, a formidable defender set to become one of the big names in Coventry soccer. Mason, who, despite the intervention of the war, went on to total 350 League and Cup games in a City career that lasted 21 years up to 1952, settled into first the centre-half position, and then the captaincy, through two unrelated off-field incidents. These resulted in Davison and full-back Charlie Bisby, Mason's predecessor as skipper, being disciplined and, soon afterwards, shown the door. Bisby, formerly of Notts County, left for Mansfield; Davison went out of the League as player-coach with Rhyl Athletic and then played his last games for Bath City before returning to Derby, during the 1937 close season, to take over the Nottingham Arms.

Davison, another who looked back on his years with Derby County as his happiest, combined running a public house with some scouting. He also regularly watched matches at the Baseball Ground, his enthusiasm for the game undimmed by the many hard physical knocks he had taken. His head injuries had necessitated a total of 20 stitches, he had lost several teeth in collisions, and a broken nose suffered while at Wolverhampton had left him with a blocked right nostril that sometimes caused severe headaches. Even so, he retained an athletic appearance and carried on for many years as a keen cricketer—mainly with the Long Eaton Spinners club for which two other former Rams footballers, George Collin and Arthur Groves, also played. He was in his 70th year when he died at Derby on the first day of 1971.

George Stephenson's stay with Sheffield Wednesday lasted a year longer than Davison's. The Hillsborough club signed him as a replacement for Jimmy Seed who was then nearing the end of his remarkable reign as captain after being discarded by Tottenham because they thought he was past his best. Seed was a very hard act to follow, having led Wednesday to an amazing escape from relegation (while Spurs had gone down) and then on to two consecutive League championships, but Stephenson opened the 1931–32 season with four goals in a 6–1 win at Blackburn

5. Davison's goal forced a 3–3 draw with Reading in December, 1932, following a 2–2 draw in the original second-round tie at Elm Park, but Reading won by an only goal in the second replay at Stamford Bridge. In the third round Reading were losing 2–0 at Millwall when play had to be abandoned because of fog, and they eventually lost by that score in a replay after a 1–1 draw. Millwall then went out to Aldershot, who were beaten by Derby County at the Baseball Ground in the fifth round. The Rams made further progress after two epic games with Sunderland, but were beaten by Manchester City in a semi-final at Huddersfield.

and went on to help the Owls to go near a title hat-trick as they finished third behind Everton and Arsenal. Wednesday were again third a year later, but Stephenson played only a minor part that time. He himself was displaced with the arrival from Newcastle of Ronnie Starling, who was soon to make up for missing the Geordies' 1932 Cup Final win over Arsenal by skippering the Owls to victory against West Bromwich Albion at Wembley.

In the summer of 1933, the cultured Stephenson, then approaching his 33rd birthday, made Preston North End his fifth League club. With that move, he set out upon the most eventful phase of his career as a member of a promotion-winning side in three successive seasons. Having been Preston's top scorer with 16 goals when they went up from the Second Division as runners-up to Grimsby Town in 1933–34, he was signed for Charlton Athletic by Jimmy Seed,[6] who had taken over the reins at the Valley after cutting his managerial teeth with Clapton Orient. In the next two seasons the hitherto unsung London club zoomed into the First Division by romping away with the Third South title and then coming second in Division Two, only one point behind champions Manchester United.

United went straight down again (to bounce back up with Aston Villa the following year) but Charlton maintained their unprecedented momentum by ending their first season in the top grade second only to the other Manchester club, City. In the remaining pre-war seasons they finished fourth and third. By then, George Stephenson was no longer in the team but on the backroom staff as Seed's right-hand man, having been promoted to assistant manager the year after first joining the coaching staff on retiring as a player in 1937 due to injury.

He remained a valued Valleyite until August, 1947, when, as the last of some 60 applicants, he was appointed manager of Huddersfield Town following the resignation of David Steele, the former Scottish international who had been a right-half regular for most of the Yorkshire club's three consecutive seasons as First Division champions in the 1920s. Thus was football history made—the first case of brothers managing the same League club. Clem Stephenson had preceded George in that post after ending an outstanding playing career in which he had claimed all the game's honours but, surprisingly, only one England cap to his brother's three—and that a belated one in a defeat by Wales at Blackburn in 1924.

Clem Stephenson became Huddersfield's longest-serving manager, holding the job from May, 1929, until his resignation in June, 1942. In his 13-year reign he piloted them to two more FA Cup Finals (lost to Arsenal in 1930 and, by a penalty at the end of extra time, to Preston in 1938) and to second and third places in the First Division in 1934 and 1936, respectively. His assistant, Ted Magner, later manager of Derby County, followed him as caretaker for just over a year until Steele's appointment.

---

6. In his book, *The Jimmy Seed Story*, Seed recalls how his appointment as Charlton's manager arose from the alphabetical arrangement for the table seating at the banquet Arsenal gave to celebrate winning the First Division title in 1933. As Clapton Orient's representative, he sat next to Albert Gliksten, the Charlton chairman, who confided that he needed a new manager. 'What about me?' asked Seed, and got the job.

Unfortunately, in contrast to his brother's term of office, George Stephenson found life in management one unrelenting battle against adversity. In his four full seasons in charge, Huddersfield were 19th, 20th, 15th, then 19th again, before he resigned near the end of his fifth, in March, 1952, with the Town inexorably tumbling towards the relegation they had been so narrowly avoiding. Only nine League games were left when he stepped down, and a week before the arrival of his successor, former Preston and Scotland full-back Andy Beattie (a war-time guest player with Derby County), the plunge into the Second Division was confirmed. It was the first time Huddersfield had been relegated.

Later that year, Stephenson[7] became licensee of the Sportsman Hotel in Halifax, and from there he moved back to Derby to rejoin the Rams as the 'A' team's coach in the early 1960s. One of the County's young players of that period was his Derby-born son, Bob, a former Derby Boys forward who played a few times for the first team under Harry Storer's management before leaving for Shrewsbury Town, and then Rochdale. Cricket was, however, the son's stronger game, and after having to desert Derbyshire because his County Championship chances were restricted by the excellence of Test player Bob Taylor, he enjoyed a most successful wicketkeeping career with Hampshire, captaining the side in the last of his 11 seasons.

Bob Stephenson, who was unable to emulate his father's success with the Rams, but enjoyed a fine cricketing career with Hampshire.
(Derby Evening Telegraph)

---

7. George Stephenson died in Derby on August 18, 1971, just over a fortnight before his 71st birthday.

Back now to Tommy Lamph, who, as recalled earlier in this chapter, was one of George Stephenson's hapless companions in that degrading auction of Leeds City players. He went straight into Manchester City's First Division side, at right-half, after his enforced move from Yorkshire in that autumn of 1919 but he played in only 11 games, all in succession, before losing his place, never to return. City were unbeaten in the first six of those games, which included an 8–2 demolition of Blackburn and the taking of three points out of four against Derby County, but then lost all but one, which was drawn, of the next five, and Lamph went out of the side after a defeat at Everton.

Lamph's opportunities with Derby were also limited—just 16 League matches and one Cup-tie—but he fulfilled the main job Jimmy Methven signed him for in helping them to avoid relegation through their last ten games of 1919–20. The Rams, who that season had engaged Sergeant Harry Curzon, DCM, a well-known local boxer, as trainer in succession to Arthur Latham, pulled clear by winning all but one of the last ten points at stake. This included a 5–0 trouncing of third-placed Chelsea, and it was the other County, from Meadow Lane, that went down with well-adrift Wednesday.

For Derby, however, it was a fate briefly deferred, and they were as good as doomed to another taste of Second Division fare by the time Lamph left for Leeds United just under a year after his arrival. The wing-half positions at the start of the dreadful 1920–21 season were entrusted to Frank Waterhouse, who was signed from West Bromwich Albion at about the same time as Lamph arrived, and Bernard McLaverty. As the changes were rung in desperate attempts to find a winning formula, one of Lamph's short-lived recalls came during the most barren spell in the club's history—eight successive games without a Derby goal—and Lamph was dispensed with in the wake of another scoring blank in a Cup replay defeat at Wolverhampton. These were the details of that depressing League sequence in 1920:

Oct 30	A	0–2	Arsenal
Nov 6	H	0–0	Bolton Wanderers
Nov 13	A	0–1	Bolton Wanderers
Nov 20	A	0–1	Middlesbrough
Nov 27	H	0–1	Middlesbrough
Dec 4	A	0–2	Blackburn Rovers
Dec 11	H	0–1	Blackburn Rovers
Dec 18	A	0–2	Huddersfield Town

In going back to Leeds, Lamph emulated another former Derby player, the amateur international Ivan Sharpe, for they were the only players to turn out for both United and their banished City predecessors. Sharpe, who in 1912 helped the Rams back to the First Division, and was also a member of the British team in the Olympic Games at Stockholm before concentrating on a career in journalism, only just qualified for that double with one first-team game for United after more than 60 with City.

Tommy Lamph's stay with Leeds United was also short—just as it had been at Leeds City and Manchester City (only 11 League games with both) as well as at Derby County. He played in only six games after joining United towards the end of February, 1921, then, struck down by ill health, he missed not only the rest of that season but also the whole of the following one. He was forced into premature retirement in the summer of 1922, and was only 32 when he died less than four years later.

The right-half (No 4) position in which Lamph made his first and last appearances for the Rams (all the others were on the left flank of the middle line) was filled after his exclusion first by Bill Morton, a former Ilkeston Town player who was subsequently with Newcastle United, Lincoln City and Wigan Borough, next by Bernard McLaverty, and then from Christmas, 1921, by the man who was to keep it in his firm grip, apart from absences through injury, for the best part of ten seasons up to September, 1931— John McMutrie McIntyre.

Glaswegian Johnny McIntyre was one of George Jobey's biggest bargains, and one of the finest of the Derby County players never to win an international cap. Costing no more than the £10 signing-on fee, he came from Stenhousemuir as an inside-forward, and scored the Rams' first goal in a 4–2 defeat at Blackpool in his debut on the opening day of the 1921–22 season. Then, after playing one match in the outside-left position which had posed such a problem between the departure of England winger Alf Quantrill to Preston and 'Spud' Murphy's signing, he then settled down to make the right-half berth his own for all but the first eight of his 349 League games for the club (plus 20 Cup-ties). The injury hoodoo which denied him deserved inclusion among the select band of players with more than 400 Derby matches to their names even spoilt his 300th

Johnny McIntyre, a £10 bargain who was a key member of
the Derby team for a decade.
(Derby Evening Telegraph)

appearance on his 30th birthday,[8] in a 2–2 home draw with Liverpool on October 19th, 1929. McIntyre, then the Rams' captain, was hurt within 15 minutes of the kick-off, and although he pluckily carried on he was little more than a passenger.

Centre-half Jack Barker also finished that match on the casualty list, and, with the visitors' goalkeeper, South African Arthur Riley, giving an outstanding display, Derby were unable to extend a two-goal lead before Liverpool staged a rousing recovery which the prolific Gordon Hodgson, another South African, crowned with a last-minute equaliser.

Although undeservedly never called upon by Scotland at senior level, Johnny Mac (as he was known) did play for his country as a schoolboy shortly before the First World War. He also represented Perthshire in the Glasgow Junior League before joining Stenhousemuir in 1918. With Derby County, he was a key member of the side that George Jobey guided out of the Second Division, and, having been an ever-present the previous season, he continued his longest injury-free run in completing a sequence of 80 appearances before being laid low again only a few matches before that belated promotion was clinched.

The parting of the ways with the Rams finally came for McIntyre in December, 1931, when, having been out of the side since the first five games of the season, he was transferred to Chesterfield—though his stay at Saltergate was contrastingly short. Derbyshire's other League club were ready to re-sign him after the 1932–33 season, but he decided not to accept a new contract as, by then, he was licensee of the Newmarket Inn at Derby and, consequently, had difficulty keeping his Saturday afternoons clear for football.

However, as he told me, 'once the game's in your blood you can't get it out' and he continued playing for a while longer in the Derby Wednesday League with the Co-op —back in his old position of inside-forward, where he showed he was still good for a few goals. Not long afterwards, he moved from the Newmarket, which was taken over by boxing promoter Jerry Shaw, on being appointed tenant-manager of the Mitre Hotel on Derby's ring road. He gave up that job early in 1944 to work as a fitter at the Rolls-Royce works, then returned to Derby County as a member of the ground staff. During the week he helped to keep everything in good order for match days at the Baseball Ground, and on Saturdays he had charge of the club's Colts side.

After the appointment of his old team-mate Jack Barker as the Rams' manager in succession to Stuart McMillan towards the end of 1953, McIntyre, along with first-team trainer Ralph Hann and joint assistant trainers Jack Bowers and Jack Poole, supervised one of the four groups of players into which the revised training programme was organised under Hann's overall control. Finally, for a few years following Barker's resignation as the Rams nosedived into the Third Division for the first time, he did some scouting. He remained in Derby in retirement until his death in June, 1974.

---

8. Other sources give McIntyre's birthdate as October 19, 1898, but when I interviewed him in 1952 he told me that he would be 53 that year. By that reckoning, he was born in 1899.

CHAPTER 6

Storer and Nicholas

*Harry Storer starts at the bottom with both Derby
County and Derbyshire – Switch to attack leads to
England place – Three promotions as manager – 'Old
Nick' follows his father into Derby's defence –
High-scoring with the Wednesday
– Luck runs against Udall and Parr*

WE NOW COME TO TWO OTHER enduring Derby County titans who have left their indelible mark on the club's history. One of them was Harry Storer, who, unlike the unhappy Barker, was a success as manager as well as player. He was McIntyre's predecessor as captain and his indomitable counterpart on the left flank of the half-back line after, like the Scot, dropping back from inside-forward. The other was Jack Nicholas, who stepped into McIntyre's boots at right-half and doubled even his long-lasting playing service before working with undiminished and unrivalled loyalty as the Rams' chief scout.

Harry Storer had the most inauspicious of starts to his careers as a Derby County footballer and a Derbyshire cricketer. He joined the Rams from Grimsby Town in March, 1921, as they were tumbling out of the First Division with results that were then the poorest in their history and he entered county cricket in 1920 as Derbyshire were going through their worst-ever season, without a win, or even a point, in finishing the limpest of lasts in the Championship table.

Yet Storer ended his eight-year stay with the Rams back in the top flight as an England international, with 274 League and Cup games, and 63 goals for the club behind him. Moreover, he had scored 13, 513 runs, taken 221 wickets, and held 214 catches in first-class cricket when he left Derbyshire as the newly-crowned champions of 1936 (after having been third and second in the previous two years).

It spoke volumes for Storer's strength of character, a quality he ruthlessly demanded from the others around him both as player and manager, that he sturdily overcame those early adversities so impressively. This was especially so on the cricket field, for, after being pitchforked into his first season of unrelenting gloom for the county, he had to battle through one that was even bleaker for him personally when Derbyshire again finished at the foot of the table without a win, but with 16 points out of 105, in 1924.

By that time, having scored the first of his 18 county centuries and gone very close to two others, he was a batsman of whom more was expected but he and Wilf Carter, a fellow footballer, were singled out for particular criticism after alarming slumps in their form, compared with the past two seasons. From being first and second in the county's averages and sharing in an eighth-wicket stand of 182 that stood as a Derbyshire record for 74 years, they declined to such an extent that Major Llewellyn Eardley Simpson, who for many years had to contend with severe financial constraints as the county's honorary treasurer, remarked in his booklet *The Rise of Derbyshire Cricket, 1919–35*, that Carter was 'a complete failure' and Storer 'was even worse.'

Storer the batsman. He helped Derbyshire to win the County Championship in 1936, his last season in a first-class cricket career that began in 1920.

(Derby Evening Telegraph)

Carter, who was a wing-half with Watford for several seasons and played in their first match at the Vicarage Road ground in 1922, fell away to average a fraction over 12, with fewer than 300 runs in 25 innings. He left the staff after that season and, although he was re-engaged in 1926, he did nothing in his five matches to warrant being kept on. He did some coaching at Repton and also spent a few years in Scotland as the Drumpellier club's professional.

If, as the good major maintained, anything could be worse than a complete failure, then the hapless Harry Storer went very close to it in 1924. Since his depressing debut season he had shown encouraging signs of upholding the high family traditions set by his father and uncle, but in 1924 he had a wretched top score of only 18 in 26 innings, scraping together 178 runs for a pitiable average of 6.84. Restricted to three innings, none notable and one runless, for Derbyshire the following season, he buckled down to rebuild his form and confidence in league cricket. He came back so resolutely that he exceeded 1,000 runs in six of the next eight years—four of them in succession from 1928.

In his most productive season of 1929, he averaged 36.71 from a total of 1,652, emulated his uncle William by hitting two hundreds in one match (119 and 100 against Sussex at Derby) and, in scoring the first of his two double-centuries (209), partnered Joe Bowden (120) in boosting the county's first-wicket record to 322, in just five minutes over four hours against Essex at Derby. An opener who could make runs on any type of pitch, and renowned for what Derbyshire's long-serving secretary W.T. Taylor called his 'terrific determination', he headed the county's batting averages in seven seasons out of nine from 1926 and was second in the two others. He twice had a final average of more than 40, and in the 1933 season, in which he was runner-up (fractionallty behind all-rounder Leslie Townsend), he achieved his highest figure of 44.36. In 1933 he also scored his second double-century, his 232, again against Essex at Derby, making him the first Derbyshire batsman to achieve that feat.

As a medium-pace bowler, he had his match to remember at Chesterfield in 1922, when he did the hat-trick as he inspired a 53-run defeat of Northamptonshire with 7–26 in 15 overs. Four years later, when Storer's final batting average of 36.54 was the best by a Derbyshire regular for more than 20 summers, he scored 132 against Somerset at Derby. He partnered Jim Hutchinson[1] (81) in a stand of 206, after the first three wickets had fallen for 48, and then took 6–48 as they dismissed the visitors for 129.

---

1. Hutchinson became the oldest living former county cricketer when Willis Walker, a batsman who played for Notts from 1913 to 1937, died on December 3rd, 1991, only a few days into his 100th year. Hutchinson had then just turned 95, the year of his November 29th birthdate having been amended from 1897 to 1896 in the 1981 edition of *Wisden*. In 1996, Hutchinson became only the fourth English first-class cricketer to reach the age of 100. He was then living in the village of Thurnscoe, between Barnsley and Rotherham, having moved to South Yorkshire on ending his career with Derbyshire. He was appointed safety officer at Hickleton Colliery shortly after being involved in the opening of a new pit at Markham Main. He first worked underground at the age of 14, at the Oxcroft colliery near Chesterfield where his father was under-manager.

He did not bat again in that game, nor did he repeat his first-innings success with the ball, but he still had a vital part to play. Derbyshire, having decided not to enforce the follow-on, declared nearly 400 ahead, but Somerset's defiant last-wicket pair, Guy Earle (43) and Jim Bridges (15 not out), threatened to deny them victory. Stan Worthington bowled the last over and, off his second delivery, Storer held the slip catch that ended Earle's resistance.

In playing such a prominent part in both football and cricket, Harry Storer outdid his famous relatives. Soccer came second to cricket for uncle William, and the opposite was true in the case of his father, also Harry. When William Storer died, in only his 45th year in March, 1912, *Wisden*, which in 1899 had made him the first Derbyshire player to be among the Five Cricketers of the Year, said in his obituary that the county had 'perhaps never produced a more remarkable player'. He was already an established batsman when he took over as Derbyshire's regular wicketkeeper at the beginning of the 1890s, and, in addition to winning representative honours on the strength of his batting alone, he took more than 200 wickets as a bowler. He played for England in all five Tests of the 1897–98 series in Australia, and in the opening game against the Aussies at Nottingham in 1899.

Harry Storer's father played in only half-a-dozen games for Derbyshire, all of them during their first season back in the County Championship in 1895, after their seven years in second-class exile, but he made nearly 200 appearances as a goalkeeper in League football. He became the first Woolwich Arsenal player to gain senior representative selection (for the Football League against the Scottish League in Glasgow) before helping Liverpool to win the Second Division title in 1896 and to finish runners-up in Division One in 1899.

Both Storer brothers started out in soccer with Derby Midland, both also had spells with Derby County and Loughborough Town. The Rams fielded William in all five forward positions, and also at full-back, but gave him only limited first-team opportunities. Harry, whose last League game for Liverpool was at the Baseball Ground on Christmas Day, 1899, did not get beyond the reserve team during the season he spent on Derby County's books after the club's merger with the Midland.

Harry Storer's son on the other hand, combined his long and rewarding service as a Derbyshire cricketer with a football career in which he excelled in the League. He played for Grimsby, Derby and Burnley, winning two England caps, and then, as a manager, guided Coventry City, Birmingham and Derby County to promotion. Having moved from Merseyside (he was born at West Derby during his father's days with Liverpool) at the age of four, when his parents returned to their home county of Derbyshire, he played for Ripley Town and Eastwood, and was then an amateur with Notts County before entering League football as Grimsby Town's centre-forward in a 3–0 home defeat by Stockport County on the first day of the 1919–20 season.

That setback sadly set the tone for one of the grimmest seasons in Grimsby's history. Storer was their top scorer with a dozen goals, but they managed a mere 34 in their 42 games and finished two points adrift at the foot of the Second Division. They had, however, a lifeline, one that temporarily eluded Lincoln City, the club immediately above them, who were voted out in favour of Cardiff City from the Southern League. By a happy coincidence this was the year the Third Division was formed, and Grimsby were elected to it along with the 21 other clubs from the First Division of the Southern League—an astute incorporation which solved the worrying problem of players being poached from the Football League without the bothersome business of forking out transfer fees.

The new section was officially known as 'Division III (South)' regardless of the fact that the Humberside home of one member was well north of Watford Gap, but that small matter was resolved the following year when Division III (North) came into existence. The Mariners were switched to it and Lincoln were brought back into the fold as another of the founder members.

In the meantime, Harry Storer Junior, who was always proud to claim that 'except for a freak of birth I am a Derbyshire man' had made his move back to his adopted county, a bargain buy at £2,500 by Derby County. The last dozen or so of his 68 appearances for Grimsby, who had no wish to lose him but needed the money, were made as left-half, a position to which he was to revert with the Rams after being switched to inside-forward. His hardworking and strong-tackling attributes were best suited to a defensive role, but his natural aggression and power of shot combined to leave his eye for a scoring opportunity undulled. It was entirely fitting that the last of his 20 goals for the Town was a winner—the only one of a game at Millwall.

Storer began with Derby County at wing-half but, after dropping out through injury and finding that Syd Plackett had been playing too well there in his absence to be displaced, he was pushed forward into attack. This move had such a telling effect that he was the club's leading scorer with 24 goals in 37 matches in the first of the two successive seasons in which they so narrowly missed promotion—plus three more in the Cup run that went to three replays against Newcastle.

That prosperous period, which included his four-goal sprees against Bristol City (in succession in 39 minutes) and Nelson, led to his first call-up for England—against France, in Paris, on May 17th, 1924. He played at inside-left in a forward line that included his right-wing clubmate, George Thornewell, and scored in a 3–1 victory. The two other goals came from schoolmaster Vivian Gibbins, then of Clapton Orient and later of West Ham, an amateur international also making his debut in the full England side and who, again like Storer, was to be given only one more chance at that level.

Storer's second cap was awarded in October, 1927, when, along with another Derby team-mate, Tommy Cooper, he was in the team, at left-half, which was beaten 2–0 by Ireland in Belfast. In their absence, the Rams[2] suffered their heaviest defeat of that season, conceding five goals without reply at Old Trafford, but they exactly reversed that result when Manchester United visited them for the return fixture, and they recovered from an inconsistent start to finish fourth in the First Division.

---

2. Gavin Malloch, a £140 signing by George Jobey from Benburb, a Glasgow junior club, made his League debut in this match, and, with the unfit Harry Bedford also absent, Arthur Bacon, an inside-forward from Chesterfield, led the attack for the first time. Bacon made only eight other League appearances for the Rams before moving to Manchester City, but Malloch went on to reach almost 100 before following Jackie Whitehouse, Tommy Davison and George Stephenson to Sheffield Wednesday. He spent nearly five years at Hillsborough, again getting near a century of first-team games, then assisted Millwall and Barrow. Bacon had a second spell with Chesterfield and also played for Reading, Coventry City and Burton Town.

That was Storer's first full season in Derby's half-back line, and, for once free from the injuries that had caused frequent interruptions to his forceful progress—most notably when he missed the last dozen games of the 1925–26 promotion season—he also played there in the Rams' first 30 matches of 1928–29 before his sudden transfer to Burnley, at a fee of £4,250, in late February. But for the fact that four of his enforced absences from the team were quite lengthy ones, he could have got well beyond 300 appearances for Derby instead of making 26 fewer.

Probably the most memorable of his 63 goals for the club was the matchwinner, to which reference has already briefly been made, against close challengers Chelsea on the run-in towards the promotion near-miss of 1925. Back in the side after a three-month lay-off, he was injured again early in the game, but, in typically indefatigable fashion, he carried on until he had to be taken off on a stretcher with torn rib ligaments after delivering his scoring shot from some 20 yards.

Storer helped Burnley to avoid relegation from the First Division with his resolute performances in their last dozen games of 1928–29, beginning with a 5–0 home win over Leeds United, and a 2–2 draw with Derby County also at Turf Moor. They then suffered three successive defeats, but Storer was among the scorers as they steadied themselves with another emphatic home victory, by 4–0 against Birmingham. They lost only one of their remaining six matches to end in 19th place—seven points above Bury, who accompanied bottom-of-the-table Cardiff into Division Two.

However, having conceded more than 100 goals that season—the worst defensive record in the top two divisions—and having survived by only one point the year before, Burnley were bedevilled with warning signs that spelled their undoing in 1929–30. Down they went with Everton, Sheffield United delaying their own descent for a few more years but only on goal average. The Goodison club bounced straight back, but it was to be 17 years before First Division football was again seen at Turf Moor.

The opposition for that long-awaited return was provided by Derby County, and therein lay one of those freaks of coincidence that fixture lists are prone to produce, for it was the Rams who were the visitors for Burnley's farewell to the First Division in April, 1930. But, whereas Derby were convincing 2–0 winners in August, 1947, on the former occasion Burnley slightly softened their fall with a resounding 6–2 triumph—an astonishing result which, however, had no more of a beneficial effect on the Lancashire club's goal figures than it had a damaging one on the County's position as runners-up. Derby finished three points ahead of third-placed Manchester City, who on that final day were themselves crushed, 5–1, by a Sheffield Wednesday side which ended ten points clear as champions. Burnley, with 97 goals against, again had the most porous defence of the first two divisions—a marked contrast to their promotion-winning record of 1946–47, when they conceded only 29.

Burnley's big win over Derby in 1930 was gained in only the third League game that Harry Storer played for them that season. Out since September, under the renewed influence of his injury hoodoo, he made his comeback at inside-left and, although he did not score against his old club, he enlivened an attack in which centre-forward Joe Mantle did the hat-trick. He continued in the forward line at the start of the club's first season back in the Second Division, but then, apart from a couple of games on the left wing and another at full-back, he reverted to wing-half. He remained a first choice until, aged 33, he was appointed manager of Coventry City in April, 1931, in the last weeks of the season his new club ended in an undistinguished 14th place in the Southern Section of the Third Division. Storer's 54 appearances and five goals for Burnley took his career League and Cup totals with three clubs to 396 and 88.

Having already been associated with one McIntyre, Johnny, as a player at Derby, he succeeded another, Jim, in securing the Highfield Road job from a host of applicants. In view of the forthright, authoritative manner for which he became so noted as one of the most intimidating, though widely respected, personalities in football, it is not surprising to learn that at his interview he so impressed chairman Walter Brandish, another strong character and recent winner of a power struggle within the boardroom, that he was offered the post on the spot.

Jim McIntyre, a former Coventry player who had been among Herbert Chapman's team-mates at Northampton, immediately guided Fulham to the Third South title after being dismissed by Coventry. Again however, he fell foul of his directors and was sacked at Craven Cottage more than two years before Storer followed him as manager of a promotion-winning side by getting City back into the Second Division in 1936. That first of three promotions as a manager, which Storer added to the one he had shared as a player with Derby County, was a mighty close-run thing, for not until the very last day did Coventry gain the narrow home win over Torquay United that kept them one point clear of Luton Town.

The springboard to that success was provided by a player whose scoring achievements for Blackburn Rovers had so caught the attention of Storer, when he was at Burnley,

Harry Storer won promotion as both player and manager.
(Derby Evening Telegraph)

that he went straight after him for his first Coventry signing. This was the bustling Bristolian Clarrie Bourton, whose £750 transfer fee was made to look ludicrously low, even for those days, as he went on to set club records that still stand of 50 goals in one season, his first, and 180 in six. It was largely through his wholehearted efforts that Coventry collected a century of goals in four of those six seasons, breaking another club record with 108 in 1931–32.

Goals were harder to come by in the Second Division, but, as Bourton faded from the scene, Storer came up with another bargain by going back to Derby early in 1937 to sign Ted Roberts, an enterprising forward from Glapwell Colliery. Roberts had only four first-team chances with George Jobey's star-studded Rams, but he rendered Coventry yeoman service over the next 15 years, less the war period that cost him his best footballing days. Typical of the spirited displays that made him one of the club's most popular players was the hat-trick he scored against Nottingham Forest, despite a broken nose, during his last season of 1951–52 before he left the League for King's Lynn, and a reunion with their player-manager and former Derby full-back, Jack Howe. The Forest centre-half who was given such a difficult time when Roberts scored those three goals, in a 3–3 draw, was Bob McKinlay, who had to wait nearly three years after that debut to gain the regular place in which he set his club's record of more than 650 appearances.

Harry Storer kept Coventry comfortably in the top half of the table through the last three full seasons they spent in the Second Division before the 1939–45 war. Indeed, they were in first place, and Derby County were leading the way in the First Division, when the clubs met in a friendly at Highfield Road on New Year's Day, 1939. Ted Roberts scored against his old club in the 2–2 draw, and one of Derby's goals was credited, on his debut, to Tom Hinchcliffe, a recruit from Huddersfield. Coventry finished fourth for the second consecutive season; the Rams, as will be recounted in greater detail later, fell away to sixth.

There was considerable surprise when Storer abandoned Coventry in the summer of 1945 to take charge of Birmingham, who that year added 'City' to their name. Later he was to admit the move was a mistake and one he regretted, even though he immediately led this new City to the transitional League South title and the FA Cup semi-finals (in which they lost to Derby in a replay after being reduced to ten men by injury), then to promotion as Second Division champions in 1947–48.

Within a few months of that return to the top section—gained mainly through the strength of a defence that was pierced only two dozen times while the attack mustered fewer goals than the team garnered points—he answered another call from Coventry. This followed the first of two unhappy managerial spells at Highfield Road for Billy Frith who had been one of Storer's favourite players, a stylish wing-half, after being signed on a free transfer from Chesterfield. Having rejoined Coventry as assistant manager, following a fraught player-manager experience with Port Vale, Frith had been as obvious a choice to fill the vacancy caused by the untimely death of Dick Bayliss[3]

---

3. Alfreton-born Bayliss, already having health problems, caught a chill on a difficult drive back from a scouting mission in Scotland during the severe winter of 1947, and collapsed soon afterwards. An incurable kidney complaint was diagnosed, and he died at the early age of 47.

Traumatic Travel for Capped Pair

In direct contrast to the molly-coddling arrangements for current football tours, Sammy Crooks and Tommy Cooper had quite a trautmatic experience in travelling to join the Derby County party for the last match of their visit to Germany during the 1934 close season after being with the England squad in Hungary and Czechoslovakia.

Arrangements were made for them to fly from Prague to Cologne in a small four-seater aeroplane, but when they landed near Leipzig the pilot told them that was as far as he went. No other aircraft was available, so they were told to go to Leipzig and complete the journey by train. Having changed some of their money into German currency, they ran into their next snag when the train was stopped by an attendant who brought along three policemen and an interpreter after they had waved him away because, not knowing German, they could not understand what he was shouting about as they settled into two sleeping berths. That little difficulty was cleared up when it was explained that an extra payment was required, but when they reached Cologne at 9.30 in the morning they learned that they had only half-an-hour in which to have breakfast and catch the club's bus to Dusseldorf—a city at which their train had stopped when they had woken up several hours earlier. To complete their ordeal, the bus broke down, they were nearly late for the match, and they did not get back to Cologne until three o'clock the next morning.

as Bayliss himself had been to succeed Storer through working with Harry as chief scout and right-hand man since 1931. A run of poor results was, however, to bring about Frith's downfall, and, on being reappointed nine years later, he was unable to halt another decline after getting the club out of the new Fourth Division at the first attempt.

Even Storer ran into difficulties after his return in November, 1948. This was a time of upheaval behind the Highfield Road scenes, during which he was just one of nine managers in the 16 years between his original departure and the arrival of Jimmy Hill that heralded the most spectacular phase in the club's history before their 1987 FA Cup win, with First Division status at last achieved. Storer's second coming lasted for five years, and ended amid confusion as the club's secretary, Bernard Hitchiner, issued an official statement that he had resigned, whereas W. Erle Shanks, who quit as president in protest but quickly popped up again as chairman of a new board, claimed that the manager had been sacked.

Storer remained a Coventry shareholder, but he stayed on the soccer sidelines until he blazed back into the Baseball Ground in 1955, recalled in one of the times of Derby County's direst need as they contemplated having to traipse around the northern outposts of the Third Division for the first time. Appalled, but undismayed, by the much-mauled morale of his new charges, he set about the daunting task of reviving a deflated giant with characteristic steely resolve. Making it perfectly clear that he wanted players who would 'roll up their sleeves and earn their pay', he straightaway turned to two on whom, from past experience, he knew he could depend. He brought in former Coventry junior Reg Ryan from West Bromwich to provide the main midfield driving force as an inspiring captain, and Martin McDonnell, whom he had previously signed for both Birmingham and Coventry, to stiffen the centre of his defence. Delving astutely into the transfer market along the way, Storer raised the Rams to runners-up at the first attempt, then to promoted champions at the second, breaking the club's scoring record for a League season with three-figure totals on both occasions.

That, though, was to be as far as he could take them. After having had something of a struggle to preserve Second Division status, Derby were close behind the pacemakers up to the New Year in what was to be Storer's last season before retirement, 1961–62, only to fade away into the bottom half of the table again. His main achievement after getting the club out of the Third North was to leave them with an overdraft reduced to nearly a third of the £60,000 with which they had been saddled when he had taken over. The impetus that at long last led to the League championship pennant being flown above the Baseball Ground was to be provided by Brian Clough, the brash young man from the North-East whose appointment as the Rams' manager came in 1967— the year in which Harry Storer died at the age of 69. The outspoken, often belligerent, but highly regarded Storer lived more than 30 years longer than his father, who was only 38 when he died of consumption in the first week of May, 1908.

As a player with Derby County, the career of Harry Storer Junior overlapped that of Jack Nicholas in the first team by just two matches, the first two of more than 500 (including war-time) in which Nicholas took part over 18 years with the club before extending his service as chief scout. 'Owd Nick' was the fans' affectionate nickname for this rugged defender. It might just as well have been 'Owd Faithful' for Nicholas was not only one of the most durable players the Rams have ever had but also one of the most loyal. It was indeed a richly-deserved reward, and the realisation of an ambition, when, as captain, he climbed Wembley's 39 steps to receive the FA Cup from King George VI after a clear-cut victory in the first final after the 1939–45 war. This earned Derby the trophy for what, regrettably, still remains the only time.

Nicholas never played for England, nor for the Football League, but he was the ideal club man. Statistics alone reflect his worth. From September 16th, 1931, when he was brought back into the side for a home game against Everton which Derby won with one of Jack Bowers's hat-tricks until war began in September, 1939, he missed only three League matches out of 331 and only one Cup-tie out of 25. And, when the Cup competition was resumed in 1945–46 he took part in all 11 games the County played to claim the trophy. In half of the last eight pre-war seasons he was an ever-present;[4] in each of three of the others he was absent from the First Division team just once. The

---

4. From January 23rd, 1937, when he returned to the side at Preston after missing just one match, until September 7th, 1946, when he was injured in a home game against Aston Villa, Nicholas had an unbroken sequence of 104 League appearances—not counting the three he also made at the beginning of the aborted 1939–40 season. With FA Cup-

Jack Nicholas at the pinnacle of his career—receiving the FA Cup from His
Majesty King George VI after the 1946 final.
(Derby Evening Telegraph)

lone exception was his first as a regular, in which he kept his place for the remaining
40 League and Cup games after missing the first five fixtures.

Such an imposing record says much for the consistent excellence of his form, both
footballing and physical. Nicholas was a hard man, fearsome but fair, reputedly with
a predilection for taking a cold shower on even the bitterest of days. In his last full
season, the Cup-winning one of 1945–46 during which he celebrated his 35th birthday,

ties included, but not war-time matches, and those three in August/September, 1939,
he had a run of 120 consecutive games during that period. From January, 1933 to April,
1935, Nicholas made 109 successive League and Cup appearances. The club record in
that respect was set by Archie Goodall, with 167 matches (151 of them in the League)
from October, 1892 to September, 1897. Two other players besides Nicholas have twice
had three-figure sequences: goalkeeper Colin Boulton (131 from January, 1971 to April,
1973; 115 from April, 1973 to September, 1975) and full-back Steve Buckley (127 from
January, 1978 to November, 1980; 119 from November, 1983 to January, 1986).

he alone played in all the Rams' games—53 of them—culminating in a stamina-testing seven in the last 16 days. This comprised the Easter rush (Friday, Saturday, and Monday) plus matches on the Monday, Wednesday and Saturday of the week following the Cup Final, which itself went to extra time. All that for nowhere near the outlandish pay packets pocketed by the pampered prima donnas of today.

Jack Nicholas, like Harry Storer, came from sound sporting stock. His father, William Joseph Nicholas, also known as Jack, was a dogged Derby defender himself, though one haunted by two penalties he conceded which resulted in an unfortunate Cup exit at the hands of Bristol City. Jack Nicholas Senior joined the Rams from Staines, where he was born, in 1905, and stepped into the right-back position when Jimmy Methven moved up to manager, making almost 150 appearances before his transfer to Swansea Town in 1912. That was how his Derby-born son, not quite two years old at the time of the move, came to win his schoolboy international honours in Wales, and also to be signed by Swansea, as a junior, before the family returned to Derby in time for young Jack to be taken onto the Baseball Ground staff shortly after turning 16.

The first of those two games in which he was introduced to the First Division, on the right flank of a half-back line that also included Harry Storer, came less than two

Jack Nicholas, a schoolboy international in Wales before returning to Derby, where he was born. He became one of the Rams most faithful servants.
(Derby Evening Telegraph)

years later, on December 29th, 1928. With Johnny McIntyre and two of his more experienced deputies, Alex MacDougall and Archie Scott,[5] all injured, Nicholas made his debut at Ewood Park, against a Blackburn side that included former Rams winger George Thornewell. He gave a useful display despite a 3–1 defeat, but he was omitted after the Rams lost again on New Year's Day, by 4–0 at Everton. He was given only eight further opportunities over the next two seasons before starting his remarkable run of appearances by supplanting McIntyre after the first five matches of 1931–32.

Eleven other youngsters made their League debuts during the season in which Nicholas was given his first chance, but only one of them, Jack Barker, was allowed an extended stay in the side at that time. The others, besides Nicholas, were Jack Bowers, Peter Ramage and Bobby Barclay, who were also to make their mark, and Albert Alderman, Jack Robson, Tom Ruddy, David Fereday, Alex MacDougall, Bert Mann and Billy Robson, who all failed to progress beyond reserve roles.

Barclay was one of George Jobey's discoveries in the North-East, which was such a profitable hunting ground for the Rams' manager. So much so that there was one match at Newcastle, shortly before Christmas in 1928, in which Derby's team included seven players from that part of the country (Collin, Davison and the complete forward line

Bobby Barclay. Capped by England after leaving the Rams, and twice a losing Cup finalist.
(Derby Evening Telegraph)

---

5. MacDougall made only two League appearances for the Rams after being signed from Wolverhampton Wanderers. Scott arrived from Airdrieonians as cover for the right-half and centre-half positions and played 32 times in the first team in seven seasons before leaving for Brentford, with whom he played a couple of League games during the 1934–35 season in which they won the Second Division title.

of Crooks, Barclay, Ruddy, Stephenson and Jack Robson), whereas the home club's side contained only two locals—and, for one of them, Jack 'Ginger' Hill, an England central defender, Newcastle had recently had to fork out a record fee of more than £8, 000 to bring him back from Burnley. Eight members of the United side that day were Scots, two of whom, right-winger Jimmy Boyd and centre-forward Hughie Gallacher, would later join Derby. Both these players were among the scorers in a 4–1 victory that day; Tom Ruddy, who was deputising for Harry Bedford, replied for Derby.

To find recruits from his home North-East, George Jobey followed up recommendations from his keen-eyed scouts in that area, Charlie Benson and 'Tadger' Stewart. Of those finds, Sammy Crooks (who will feature in the next chapter) George Collin and Ike Keen were the greatest, but Bobby Barclay, who made his League debut as Crooks's partner at inside-right in that game at St James's Park (not far from his Scotswood birthplace), was another to hit the high spots, though he really did so only after moving elsewhere.

Barclay's most successful season with Derby County was that of 1929–30, during which he made 35 of his 64 first-team appearances for the club and scored 17 of his 26 goals. On the Easter Monday he did the hat-trick in a 4–1 home win over Sheffield Wednesday, though the visitors were handicapped by an early injury to Billy Marsden, the man who was marking Barclay. The career of this powerful left-half was ended only a few weeks later when, in the most unfortunate of circumstances, he suffered a spinal injury resulting from a collision with one of his international team-mates, Huddersfield's Roy Goodall, while winning his third England cap in a 3–3 draw with Germany in Berlin.

Barclay scored again in Derby's return game at Hillsborough on the Easter Tuesday, but the Wednesday won that one 6–3. Seven of the goals came in 25 second-half minutes —the first four of them to the home side in ten minutes, the three others, after a slight lull, to the Rams in five minutes. It was but one of a series of high-scoring matches between the clubs since their return to the First Division together in 1926. This was the sequence:

1926–27:   Derby 8 (Whitehouse 4,Bedford 3, 1 pen, Gill); Wednesday 0
1927–28:   Derby 4 (Whitehouse 2, Mee,Stephenson); Wednesday 6 (Harper 3, Hill, Wilkinson, Collin, og)
Wednesday 2 (Trotter, Seed); Derby 2 (McIntyre, Stephenson).
1928–29:   Derby 6 (Stephenson 3, Bedford 2, Whitehouse); Wednesday 0
Wednesday 5 (Harper 3, Gregg, Strange); Derby 0
1929–30:   Derby 4 (Barclay 3, Robson, JC); Wednesday 1 (Hooper)
Wednesday 6 (Allen 3, Hooper, Millership, Rimmer); Derby 3 (Barclay, Bedford, Robson. JC).

The reversal of those 1928–29 results was the most exaggerated for the Rams since 1890–91. They had opened that season with an 8–5 home victory against Blackburn Rovers, but, reduced to ten men by an injury to inside-forward Lewis Cooper, had lost the return 0–8 just a week before walloping Wolverhampton Wanderers 9–0 for a club record League victory that was equalled against the Wednesday in 1899.

Ted Harper, who played only once for England (in a 1–0 defeat by Scotland) despite amassing 260 goals with four clubs, was certainly Derby's bogeyman, for his two hat-.

tricks against them, the first on his Wednesday debut, followed the brace of goals he had scored on each of the two occasions he had faced them while with Blackburn in 1926–27. Wednesday were 1–3 down at half-time when Harper played his first game for them on the last Saturday of November, 1927. The five goals they scored after the interval to win 6–4 were the most Derby conceded in the second half of a home game until promotion-bound Everton shocked the Rams with six as they rallied from 0–1 to 6–2 on a Second Division visit in February, 1954.

Harper netted five in a match for Blackburn Rovers (against Newcastle) and also for Tottenham (against Reading), breaking both clubs' scoring records for one season, but his stay at Sheffield was short—only 22 games and 16 goals—before his transfer to Spurs.

For Wednesday, the bogeyman was Jackie Whitehouse, with his four goals against them in one game, and nine altogether during his time with Derby (plus a previous three for Birmingham). This no doubt influenced them in their decision to take him from the Baseball Ground in February, 1929, but by then almost 32, he, too, did not stop with them for long. He only just took his League appearances with the Sheffield club into double figures before going to Bournemouth. It was Whitehouse's departure from Derby, after exactly 200 League and Cup games and 86 goals to add to his 115 and 35 for Birmingham, that opened the way for Barclay to be a Rams regular until a series of injuries interrupted his stylish progress and led to his leaving for Sheffield's other club at Bramall Lane.

With Sheffield United Barclay settled in so smoothly to justify their £3,500 outlay that he quickly established himself as a firm favourite with the fans and became the club's first inside-forward to play for England for more than 20 years. He resumed his partnership with Crooks in victories over Scotland at Wembley, and Ireland at Blackpool in 1932, then in a draw with the Scots, again at Wembley, in 1936. He and Crooks both scored, along with 'Pongo' Waring, the Aston Villa centre-forward, in the 3–0 defeat of Scotland, and he obtained the only goal of the game against the Irish.

Wembley, however, also held two bitter memories for Barclay. Three weeks after gaining the last of his three caps, he was back there with the Blades for the 1936 FA Cup Final in which they were beaten by a 74th-minute goal from Ted Drake, Arsenal's battering ram of a centre-forward. Two years after that, United having decided to part with him much to the dismay of the Bramall Lane faithful, he was in the Huddersfield Town side that also lost in the final to an only goal. This was scored in the last minute of extra time by Preston's George Mutch, from a very dubious penalty, so reversing the outcome of the final between these clubs 16 years earlier.

Barclay carried on playing for Huddersfield through most of the war years, but, rising 40, he was too old to contemplate continuing his League career after the war. Shortly before being released by the Town, he went back to Sheffield United as a guest player, and it was with the Blades that he met his other former club for the last time, at the Baseball Ground, in the transitional season of 1944–45, a few weeks before the war ended. As in one of his first games for Huddersfield, when he scored both goals in a 2–0 win at Leeds Road, he was on target against Derby County, equalising with a typically neat header, but once more his team were undone by a penalty. Irishman Peter Doherty, the guest from Manchester City who was soon to sign for the Rams and help them to a long-overdue triumph in an FA Cup Final, converted it to seal a 3–2 victory.

Ted Udall, whose persistent shoulder injury necessitated a
dozen operations after he had left the Baseball Ground.
(Derby Evening Telegraph)

The well-dressed footballer of the 1930s.
Jack Nicholas off duty.
(Derby Evening Telegraph)

Derby's right-back that day was the muscular, 13 stone six-footer Jack Nicholas, who
from the start of the last full pre-war season of 1938–39 had been as much at home there
as he had in the right-half position he had filled in nearly 300 games. He had already
shown his versatility by standing in at full-back a few times in an emergency, and also
by deputising at centre-half during some of Jack Barker's rare absences. During the war
he even turned out occasionally at the head of the attack—notably when he scored twice
in a 7–3 home win over Notts County—and in another match he played throughout in
goal. This happened at Barnsley, where hurried changes had to be made when Frank
Boulton, the Rams' former Arsenal goalkeeper and Charlton's Bert Brown, who was to

have guested at inside-forward, missed their train connection and were stranded at Birmingham. The young reserve goalkeeper named Vanham who was summoned reached Derby's bus station just too late to catch the team's motor coach, so Nicholas had to don the green jersey. Although his hesitation contributed to the first of the two goals Barnsley netted without reply, he 'did quite well in his unaccustomed role', to quote from the report in the *Derby Evening Telegraph*. The scorer of that opening goal was the Chilean George Robledo, who was to get one that won the Cup for Newcastle.

Kinnerley, an inexperienced 'A' team player, was brought into a reshuffled forward line to plug the gap left by the absence of Bert Brown, who had made what was to be his only appearance for Derby County in their home defeat by Barnsley the previous Saturday. Less than two years later, Brown was in the Charlton team that lost to the Rams at Wembley.

The conversion of Jack Nicholas to full-back solved a problem that had been worrying manager George Jobey. Ever since an injury to Ted Udall, and a loss of form by his first-choice deputy, David Bell, Jobey had been compelled to experiment in the previous season with Tom Alton, a Chesterfield-born youngster from New Tupton Ivanhoe, and George Wilcox, who arrived from Jack Barker's former club Denaby United but soon left for Rotherham after Nicholas had closed the first-team door on him.

Ted Udall's[6] first game for the Rams, as an emergency winger, was in Germany, for he accompanied them on their close-season tour immediately after his transfer from Leicester City in May, 1934. In fact, he was still a Leicester player on the first stage of that journey, completing the forms in London after joining his new clubmates when their train reached Leicester. Udall stepped into the League side at full-back straight after Tommy Cooper's departure to Liverpool, but his injury troubles began in an Easter Monday match with Everton at the Baseball Ground the following year, when he fell heavily tackling Jimmy Stein, the visitors' left-winger, and dislocated his left shoulder.

During the next season he aggravated the injury in an FA Cup-tie at Fulham, and several months later suffered another dislocation while playing against Stoke City. The final blow for him came in January, 1937, at Old Trafford. In attempting to avoid a fall on his shoulder, and risk further injury to it, he struck the ground with the back of his head, damaging an optic nerve and suffering tempory blindness. Udall made only one more League appearance after that, in a 5–0 home defeat by Manchester City. He was then forced to give up playing at the early age of 28. His shoulder, which he dislocated 13 times altogether, was too vulnerable, and the risk of more serious injury too great.

---

6. Udall played not at full-back but at outside-right, a position he had been filling in Leicester's reserve side, when he made his Derby debut in the first match of a German tour, in a 5–2 defeat by a German FA team in Frankfurt. The Rams' line-up was: Kirby; Reid, Collin; Nicholas, Barker, Keen; Udall, Hann, Bowers, Ramage, Randall. Collin was the captain in the absence of Tommy Cooper, who, along with right-winger Sammy Crooks, was on international duty in Hungary and Czechoslovakia, and took part in only the last game of Derby's tour, a 1–1 draw in Dortmund. In the other games (all four were against German FA sides) the County lost 5–0 in Cologne, but won 1–0 in Dusseldorf.

Goalkeeper Jack Kirby is the defiant odd man out as Derby's players reluctantly give the Nazi salute as they line up before a game during their 1934 tour of Germany.
(loaned by David Halford)

Derby's players, immaculately turned out for a function during the German tour, are all smiles as manager Jobey, so often the strict discipinarian, is in jovial mood.
(loaned by David Halford)

Tommy Cooper leads out the Rams through lines of Nazi salutes for the last match of their tour of Germany in May, 1934.
(loaned by David Halford)

David Bell, a former Scottish schoolboy international who himself had been unlucky with injuries while at his previous club, Newcastle United, reached almost a half-century of consecutive appearances after Udall had dropped out. He was then temporarily replaced by Wilcox and left for Ipswich Town just in time for the Suffolk club's first Football League season of 1938–39. He made good there as centre-half and captain, staying at Portman Road for a dozen years.

Ted Udall, meanwhile, went back as manager to Atherstone, the Birmingham Combination club from which he had graduated to Leicester. The first two players he signed were his former Derby team-mates Arthur Groves and Peter Ramage, inside-forwards who at one stage flanked Ray Freeman, a centre-forward who had been with Manchester City. From this nucleus, and using several ex-Derby reserve players, Udall built up a side that completed a treble in 1947–48 by adding the Birmingham Senior Cup and the Atherstone Nursery Cup to the Combination title they had gone close to claiming in the previous two seasons. Udall then refused a new contract because he had lost much of his direct control owing to the club's conversion to a limited company, but he did return for a second spell as their manager, reviving them from a slump, before leaving again to accept a similar appointment with Birch Coppice, a nearby colliery club then newly elected to the Birmingham Combination.

The last full-back partner Udall had in the Derby County side was Jack Howe, the former Hartlepools defender alongside whom Jack Nicholas struck up the formidable combination that was to reach its high point in the Cup Final success of 1946 through the coincidences of Howe's timely return from Army service abroad and the injury that kept out the young man who had been filling the left-back berth so ably in his absence. The unlucky Jack Parr not only missed that winner's medal but also the international recognition for which he was being tipped—and which Howe received instead—until he broke his right arm in a league game only a week after helping the Rams to reach Wembley in a semi-final replay.

After guesting for Notts County[7] during Derby County's close-down for the first two years of the 1939–45 war, Jack Nicholas was mainly responsible for starting things up again at the Baseball Ground, and for keeping them going until Ted Magner was appointed in 1944 to fill the managerial void left by George Jobey's sad exit. In the difficult job of cobbling teams together with the aid of guest players and untried youngsters, Nicholas had the enthusiastic assistance of Jack Webb, a doughty North-Easterner who had spent ten years as a reserve Derby defender before helping Newport

Jack Webb, pictured while on the ground staff at the Baseball Ground.
(Derby Evening Telegraph)

---

7. More than a dozen past, current and future Derby County players guested for Notts County during the 1939–40 and 1940–41 seasons in which the Rams were inactive. In some games there were as many as seven of them at the same time: Wilcox, Nicholas, Barker, Hann, Crooks, Walsh, and Duncan. Others included Groves, Keen, Musson, Parr, Ward, Carter and Broome. In 1941–42, when Derby County started up again on Christmas Day with a match against an RAF XI in aid of the Mayor of Derby's War Fund, Notts themselves were out of action because of the extensive damage to the pitch and main stand at Meadow Lane caused by enemy bombing.

County out of the Third Division South in the last pre-war season. Webb was to have a few more years back on Derby's ground staff shortly after playing one of his last games for the South Wales club against the Rams in the transitional League South of 1945–46.

The Nicholas-Howe pairing lasted only a third game into the resumption of First Division football after the war before 'Owd Nick', then nearing his 37th year, appeared to have at last come to the end of his League career when he was carried off with a wrenched knee in the closing stages of a home defeat by Aston Villa[8] early in September, 1946, but he made a comeback at Blackburn five months later and finally bowed out during Easter, in a 3–0 defeat at Chelsea on April 5th, 1947. That took him to a total of 347 League appearances, plus 36 in the FA Cup and just over 120 in war-time matches.

On the boat returning from the tour of Germany. The two at the back are Tommy Cooper and trainer Dave Willis. *Standing (left to right):* Jack Kirby, Sammy Crooks, Jimmy Randall, Sid Reid, Ike Keen, Ossie Bowden, George Collin, David Halford, Jack Nicholas, the Derby Evening Telegraph reporter who covered the tour, Freddie Jessop, Ted Udall, Jack Webb, Ralph Hann. *Centre:* George Jobey (wearing hat) and Councillor H.G. Pattison (director). *Front:* Syd Wileman, Jack Bowers, O.J. Jackson (director), Jack Barker, Peter Ramage. Mr Jackson is holding the metallic plate, framed in oak and suitably inscribed, that was presented to the club as a memento of their visit.

(courtesy of John Bowers, son of Jack)

---

8. The fixture list for the 1946–47 season was the same as that for the 1939–40 campaign which had to be abandoned because of the war. In the home game with Villa on September 2, 1939, the day before hostilities started, Derby won 1–0 with a penalty converted by Nicholas.

The strength of his kicking made him a reliable taker of penalties, these accounting for a third of his 30 goals—15 in the League (including the nullified 1939 winner against Villa mentioned in the footnote on the previous page), two in the Cup, and 13 during the war. However, his most important scoring shot was not from the spot. It forced a replay, which the Rams won narrowly, in a third-round Cup-tie at Ashton Gate in January, 1933, when Bristol City held the lead until he lashed the ball home on the hour from fully 30 yards. The man he left helpless was Ken Scattergood, who was to follow his father, Ernald, as guardian of the Derby goal but had a shattering experience on his debut which we shall be coming to in the chapter on Rams 'keepers.

As a scorer, Jack Nicholas enjoyed his most productive day as a war-time member of the Derby Borough Police force. He led the Derby Police attack against Nottingham City Police, and scored all their goals in a 4–4 draw. It was to Nottingham that he moved to live after his work as chief scout had increased his overall service with Derby County to some 30 years. He was fewer than three months past his 66th birthday when he died there in February, 1977.

Ted Udall, pictured during his days in
management in Birmingham district football.
(Derby Evening Telegraph)

CHAPTER 7

Wings for Victory

Jobey beats five rivals to Crooks deal – 'The gentleman from Derby' reaps rich dividends from his shillings – Sammy reprieved by Durham after hush-hush trial – Late rally just fails to avert semi-final defeat – Thornewell a Cup winner after leaving Derby for Blackburn – Crooks excels in England debut as defeat by 'Wembley Wizards' is avenged – Duncan and Ramage in ideal partnership — Unlucky Stockill

DURING THE 1930s, long before orthodox wingers were put out of fashion by Alf Ramsey's 'wingless wonders' who won the World Cup for England, there were some outstanding pairs of flank forwards in the top echelons of the Football League.

To name a star selection, Arsenal had Joe Hulme and Cliff Bastin; Aston Villa, Frank Broome and Eric Houghton; Everton, Ted Critchley or Albert Geldard and Jimmy Stein, then Torry Gillick and Wally Boyes; Manchester City, Ernie Toseland and Eric Brook; Sheffield Wednesday, Mark Hooper and Ellis Rimmer; Sunderland, Bert Davis and Jimmy Connor, then Len Duns and Eddie Burbanks. And Derby County arguably possessed the best of the lot in Sammy Crooks and Douglas ('Dally') Duncan.

George Jobey, having been tipped off about Crooks by Frank Keetley,[1] the former Derby forward who was impressed while playing against him for Doncaster, took his first step towards forming that famous wing pairing for the Rams in April, 1927, during the closing weeks of their first season back in the First Division. Learning that five other clubs were on the trail of Durham City's nippy little outside-right from the nearby coal-mining village of Bearpark, he forestalled them all by travelling up to sign Crooks a few days before the Third Division North match in which Arsenal, Chelsea, Huddersfield, Preston and Tottenham had planned to have him watched. For a fee of £300, the County's canny manager landed one of his biggest bargains, a penetrating raider who, with 26 international appearances, was to become England's second most-capped player between the wars—just one behind Eddie Hapgood, the Arsenal full-back who captained both club and country.

---

1. Keetley recommended to the Rams two other future internationals, centre-half, Jack Barker, whom he spotted with Denaby United in a midweek game, and Tim Ward. He was also instrumental in Lincoln City, another of his clubs, signing Bob Iverson, who went on to make good with Wolves and Aston Villa.

This was how Crooks looked back on the day he decided to join Derby County, influenced, it could be said, by the wily Jobey bobbing up to give him a timely nudge:

> The first idea I had of Mr Jobey's arrival was at about two o'clock on the Thursday afternoon. I was riding in a lorry with my mate, looking almost as black as the coal we were carrying, when I suddenly spotted Dickie Jackson, our manager, coming towards me with a stranger. 'It's you I want' he said, pointing to me. Then he introduced me to Mr Jobey, explaining that the Derby County manager wanted to have a chat with me.
>
> I arranged to meet them at my home at about four o'clock, and what a homecoming it was! I think nearly every boy and girl in Bearpark had gathered around our house that afternoon, and nearly every one of them had a shilling to show, and a shilling in those days of depression in the North-East was a big sum for a grown-up, never mind a youngster! It was Mr Jobey who paid out the shillings, and, believe me, everybody round our district of Durham looked upon him as a fairy godfather.
>
> After all that 'sudden wealth' had been showered on it by 'the gentleman from Derby' Bearpark had transferred me to Derby County before I had a chance to talk things over with Mr Jobey. Everybody had taken it for granted that I should sign for Derby County, and even if I had wanted to refuse I don't think I could have found it in my heart to have done so, especially when thinking of those kiddies outside, clutching their shillings.

Crooks, craftily coerced or not, never had cause to regret his decision to throw in his lot with the Rams. He also came to consider George Jobey to be, in his words 'the greatest manager of his day'—praise indeed, considering that the others included a certain Mr Chapman. There was satisfaction all round from the Crooks deal, for although the fee Durham received was far from fat, Sammy thought it was 'not a bad figure considering I was an amateur with City' and it gave them a reprieve, if not long-lasting, in clearing their most urgent debts. Sadly, their tentative hold on League status was to be broken after only one more season, when they finished next to last in the Northern Section table and were voted out in favour of Carlisle United. Nelson, the bottom club, survived for another three years.

Of the clubs on whom Jobey jumped the gun, Preston probably had most reason to feel aggrieved, for it was the second time they had been frustrated in their quest for Crooks. While he was still in Durham's second team he was invited to Deepdale for a hush-hush trial, only for it to be called off when City officials got to hear of it and informed North End that he was ineligible because he had already signed amateur forms for them. But for the intervention of manager Jackson, he might have been lost to Durham there and then, so heated a reception did he get when he arrived back home from that aborted trip. One annoyed City director said the club had no further interest in him because he had gone behind their backs, but Jackson, well aware of his protégé's potential, successfully argued for him to be forgiven.

Sammy's Debut Memories

Sammy Crooks admitted that he felt far from confident when he was called to George Jobey s office on Thursday, September 8th, 1927, after playing in just one Colts game and three reserve matches since turning professional with Derby County. With no thought of being given his first chance in the First Division side, and fearing that he was going to be told he needed to improve a lot if he wanted to make progress, he was, to use his own words, 'stunned into silence' when the Rams manager told him that he was to deputise for the injured George Thornewell for that Saturday's visit of Leicester City.

> *Perhaps it was as well that I had to wait only two days for the match', he recalled. 'I was not nervous, but I might have been if I had been given a week to think about it. After telling me I was to play, the manager spent the next half-hour in giving me some very good advice. I listened to every word of it, but if I didn't take it all in it was only because I was so excited at the prospect of taking a place among stars of the football world. One thing I do remember him telling me was to take notice of what the other players said to me on the field. We also had a number of talks on team tactics.*
>
> *On the Saturday morning I was supposed to be resting in my digs, but, as I lived near the Baseball Ground, I found it almost impossible to control my excitement after lunch. I repeatedly wandered to the window to watch the crowds gathering round the gates, and it came as a great relief when it was time for me to report at the ground. The lads were quite lively in the dressing room, and it was then that I heard for the first time the famous motto of the Derby County defenders. 'You forwards put 'em in', said one of the full-backs, 'and we ll keep 'em out and win the match for you'.*

Although it did not work out exactly like that on Sammy's debut day because Arthur Chandler scored for Leicester, Derby did win and Crooks was closely involved in both their goals. This was how he remembered the first one:

> *The ball was sent out to me, and, in my customary way, I pulled it back a little and then slipped Jimmy Gill an inside pass. Before I realised what had happened, Jimmy had cracked it home from about 20 yards. I had done nothing out of the ordinary. In fact, I was still waiting for a return pass when it suddenly dawned on me that my partner had scored. It was certainly Gill's goal, but anybody walking into the Baseball Ground at that particular moment would have thought that I had netted. My team-mates rushed over to me, patted me on the back, shook hands with me, and almost bore me to the ground with their vigorous congratulations. If anybody tells you that it is a lot of nonsense for players to shower their congratulations on a scorer or a player who has helped in the scoring of a goal, don t believe them. Those pats on the back encouraged me no end. I was brimful of confidence for the rest of the game, and it was from my centre that Harry Bedford scored our second goal.*

These were the teams that afternoon **Derby County**: Olney; Cooper, Crilly; McIntyre, McLaverty, Storer; Crooks, Gill, Bedford, Whitehouse, Murphy. **Leicester City**: McLaren; Black, Osborne; Duncan, Carrigan, Findlay; Adcock, Hine, Chandler, Lochhead, Bell.

Sunderland, for whom Jackson had played at half-back, were another club to rue the day they missed the chance to sign Crooks. Although he was unaware of it at the time, he was offered to them because Durham so desperately needed the money, but the Sunderland manager, Bob Kyle, turned him down for being too small. It was mainly due to his lack of height (he was 5ft 7in at his tallest) that he became an outside-right, originally very much against his wishes. Dickie Jackson did not take long to decide that he could make more use of his speed on the wing than at inside-right, even though he had scored 98 goals from that position before Christmas one season while playing for Brandon Juniors in the Durham Junior League. It was a switch for which Crooks was to be grateful, though there were to be several occasions on which Derby County benefited from his habit of moving back inside when they were up against it late in a match.

Unfortunately for the Rams, the most important game in which he tried that ruse was one they narrowly lost, even though it inspired a two-goal revival. This was in the 1933 FA Cup semi-final against Manchester City at Huddersfield where Derby, the favourites, fell three goals behind after missing some good early chances and also being handicapped by injuries to the Jacks, Bowers and Nicholas. It was while Nicholas was

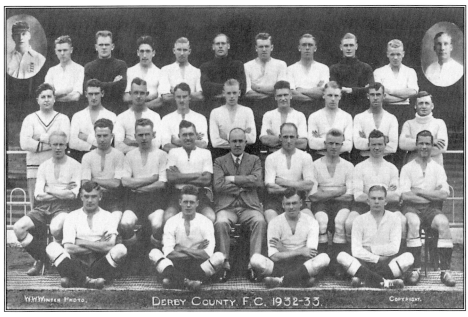

The line-up of 1932–33. *Inset (left):* Tommy Cooper, and *(right):* Albert Alderman. *Back row (left to right):* Syd Wileman, Harry Wilkes, Ralph Hann, Ossie Bowden, Jack Kirby, Jack Nicholas, Jack Robson, Frank Eckersley, Keith Hague. *Second row:* Laurie Edwards (trainer), Jack Bowers, Archie Scott, A.H. Fabian, Arnold Robinson, Jack Barker, Eddie Green, George Collin, Bill Bromage (assistant trainer). *Seated:* Ike Keen, Sid Reid, Norman Robson, Freddie Jessop, George Jobey (manager), Billy Carr, Jimmy Randall, Duncan Hutchison, 'Dally' Duncan. *On ground:* Jack Webb, Sammy Crooks, Peter Ramage, Eddie Dickenson.
(W.W. Winter)

off the field receiving treatment that Eric Brook, City's outside-left, put over the centre from which right-winger Ernie Toseland opened the scoring with a header two minutes before half-time. Bowers, dazed in collisions with goalkeeper Len Langford and centre-half Sam Cowan, had cold water poured over him from a hosepipe by trainer Laurie Edwards during the interval, but although he played on he was still in what one report called 'a state of coma' throughout the second half. Sammy Crooks said he had 'rarely seen a player knocked about as much as Bowers was in that match'.

Fred Tilson, who a year later followed Bowers as leader of England's attack, headed City further in front when Brook lobbed the ball across soon after the break, and 20 minutes from time skipper Jimmy McMullan, who had been switched from left-half to inside-left to retain his place in the side in his last season with the Manchester club, wriggled through to score their third goal. That was when Crooks swapped places with his inside partner, Howard Fabian, an England amateur international and newly-appointed sports master at Highgate School[2] whose lack of full-time training was beginning to show. The effect was immediate. Whereas Fabian had tired himself out chasing McMullan, Crooks ('rarely had I put so much into a game') made McMullan chase him, and City faded as an attacking force as their 'general' was run almost to a standstill.

Fabian caught Langford off his line to reduce the deficit, but Derby's second goal, from Crooks, came too late to prevent the men from Maine Road holding on to make the first of two successive appearances at Wembley. Beaten by Everton in the 1933 final, they returned the next year and staged a winning recovery against Portsmouth. For Fabian, compensation for falling at the semi-final hurdle came when he helped the Casuals to win the Amateur Cup in 1936. Alas, there was to be no such consolation for Crooks. He scored a late winning goal when the Rams next reached the Cup's last four in 1946, but injury cost him the chance to crown his magnificent career by being in the team that at last claimed the trophy for Derby in the first post-war final.

The First Division title medal which several times seemed so tantalisingly close also eluded this most popular of players who devoted so many years of cheerful, uncomplaining service to Derby County. He was, however, an enduring international, called upon by his country more times than anybody else while with the club until his record was overtaken first by Alan Durban, next by Roy McFarland, and then by Peter Shilton, who made 34 of his record 125 appearances for England as a Derby player. Durban inched ahead of Crooks with 27 games for Wales, one of them as a substitute; McFarland reached 28 for England, and would undoubtedly have played in more if he had not snapped an Achilles tendon during the 1974 match with Northern Ireland

---

2. While a student at Highgate, Fabian played in the School's soccer team along with R.W.V. Robins, who went on to play cricket for Middlesex and England. He was also with Robins at Cambridge University, where he won cricket and soccer Blues, captaining the soccer side in his third and final year, 1931. From 1931 to 1934 Fabian gained six England amateur soccer caps, and he was also in the Casuals team that defeated Ilford 2–0 in an Amateur Cup Final replay after a 1–1 draw. He twice won the Public Schools' threequarter-mile steeplechase, and four times won the amateur championship for the Kinnaird Cup at Eton Fives.

at Wembley. Colin Todd, twice a sub, also edged one appearance past Crooks in equalling Durban's total, though he, too, could have progressed beyond that but for temporarily being banned from consideration after declining to make himself available for a close-season England tour.

From the day, September 10th, 1927, when he made his First Division debut in a 2–1 home win over Leicester City, Sammy Crooks never looked back. An injury to George Thornewell gave him that early opportunity, in Derby's fourth game of the season, and he made such an instant impression that Thornewell got back for only three more matches, taking him to within five of 300 for the Rams (26 goals), before leaving for Blackburn. Five months later, Sammy's predecessor was doing what Crooks himself was never destined to do—playing in a Cup-winning team at Wembley. Thornewell broke a collar bone in Rovers' fourth-round tie at Exeter, but he recovered in time to return for the semi-final against Arsenal at Leicester. In the final—only his 12th game for the Lancashire club—he helped to upset the form book in a 3–1 defeat of Huddersfield Town, who also finished runners-up for the League title (for the second consecutive season, after being champions in each of the previous three years).

The newcomer from Derby was prominent in the move that led to Jack Roscamp, scorer of the goal that knocked out Arsenal, bundling the Huddersfield goalkeeper, Billy Mercer, into the net with the ball in the very first minute. What was more, on the following Thursday, Thornewell shared in a 3–2 win at Ewood Park (Crooks scored

Sammy Crooks who made his first-team debut after
one game with the Colts and three in the Reserves.
(Derby Evening Telegraph)

one of Derby's goals) that ended his old club's run of ten League matches without defeat.

Years later when I met George Thornewell while he was licensee of the White Hart, at Duffield, just outside Derby, the match that still stood out most in his memory was not that 1928 Cup Final, but the Baseball Ground nail-biter in which the Rams fell one goal short of the 5–0 victory against Leicester City that they needed for promotion. He said:

> That was very, very disappointing. And, to add insult to injury, Bill Barrett, the Leicester right-back, booted the ball into his own net immediately after the final whistle, just to show us how it was done! Because I had been a member of the side that had been relegated several years before, I derived great satisfaction from staying with the club long enough to have the honour of helping them back to the First Division a couple of years after that bitter disappointment against Leicester.

After almost 50 League and Cup games for Blackburn, and having by then taken over the White Hart, Thornewell moved to Chesterfield. In 1930–31, his second season at Saltergate, he collected another medal in the team that carried off the Third North championship. Finally, he was briefly with Newark Town as player-coach, then hung up his boots to concentrate on his work as a publican. He maintained an interest in

George Thornewell with his football trophies, displayed in the public bar while he was the licensee at the White Hart, Duffield.

(Derby Evening Telegraph)

football right up to his death, aged 87, at Derby in 1986, serving for a time as president of Duffield United, and on the committee of the Derby County Supporters' Association.[3]

Sammy Crooks, whose integration into his new life at Derby was strengthened by his marriage to Freda Stone, a swimmer well-known locally, proved such an admirable replacement for Thornewell that the Rams gained the enviable record of having only those two players as regular holders of their outside-right position during the 20 years between the two world wars. After playing for the FA against a Lancashire FA side,

Sammy Crooks with his wife Freda, a well-known Derby swimmer.
(Derby Evening Telegraph)

3. The Derby County Supporters' Association was formed in 1956. The Rams' first Supporters' Club was launched on a great wave of enthusiasm in June, 1923, but membership fell from a first-year figure of about 2,500 to just under 500. This, combined with a feeling that there was 'a lack of sympathy and support among the Derby County directors', culminated in the decision to disband at the fourth annual meeting in August, 1927. The Rams had obtained, in cash or kind, some £2,200 annually from the Supporters' Club, including the provision of cover for part of the Baseball Ground's popular side terracing at a cost of £825. A second Supporters' Club was formed a few years before the third one, but was not recognised by Derby County and ceased to function after only a few years.

Crooks took his first big step towards following Thornewell as an England winger when, in March, 1929, he was chosen for The Rest against an England XI in an international trial at Tottenham's ground. The teams for that game make interesting reading, representing the pick of home talent on the threshold of the Thirties:

ENGLAND: **Hacking** (Oldham Athletic); **Jackson** (Liverpool), **Blenkinsop** (Sheffield Wednesday); **Edwards** (Leeds United), **Hart** (Leeds United), **Campbell** (Blackburn Rovers); **Hulme** (Arsenal), **Brown** (Huddersfield Town), **Watson** (West Ham United), **Walker** (Aston Villa), **Ruffell** (West Ham United).

THE REST: **Hibbs** (Birmingham); **Smart** (Aston Villa), **Shaw** (Wolverhampton Wanderers); **Kean** (Bolton Wanderers), **Sneddon** (Bolton Wanderers), **Marsden** (Sheffield Wednesday); **Crooks** (Derby County), **Hine** (Leicester City), **Hodgson** (Liverpool), **Price** (Fulham), **Page** (Burnley).

In being selected as a reserve for The Rest along with Harry Storer, who was then with Burnley, George Collin, the Rams' left-back, received his only representative call-up. There was no further upgrading for him—well deserved though it was—but in the case of Crooks it was only an honour deferred when his hopes were dashed of being chosen for the following month's match with Scotland in Glasgow. Neither did Joe Hulme, the Arsenal flier, keep the right-wing place he had held in England's last two matches, despite scoring in both, in narrow wins over Ireland and Wales. Instead, there was a recall for another pacey player, Jack Bruton, of Burnley, who in turn had to give way to Leicester's Hughie Adcock for the ensuing five England games before Crooks was brought in for the next clash with the Scots at Wembley on April 5th, 1930.

Sammy earned that opportunity with an outstanding display in that year's international trial, at Liverpool's ground, in which two other Derby players, Tommy Cooper and George Stephenson, also took part. Crooks and his inside partner, David Jack (Hulme's club colleague at Highbury) were the men of the match in helping The Rest to an astonishing 6–1 victory against an England XI. This left the selectors with no option but to award the Derby winger his first cap, and also give a fifth one to Jack, the Arsenal stylist who had been overlooked since helping to beat Belgium at Antwerp two years earlier, while with Bolton Wanderers. Crooks recalled:

> After the team had been announced I just lived for Wembley. I decided that if fitness meant success then I was going to be the 'hit' of the match. Although I was too excited to sleep the night after I had been selected, I made up my mind that sleep, and plenty of it, plus hard training, would be the order for me until the day of the match. And, though you may not believe it, I can truthfully say that I went to bed between 8.30 and 9.00 each night until the big day. When April the fifth came I was as fit as it was possible for a footballer to be.

How magnificently that super-toned fitness paid off! Again, the 21-year-old Crooks, and Jack, who was ten years his senior (he celebrated his 31st birthday two days before the game) were the stars as England avenged their 5–1 humiliation by Scotland's 1928 'Wembley Wizards' with a sparkling 5–2 triumph. It was only the second success they had achieved against the old enemy in ten meetings, since the Scots had lost by the odd goal of nine in the Sheffield thriller of 1920 which had marked the official resumption of the annual series interrupted by war.

Thriving on the excellent support he received from Jack, who repeatedly drew the opposition by holding the ball before providing the pass that gave him a clear opening, Crooks contributed directly to all four first-half goals that put England in command— and he went very close to scoring twice himself. Tommy Law, the stocky and shrewd Chelsea full-back who was one of the five 'Wizards' of 1928 in the Scottish line-up, had the most harrowing afternoon of his distinguished career as shock-haired Sammy tormented him with his direct and incisive methods. These were the teams on that memorable day:

ENGLAND: **Hibbs** (Birmingham); **Goodall** (Huddersfield Town), **Blenkinsop**; **Strange** (both Sheffield Wednesday), **Webster** (Middlesbrough), **Marsden** (Sheffield Wednesday); **Crooks** (Derby County), **Jack** (Arsenal), **Watson** (West Ham United), **Bradford** (Birmingham), **Rimmer** (Sheffield Wednesday).

SCOTLAND: **Harkness**[4] (Hearts); **Gray** (Rangers), **Law**[4] (Chelsea); **Buchanan**, **Meiklejohn**, **Craig** (all Rangers); **Jackson**[4] (Huddersfield Town), **James**[4] (Arsenal), **Fleming** (Rangers), **Stevenson** (Motherwell), **Morton**[4] (Rangers).

Watson and Rimmer both scored twice for England, whose other goal came from Jack. James Fleming obtained Scotland's two replies.

Widespread as was the the praise heaped upon Crooks in attaining the peak of the footballing ambition that it had been left to him, the youngest of four brothers,[5] to fulfil for their father, that display against the Scots was not the one he personally rated as the best he ever gave. It was not even the second best. For what he considered the top performance of his career he looked back to a November afternoon in 1930 at Tottenham, where he scored twice in the Football League's 7–3 defeat of the Scottish League. The other game in which he felt he also fared even better than he did during the revenge win at Wembley was played against Belgium, who were beaten 4–1 in Brussels a few months after that second of his five appearances for the League.

Derby County were well represented on that England visit to the Continent in the spring of 1931, for Tommy Cooper was also in the party, and the club's trainer, Laurie Edwards, was the 'team attendant' to give his official title. One of the other players was George Stephenson, who had only recently left the Rams for Sheffield Wednesday.

---

4. Survivors from the team that won 5–1 at Wembley in 1928.
5. Sammy's father, who never played for a League club because he received more money from the collections the big amateur clubs in the Durham area made for him, was bitterly disappointed when his two older sons, Harry and Fred, failed to make football a career. Harry, a centre-forward, was sought by several clubs after his demobilisation from the Royal Navy at the end of the 1914–18 war, but, like his father, was not interested in playing professionally. Fred, a centre-half, was discouraged by a succession of injuries. The third brother, Robert, had no interest in soccer. According to Sammy 'he just didn't know how to kick back-doors, never mind footballs!'

Several months later, there was another international match which Sammy Crooks had particular reason to remember. It was the eagerly-awaited Highbury clash with Spain, whose 4–3 win in Madrid two years earlier had broken England's unbeaten record against overseas sides. When Crooks was slightly injured during the first half, Zamora, the Spaniards' much-vaunted goalkeeper, immediately rushed to his aid and carried him to the touchline for treatment. On his recovery, Sammy proceeded to show his 'appreciation' of such a sportsmanlike act by twice slamming the ball past his benefactor as England romped to a 7–1 victory. He confessed:

> I could not help feeling sorry for Zamora, a great-hearted player, as we left the field at the final whistle. Evidently, Zamora felt sorry for himself too, for tears of anguish flowed down his swarthy cheeks as he made his way to the dressing room.

One of the linesmen that day was Stanley Rous, the schoolmaster referee who became secretary of the Football Association, then president of FIFA, and who was knighted for his services to soccer.

Crooks played in 15 successive games for England before his 1932–33 season was prematurely ended by a pulled leg muscle suffered in an international trial at Portsmouth on the Wednesday after his strenuous efforts in the Cup semi-final against Manchester City. The injury kept him out of the annual tussle with the Scots, who won 2–1 in Glasgow, but after also missing England's following visits to Rome and Berne he won six more consecutive caps before he first had to give way to Stoke's own 'Wizard' Stanley Matthews. Sammy's subsequent appearances for his country were spasmodic as, apart from Matthews, he had to contend with strong competition from Albert Geldard (Everton), Freddie Worrall (Portsmouth), Wilf Birkett (Middlesbrough), Dick Spence (Chelsea) and Alf Kirchen (Arsenal), but he missed two close-season tours only through injury. He at least had the satisfaction of going out on a high note. It was not until after the 6–2 humbling of Hungary, back at Highbury on December 2nd, 1936, that he finally faded from the international scene as, following the brief intervention of Kirchen and Geldard, Matthews eventually emerged in all his baffling glory.

Over his six years as an England winger, during which he also started his 14 years as chairman of the Players' Union (now PFA), Crooks had a dozen partners at inside-right. Two of them were former Derby clubmates, George Stephenson and Bobby Barclay, and another a future colleague at the Baseball Ground, Sunderland's Raich Carter. The others after David Jack were Gordon Hodgson (Liverpool), Henry Roberts (Millwall), J.W. Smith (Portsmouth), Tom Grosvenor (Birmingham), Joe Beresford (Aston Villa), Jackie Bestall (Grimsby Town), Ray Bowden (Arsenal) and Billy Scott (Brentford).

With Derby County, Crooks had almost 50 partners, ranging from Jimmy Gill to Frank Broome, who, while with Villa, was one of Sammy's successors as England's outside-right (he occupied four forward positions in his first five internationals, with inside-left the exception). Those who played most frequently at inside-right to Crooks in Derby's attack were Arthur Groves, Barclay, Whitehouse, Reg Stockill, Ronnie Dix, Dai Astley and, during the war years, local boy Tommy Powell.

In one season alone, 1931–32, Crooks had eight different partners, among them Wilf Lewis, who had been capped by Wales while with Swansea and Huddersfield, but who was unable to solve Derby's problem. Lewis was one of the four partners Sammy had in the Rams' first five games that season—and in the other match he played at inside-right himself! No wonder he admitted to feeling 'a trifle envious' when, as he put it, 'Dally' Duncan 'had the good fortune to find a perfect partner in his first season with Derby County'. The man he assessed so highly was Bonnyrigg-born Peter Ramage, who played at inside-left to Duncan in more than 160 matches. There were only rare look-ins, when either of them was unavailable, for half-a-dozen deputies before another fellow Scot, Charlie Napier, settled in alongside Duncan after appearing in all five forward positions with the Rams. In Sammy's opinion:

> Ramage and Duncan formed the greatest left-wing partnership I ever saw at Derby. I have nothing but praise for the sturdily-built inside-left. An ideal team man, both on and off the field, Ramage was what we footballers term a 'spade' man. He was a great forager, a glutton for work, and one of the best clubmen Derby have ever possessed. He was always there to help you out of trouble, and if he had been with a London club he would have been hailed as a second Alex James. His positional play and ball distribution were second to none. I can honestly say that, at times, I have stood still on the right wing and marvelled at some of the brilliant triangular movements Duncan and Ramage worked with Ike Keen on the opposite flank.

Duncan looked upon Bob McPhail, of Rangers, with whom he linked up in the Scotland side, as the best of all his partners, but he shared Sammy's Ramage rating in putting

Peter Ramage, an ideal team man, a great
forager and a glutton for work.
(Derby Evening Telegraph)

Peter at the top of his list at club level—and that was some rating considering that another Peter, the impish Irishman Doherty, later also played inside to Duncan, if at an advanced stage of both their careers. The other Derby players of 'Dally's' early days at the Baseball Ground also readily recognised Ramage's worth. One of them, Jack Barker, considered that 'he helped more men to an international cap than any player I have known'. Unfortunately, however, his ability was never fully appreciated by many of the club's followers, chiefly because he did not get many goals. He scored just 60 in 255 League and Cup games for the Rams—from their first match of the 1928–29 season, when he deputised for George Stephenson, who had been injured in the public practice match, and did score on his debut in a 5–1 beating of Cup holders Blackburn, until their last game of 1936–37, when he bowed out scoreless in a 3–1 defeat at Wolverhampton.

The undiscerning failed to acknowledge the hard-working and unselfish value of Ramage as a provider. His scheming, positioning and anticipation made him a first-rate creator of openings for others, and it is interesting to note, in view of one comment from Crooks, that his style was likened in some quarters to that of the illustrious James. Ramage's signing was yet another of George Jobey's master-strokes. He entered English football with Coventry City, who spotted him playing for Newtongrange Star in the Midlothian League. After quickly gaining a place in City's Third Division team, he chanced to come to the attention of the Rams' manager when, due to Coventry's heavy casualty list, he was needed for a Midland Midweek League match at Derby in January, 1928. Wolves had an option on the then 19-year-old Ramage until the following August, but he did not wish to go to Molineux, and within a week of that arrangement expiring the impressed Jobey made him a Derby County player.

Scarce as Ramage's goals were, it is for one of them that he is best remembered. It was the extra-time winner in a sixth-round FA Cup replay at Sunderland, on March 8th, 1933, a match among the most dramatic ever staged in the North-East's soccer cauldron. It attracted the record Roker Park crowd of 75, 118[6] with thousands more locked out. One spectator was carried out of the ground, dead, after a goal by Sunderland's centre-forward, Bobby Gurney, had been disallowed for offside. Another man died in the crush outside after the gates had been closed. Four trainloads of Derby supporters were turned back several miles short of their destination when it became clear that they could not get to the stadium in time—especially as so many people were already packed in that it was deemed advisable to bring the kick-off forward.

For those Rams fans who did manage to gain admission, it was a game never to be forgotten, even though it was to lead to the bitter disappointment of defeat in that ill-starred semi-final at Huddersfield as Manchester City knocked Derby out for the second successive season. With the County's defence in superlative form, and their formidable half-back line of Nicholas, Barker and Keen excelling, the only goal of the Roker replay came in the 11th minute of the extra half-hour. Nicholas swept the ball out to Crooks, who took it in his stride, swerved round left-back Harold Shaw, and sent over a deceptive,

---

6. The receipts were £4,566, a Roker record broken when 44,820 paid £4,631 to see the first leg of Sunderland's fifth-round FA Cup-tie against Birmingham City on February 9th, 1946. The final receipts record at Roker Park was £187,000, for a third-round FA Cup replay against Manchester United, watched by a crowd of 21,378, on January 16, 1996.

curling centre. The ball eluded the Rams' centre-forward, Jack Bowers, and his marker, Scottish international Jack McDougall, but not the leaping Ramage, who steered it just inside the far upright with a marvellous header.

Surprisingly, although Ramage naturally retained an indelible memory of that magnificent, decisive effort, he did not store it away as his most outstanding footballing experience. Instead, he gave pride of place to the First Division match in which Derby fielded an all-Scottish forward line at Villa Park, on the last Saturday of September in 1935. He told me:

> I put that game first because of the high standard of football it produced. Our forward line really clicked that day, and we fully deserved the win we gained, with goals from Jimmy Boyd and Hughie Gallacher. Boyd, who picked up a Cup winner's medal with Newcastle, was playing his first match on our right wing because Sammy Crooks was unfit. We had Charlie Napier at inside-right, and myself and 'Dally' Duncan on the other side of Hughie on the left wing.

The Roker replay Ramage so spectacularly Ram-raided arose from an even more gripping thriller—the original tie, watched by a then record Baseball Ground crowd

'Dally' Duncan, alert for another attacking chance, with his inside-left partner Peter Ramage looking on and Ike Keen deeper in the background.
(Derby Evening Telegraph)

of 34,218, in which Duncan was the scoring hero. Jimmy Thorpe, the Sunderland goalkeeper whose death at the age of only 22[7] so shocked the soccer world during his club's title-winning season of 1935–36, had been forewarned about the swerving shot 'Dally' had perfected, yet he was twice beaten by it as the winger flighted the ball across from out near the corner flag. The first of those Scottish specials helped Derby to a two-goal lead in the opening 20 minutes, the other conjured up a sensational last-minute equaliser at the Normanton end after Sunderland, inspired by Ram-to-be Raich Carter, had fought back to go 4–3 ahead. The first six goals came in 36 minutes.

There was another match, at Highbury earlier that season, in which Duncan's deceptive crosses were also too much to bear for a defender considerably more experienced than Thorpe. Derby seemed set for defeat when, with Arsenal well on top, they trailed by 3–1 shortly before half-time. Suddenly, however, Duncan broke away and put over a low centre. Herbert Roberts, king of the stopper centre-halves and known as 'The Policeman' moved calmly and unhurriedly to deal with it, but, to his consternation, it skidded off his right boot as he swung confidently for the clearance and went behind him into his own net.

Three minutes later, Duncan again drifted languidly down his wing and crossed the ball in identical fashion. Amazingly, Roberts repeated his reaction, his attempted clearance slicing past goalkeeper Frank Moss for the equaliser. The whistle had still to be blown for the interval when Duncan got in another centre, hit more powerfully this time. The anguished silence in which the home crowd watched their centre-half shaping to deal with the cross gave way to a collective sigh of relief as he made it a case of third time lucky, steering the ball away to safety. There was no further scoring, the Rams' salvaged point maintaining an impressive start in which they lost only two of their first 14 matches.

In the opinion of Sammy Crooks, that 1932–33 season was the one, above all the others he spent with Derby County before the Second World War, in which they should have won some of the game's honours, but the hopes they had of doing the double faded away as they faltered to finish seventh in the First Division after so narrowly losing their first Cup semi-final for ten years. Again as Sammy saw it, the main reason they fell short was the continued weakness at inside-right, and it was in an effort to solve this pressing problem that George Jobey went into the transfer market during the following close season to bring back to Derbyshire the forward who became Crooks's most frequent partner. For a fee of £550, he signed Arthur Groves, who found his way back to his home county from Blackburn Rovers after leaving his local Langwith Colliery club to make his first foray into League football with Halifax Town.

Groves, who was born at Killamarsh, near Chesterfield, in 1907—on September 27th, which, by a sad coincidence, was also the date of his death in 1979—gave some notable displays for Derby. He also brought them a handsome profit, valued at £1,500, when early in 1936 he reluctantly departed to Portsmouth, against whom he had played the last of his 64 League games for the Rams at Fratton Park the previous Christmas Day. Like Peter Ramage, this skilful stylist was a maker, rather than taker, of goals, and there

---

7. A coroner's jury found the cause of Thorpe's death to be diabetes, accentuated by the rough usage he received during a home game against Chelsea a few days earlier.

was some justification for the complaints that they were too similar in their methods to provide the required blend.

In opening his account for Portsmouth, Groves accomplished something he never did for Derby by getting two goals in one match. He scored only 18 for the Rams, but among them was one of the most explosive ever seen at Villa Park, a real humdinger that clinched a lead gained by Crooks. This is how Arthur described it to me:

> Jack Bowers pushed the ball back to where I was standing, about 35 yards out, and I hit it first time. Helped by the wind, it went past Villa's keeper, Harry Morton, into the top corner of the net like a rocket—but it might easily have gone near the corner flag instead!

When I met Arthur Groves, he was back in the Derby area, living at Spondon only a few minutes' walk from George Collin's home, after completing his League career with Stockport County on the outbreak of war, and then rejoining two other former Rams team-mates, Ramage and Ted Udall, at Atherstone. From there he went into the Central Alliance as Heanor Athletic's player-coach, finally packing up playing after helping to win the inter-departmental trophy at the British Celanese works where he was employed. As he jokingly put it 'after that my back legs really went!'

Arthur Groves, an infrequent scorer but a
memorable marksman at Villa Park.
(Derby Evening Telegraph)

Arthur still had a few years left in him, though, as a cricketer. Before the war he was an opening batsman with Heanor Town CC when they won the Notts and Derbyshire Border League championship. He later assisted Long Eaton Spinners and Spondon before winding up with General Industrial Cleaners, a Borrowash firm he joined from Celanese—and for whose cricket team Alf Pope, the former Derbyshire all-rounder, also played. In addition, Groves kept up his interest in football as a regular attender at the Baseball Ground, and occasionally did some scouting for Luton Town when 'Dally' Duncan was manager there.

One of his best 'finds' was his own son, John, though Duncan said it was only in casual conversation with his former Derby clubmate that he learned of the versatile young man's promising form. Duncan signed Groves Junior after seeing him play for Derbyshire Boys against Surrey Boys at Crystal Palace's ground, and the Derby-born inside-forward or wing-half went on to play for Luton when they reached the First Division and the FA Cup Final, both for the first time, in the 1950s.

One player who, but for being jinxed by injury, could have provided the ideal solution as a partner for Sammy Crooks at Derby was Reg Stockill. An England schoolboy international, he entered League football with his home club, York City, at the tender

Reg Stockill, who looked the answer to the inside-right problem until hit by injury.
(Derby Evening Telegraph)

age of 15 years, 280 days on the day they also did, August 31st, 1929. He had the added distinction of scoring the first of their two goals as they got off to a winning start in the Third Division North, away to Wigan Borough.

Despite that encouraging display, he played only one more first-team game before moving to Scarborough in 1931, and later that year he was snapped up by Arsenal. Having scored four times in seven senior appearances for the Gunners, he was biding his time in their reserve side when George Jobey pulled off another of his coups by beating Huddersfield, Liverpool, and Newcastle for his signature just a few weeks into the 1934–35 season. Jobey had to overcome initial resistance from both club and player to do it. The Gunners scoffed at his initial bid of £1,000, but accepted a doubled offer, and Stockill, initially, was not keen on the deal because he was reluctant to leave Highbury. It looked a bumper bargain for the County, though, when, soon afterwards, Stockill starred in a 9–3 demolition of West Bromwich Albion at the Baseball Ground. He and Crooks hit their only First Division hat-tricks as Derby ran up their biggest score since the 9–0 defeat of the Wednesday nearly 36 years earlier. Excluding a 10–0 war-time win over Mansfield, they have since raised that record with a 12–0 defeat of the Irish club, Finn Harps, in a 1976 UEFA Cup-tie.

In the next home match after the Albion's unhappy visit, Stockill scored twice in a 3–1 win over his former Arsenal clubmates, but four days later, on Boxing Day, 1934, also at Derby, he was carried off after 15 minutes' play against Wolves with right-knee ligaments so badly damaged in a hasty, misjudged tackle by Jack Dowen, a young full-back making his League debut, that more than 14 months went by before he was back in first-team action. Despite dispelling fears that he career might be over, he was never the same force again.

His confidence impaired, he was unable to fulfil the promise that had appeared so abundant, and his form fluctuated to such an extent that he was placed on the transfer list at the end of the 1937–38 season. Though reprieved in being re-signed for what was to be the last full pre-war campaign, he showed only a few flashes of his old form in several appearances at centre-forward before Scottish international Dave McCulloch's arrival from Brentford. In August, 1939, after 69 games and 30 goals for the Rams, he moved to Luton Town in exchange for Billy Redfern, an inside-forward whose two League games for Derby had to be deleted from the records when the 1939–40 season's programme was abandoned with the declaration of war. Stockill saw out his career during the war back where he had started, with York City. He died in 1995.

Redfern, who played for Wales against England early in the war, scored on his debut for Derby in a 2–0 midweek home win over Portsmouth. The other scorer in that penultimate peacetime match was 'Dally'[8] Duncan, the mesmerising left-winger who preceded Reg Stockill as a £2,000 Jobey signing when, in March, 1932, his tormenting

---

8. As a small boy, Duncan carried big brother Jim's football boots to matches played by Aberdeen Richmond. One source says that his nickname arose from the fact that he was such a little chap that his brother affectionately called him 'Dolly' and that as a schoolboy this became 'Dally'. 'I used to love dribbling with the ball, so I would hang on to it', Duncan recalled. 'The switch of nicknames was natural enough. As a boy I spent every spare moment kicking a rubber ball around on a piece of waste ground at the top of our

talents were rescued from the obscurity of the Third Division's Northern Section into which he had descended with Hull City. This deceptively nonchalant Aberdonian's famous wing link-up with Sammy Crooks had a muted start in defeat at West Ham, but it blossomed through the next five seasons, during which Derby County's final First Division placings were as high as second, and never lower than seventh. Duncan's first full campaign with the Rams was in only its third month when he added to the international selection he had gained as a schoolboy by earning his first senior call-up by his country and becoming Derby's first Scottish cap. He said it was the proudest moment of his career when he was chosen to succeed Alan Morton as Scotland's left-wing partner for Alex James.

Wales, whose team included Duncan's future Derby colleague Dai Astley, then of Aston Villa, spoiled that international debut on October 26th, 1932 with a 5–2 win at Hearts' Tynecastle ground in Edinburgh, but Duncan did score one of Scotland's goals. He and right-winger Crawford, of Queen's Park, were the only players retained for the match in which England were beaten by the odd goal of three at Hampden Park the following April. Duncan's first match for Scotland was the last with Wales for Fred Keenor, the former Cardiff City captain and one of the great personalities of Welsh football. There was also the curiosity that Wales played for Scotland—Hugh Wales, a member of Motherwell's Scottish League championship team of 1931–32, who was winning his only cap. This was how they lined up:

SCOTLAND: **McLaren** (St Johnstone); **Gray** (Rangers), **Blair** (Aston Villa); **Wales** (Motherwell), **Johnstone** (Hearts), **Thomson, J** (Everton); **Crawford** (Queen's Park), **Thomson, A** (Celtic), **Dewar** (Third Lanark), **James** (Arsenal), **Duncan** (Derby County).

WALES: **John** (Stoke City); **Williams** (Everton), **Ellis** (Motherwell); **Keenor** (Crewe Alexandra), **Griffiths** (Bolton Wanderers), **Richards**; **Phillips** (both Wolverhampton Wanderers), **O'Callaghan** (Tottenham Hotspur), **Astley** (Aston Villa), **Robbins** (West Bromwich Albion), **Lewis** (Swansea Town).

The scorers, besides Duncan, were O'Callaghan (2), Astley, Griffiths and Thomson, J (own goal), for Wales; Dewar for Scotland.

Duncan did not score when he first faced England, but when those countries met in Glasgow two years later he headed both goals of the game from right-wing corner kicks by Charlie Napier, who cost Derby County about £3,500 a couple of months later after Celtic had rejected his request for a benefit. Those goals came in quick succession—the first only seconds before half-time, the other four minutes after the interval. Another feature of that match, watched by a crowd of almost 130,000, was the keen duel between two Derby County players: Jack Barker at centre-half for England, Hughie Gallacher (winning the last of his 20 caps) at centre-forward for Scotland.

---

street. When the other boys weren't there I worked hard on little dribbling tricks with which I hoped to surprise them.' Jack Stamps, Duncan's last inside-left partner at Derby, said: 'We always knew him as 'Dally'. I occasionally heard him called Douggie, but never Douglas'.

Despite having three of their top men at Hampden Park, the Rams that day gained their first away win over Liverpool since 1902. One of their three goals was scored by Duncan's deputy, Don Bird, a Welsh junior international who had spells with Cardiff City (as an amateur) and Bury before making 80 appearances in two seasons with Torquay United. He was signed as cover from the Devon club for £250, but he found only four further League chances with Derby, also scoring in a win over Wolves, before he left for Sheffield United. From there, he went to Southend.

With 50 goals in 122 League and Cup games for Hull, Duncan had built up quite a reputation as a scoring winger after entering English football from Aberdeen Richmond, and he kept it up with Derby County by getting 21 goals in 46 matches in the 1932–33 season. He reached double figures with the Rams in only one other season, 1936–37, but he left them for Luton in 1946 with the reasonable total of 69 in 289 League and Cup games—plus just over 50 more during the war years in which he temporarily re-formed his Derby partnership with Peter Ramage after popping in ten others as a guest player with Notts County.

Ramage stayed in Derbyshire for two years with Chesterfield after ending his nine seasons' sterling service at the Baseball Ground, then had time to play only three games for Chelmsford City before the war cut short his engagement with the Essex club. On returning to Derby to work for Qualcast, the lawnmower firm, he made just a few further appearances for the Rams when they resumed their activities in the third year of the war. Subsequently he had spells with Heanor Town, Atherstone, Ilkeston Town and SS Sports, a Derby team he also coached, before finally calling it a day as captain of the Qualcast side in the 1951–52 season. One of his last matches was back at the Baseball Ground, in the final of a Derbyshire cup competition. He was 74 when he died in December, 1982.

'Dally' Duncan made the last of his 14 appearances for Scotland five years after his first, again in defeat to Wales, by 2–1 in Cardiff. When he achieved the honour denied his wing colleague, Sammy Crooks, in helping to win the FA Cup for the first time in the club's history, in 1946, he was the oldest member of Derby County's team—in his 37th year. His was the shot, which he claimed would have gone in anyway, that brought the opening goal against Charlton Athletic at Wembley. It was turned into his own net by Bert Turner, who promptly equalised with a deflected free kick to force the extra time Derby dominated as Peter Doherty and Jack Stamps (2) crowned their 4–1 triumph. Duncan's wife Dorothy, a Derby woman, proudly wore his winner's medal as a pendant on a gold chain on special occasions.

It was a case of third time lucky for Duncan in at last reaching an FA Cup Final in the twilight of his career. Before the disappointment of the Rams' 1933 semi-final defeat by Manchester City, he had first won through to the last four with Hull City in 1930. On that occasion, typically unperturbed by having to arrive aboard a later train after missing the one his team-mates travelled on, he had scored to put the Humberside club two up on the half-hour against Arsenal at Leeds, only for the Gunners to round off their revival with a late equaliser and then narrowly win the Villa Park replay against a side handicapped by the sending-off of centre-half Arthur Childs.

Sammy Crooks, who ended his ten-match injury absence in a transitional League South fixture at Charlton the Saturday before the 1946 final for which he was declared 'not football fit' was into his first spell as the Rams' chief scout when, pressed back into playing service owing to injuries and international calls, he took part in the last three of his 408 Football League games early in the first post-war season of 1946–47. He and Duncan fittingly made their last appearances in Derby's colours on the same day, September 28th, 1946, but, regrettably, not on the winning side. Weakened by the absence of their forward aces Raich Carter (from whom Crooks took over the captaincy) and Peter Doherty, who were international opponents in Belfast, the Rams lost 2–1 at home to a Blackpool team reduced by injury to ten men for most of the second half. The deciding goal came in the last minute.

Duncan, whose other sporting interests took in bowls and golf (like Crooks he had a single-figure handicap) had returned to League action in a win at Highbury only the Saturday before that game with Blackpool, after recovering from a pre-season muscle sprain. For the following match—won handsomely at Brentford with thousands locked out of a packed Griffin Park—he gave way to Kenneth Powell, [9] a young Mansfield man fresh from war-time service in the Royal Navy who had been giving some sparkling displays for the reserves. The veteran Scot then became the first member of the Cup-winning team to leave Derby, joining Luton a few weeks later.

After an inauspicious start with the Bedfordshire club, in which he was ordered off for the only time in his career following goalmouth incidents that resulted in two successive penalty kicks being awarded to Swansea at the Vetch Field, Duncan was promoted to player-manager when George Martin moved to manage Newcastle. Then, concentrating on management, he led Luton into the First Division for the first time in their history in 1955, but, early in the 1958–59 season, in which they also reached their first FA Cup Final, he ended his reign as their longest-serving manager, forfeiting his first chance to join the select few who have both played in and managed Cup-winning teams. He was tempted away to fill the managerial vacancy at Blackburn caused by the departure of former Irish international Johnny Carey to Everton. Luton's chairman Percy Mitchell, described Rovers' approach as 'a big shock to us' and he showed how highly he and his fellow directors valued Duncan by adding 'We offered 'Dally' a substantial increase in his wages, to the utmost limit of our resources'.

Deprived of Duncan's canny direction, the Luton team he assembled lost at Wembley, by 2–1 to ten-man Nottingham Forest, whose right-winger Roy Dwight (cousin of the entertainer Sir Elton John) broke a leg soon after scoring and helping them to go two up in the first ten minutes. Blackburn were also beaten there the next year, when they, too, had a player, full-back David Whelan, carried off with a broken leg. Rovers' 3–0 defeat by Wolves in the 1960 final, following their close escape from relegation, was Duncan's last match as a manager. His £2,500-a-year contract still had just over three years to run when he was dismissed after refusing to resign and, 'angry and disappointed by this first slur on my name after having a record in football of which I have been very proud' he went to live in Brighton, where he did some schoolboy coaching and scouted for Luton before concentrating on running a boarding house. He was 80 when he died in hospital at the Sussex seaside town in 1990.

---

9. Powell failed to sustain a bright start and played in only 13 League games before joining Southport during the following summer.

For Sammy Crooks, the exit from League-club management came six years before Duncan's. Having left Derby County in August, 1949, on friendly terms despite resigning as chief scout because he was refused a step up to assistant manager, he piloted Retford Town to promotion in the Yorkshire League before becoming Shrewsbury Town's first manager in the Football League in 1950. He was appointed in the month preceding the Shropshire club's election to the Northern Section of the Third Division (along with Scunthorpe United) on its extension to 24 clubs. However, he found it such hard going, as he was also helping to run the sports outfitting business he owned in Derby in partnership with Harry Elliott, the former Derbyshire and England wicketkeeper, that he decided to leave Gay Meadow in the summer of 1954, after again only just avoiding having to seek re-election. Despite the continued lack of playing success following a switch to the Southern Section, he at least had the satisfaction, by astute sales, of leaving Shrewsbury financially far better off than he had found them.

After scouting briefly for Birmingham City, Crooks had two spells with Gresley Rovers in the Birmingham League, either side of an unhappy few months managing Burton Albion on their entry into the Southern League, and it was not until after he had turned 50 that he played the last of his occasional matches, on his final day with Gresley. That was in May, 1959, when he turned out for the reserves against Newhall. That evening, he still had enough energy left to win the Mickleover Golf Club's Salt Cup medal competition, with a net return of 64 off an eight handicap, in a field of more than 60. It was a success he had been trying to achieve for the past 20 years.

Next came a season as Heanor Town's coach, after which he returned to the Baseball Ground for his second stint as Derby's chief scout. This lasted seven years up to 1967, when he and a former Rams team-mate, manager Tim Ward, were swept aside as Brian Clough and Peter Taylor breezed in from the North-East to propel the County out of the doldrums and to peaks the club had never previously scaled.

Though kept on the outside looking in, as the First Division title was at last annexed twice in four years in the 1970s, Crooks never lost his affection for Derby County. It was sad that he, one of the most popular and loyal players they have ever had, did not live to see them progress to a prolonged period of prosperity. On the contrary, they were once more in decline, heading back to the Third Division, at the time of his death in February, 1981, just over a fortnight after his 73rd birthday.

Whereas George Jobey was not averse to snubbing sentiment in dispensing with players once they had turned 30, no matter how talented or highly regarded, it was significant that Crooks and Duncan both continued on the Rams' books well beyond that age. It was not, of course, that neither was much sought after, and there was one particular occasion, around Christmas 1930, when Sammy was nearly transferred for a then record fee of some £13,000. He recalled:

> Very few people knew about that. Indeed, it was kept so secret that I did not know anything about it until some time afterwards. Arsenal had been impressed by the understanding David Jack and I had developed in representative games. Negotiations opened between the two clubs, but for some reason, of which I was not acquainted, the deal fell through.

The reason came to light when Tom Whittaker, then Arsenal's trainer and later their manager, stated in his *Arsenal Story* that Alex James refused to move to Derby in part exchange when he learned that he was being valued at only £2,000 in the proposed deal, which, according to Whittaker, also involved Tommy Cooper.

Statistics clearly show why envious eyes were so often cast in the direction of Derby's international wingers throughout most of the Thirties. Consider these figures:

	Appearances			
	Lge	Cup	War-time	Total
Crooks	408	37	108	553
Duncan	261	28	145	434
	Goals			
	Lge	Cup	War-time	Total
Crooks	101	10	27	138
Duncan	63	6	51	120

As Notts County guests in seasons 1939–40 and 1940–41, Crooks made 38 appearances, scoring 16 goals, and Duncan netted 10 times over 40 games.

But figures alone cannot tell the whole story. Consider also these quotes from some of those most in the know—their playing colleagues. Firstly Crooks:

Tommy Powell (his inside-right partner during the 1939–45 war):

> Sammy took me under his wing and acted as a father figure towards me. He was undoubtedly one of the most popular people to wear a Derby shirt.

Jack Parr (full-back):

> He was a grand man to have in your side. I believe he was one of the greatest outside-rights I have ever seen.

Jack Stamps (two-goal hero of Derby's 1946 Cup Final win):

> He was one of the most enthusiastic and skilful players in the game. He had an enormous influence on the Derby teams of his era. He was a real fun-loving person, and a marvellous character.

Tim Ward (a colleague at Derby as both player and manager):

> He was a great friend to all of us. He was one of the few players you could call a legend in his own lifetime. When I was young he was my hero. It was a great privilege to play with him. He had a great knack of lifting you up after a defeat. He was never depressed.

And Duncan:

Stuart McMillan (Derby's manager when Duncan moved to Luton):

> We felt, after the wonderful service he has given Derby County, that we could not deny him this splendid opportunity for his future in football.

Jack Stamps:

> The best outside-left I ever played alongside. He was reserved in his ways off the field. He never pushed himself forward and was very respectful to other people, always prepared to listen to what they had to say.

Raich Carter:

> 'Dally' was a very good player. When I joined Derby I could not have hoped to find a better pair of wingers than Sammy Crooks and 'Dally.' I had played against them for Sunderland in the 1930s, when Derby were always a fine side.

CHAPTER 8

The Denaby Double

Barker and Bowers reap Rams rich dividends for outlay of only £425 – Triumphant return to Derby by Bedford after transfer to Newcastle – Bowers breaks Derby scoring record and twice heads First Division goals list – Bowers scores in England debut – Barker one of outsiders as Arsenal have record seven players in 'Battle of Highbury' – Title for Reserves – Shock departure by Bowers – Unhappy return for Barker

O F ALL THE SLICK PIECES OF BUSINESS George Jobey did for Derby County, surely the slickest was the one that could truly be tagged the Denaby Double. So impressed was he by the strapping centre-half who opposed the raw and rangy Scunthorpe United centre-forward he went to watch in a Midland League match at Denaby that he signed the pair of them. Both went on to play for England and to become key figures in Derby's successes of the 1930s. Rich dividends for an outlay of just £425.

The defender, John William Barker (cost £275), an uncompromising Yorkshireman who had survived a pit disaster, rose to captain the Rams, and also his country in his last international match. The attacker, John William Anslow Bowers (£150), barnstormed through the best of defences, twice smashing the club's scoring record for one season and twice topping the First Division's individual goals list.

From Christmas1928 to the eve of war in September, 1939, Jack Barker played in 326 League games and 27 Cup-ties for Derby. From the first Saturday of February, 1929, to mid-November, 1936, Jack Bowers made 220 appearances (203 League, 17 Cup) and amassed 183 goals—overtaking Harry Bedford (152) as the County's most prolific scorer since Bloomer, and still their second highest[1] in League matches alone with 167 to the peerless Steve's 293.

Jack Barker, who was born at Denaby, a few miles from Rotherham in South Yorkshire, in February, 1907, was just over a year older than Bowers, who came from Santon, a village near Scunthorpe. They were among ten players introduced into Derby's senior side during the 1928–29 season, but only Barker was given an extended run at that

---

1. For all matches, Bloomer leads with 332 goals for Derby, followed by Kevin Hector (201) and Bowers (183). For League matches alone, Hector (155) is third behind Bloomer and Bowers.

time. Of the others, in addition to Bowers, Bobby Barclay and Jack Nicholas were to make the most progress, though another, utility forward Albert Alderman, was to enjoy a productive career as an opening batsman with Derbyshire, whom he helped to win the County Championship in 1936.

Having been pushed back into the background by Tommy Davison for much of his second season at the Baseball Ground, Barker began 1930–31 as the first choice he remained for the rest of the pre-war years, and he settled in comfortably between Johnny McIntyre and Gavin Malloch in the half-back line as the Rams got away to one of their best starts. They went unbeaten through their first eight games before conceding two goals without reply at Portsmouth, and lost only once more in their next seven matches. There was a real championship look about them at that stage, especially in their high-scoring away wins over Newcastle United (5–2) and Aston Villa (6–4), but after further impressive victories, at home, against Chelsea (6–2) and Huddersfield (4–1) they leaked two dozen goals in six games and, lacking consistency, subsided from being third in the table just before Christmas to finish 'only' sixth.

One of the reasons for that falling-off in form was a centre-half problem, brought about by an ankle injury to Barker which kept him out of the side from the beginning of November until late the following February. With Tommy Davison laid low with a septic throat, Billy Carr having broken a bone in a foot in a collision with Liverpool's lanky Tom Bradshaw, and Archie Scott needing stitches in a badly-cut cheek after crashing into George Stephenson, it was during this period that Harry Bedford had to be pressed into the central defensive role. He played just the one match there, in a 4–1 defeat at Middlesbrough in which the Rams were also depleted by the absence of Sammy Crooks. It transpired that Bedford was to turn out for the club only once more before being transferred to Newcastle.

And therein lay another cause of the Derby decline—onto which most of the blame was to be attached by supporters dismayed by the departure of a firm favourite. As Crooks remembered it 'Bedford's transfer certainly caused a stir'. This detrimental effect was aggravated when Stephenson, with Davison, left for Sheffield Wednesday two months later. What was worse, Bedford returned to the Baseball Ground to play 'old Harry' with the Rams in the match that coincided with Barker's return. Captain for the day against his recent team-mates, he led Newcastle to a 5–1 win, scoring one of their goals, as United reaped revenge for the triumph on Tyneside to which he had contributed one of Derby's five goals—three of which had come in just four minutes after winger Tommy Lang, later also a scorer from a penalty, had given the home side an early lead. On the day, February 21st, 1931, when Bedford came back to leave the Rams red-faced, Newcastle's other scorers in their heaviest defeat of Derby were left-winger Jack Wilkinson, who did the hat-trick, and a County player-to-be, centre-forward Duncan Hutchison, who gets more of a mention later in this chapter. Derby's lone reply in their biggest home setback for 38 years came from, of all people, Jack Barker—the first of the only two goals he netted in League football. The other one helped towards a win at Middlesbrough about a year and a half later.

Harry Bedford was Newcastle's joint top scorer with a dozen goals in nearly two dozen League games in his first season with them—all from the inside-right position to which he had been switched for his last few matches with Derby apart from his one appearance in central defence. He then lost a regular place to the recalled Jimmy

Richardson, the former Blyth Spartan who was soon to be caught up in one of Wembley's fiercest controversies. For Richardson it was who enabled Newcastle to overcome an early deficit in the 1932 FA Cup Final by crossing a ball that looked out of play to set up the first of Jack Allen's two goals in the defeat of Arsenal.

At the beginning of that year Bedford joined Sunderland, but he spent only a few months there before moving again, to Bradford. During his short stay with the Roker Park club, he was motoring back to his Newcastle home after a defeat by Huddersfield when he stopped to pick up a man who thumbed a lift because he had lost his railway ticket. 'I've been to the match' said his passenger. 'It was terrible, and so was that fellow Bedford.' In telling me this story against himself, Harry said that he waited until he dropped the man off before asking: 'What would you say if I told you my name was Bedford?' His departing guest was not the least bit ruffled. 'You know, I thought your face was familiar' he replied. But there was no apology.

After just one season with Bradford at Park Avenue, Bedford made Chesterfield his seventh League club before moving on as player-coach with Heanor Town and helping them, with nearly 30 goals, to win the Central Combination championship. Having been focused on football for so many years, he brought the spice of variety into his life after playing his last game for Heanor in 1936 by having spells as masseur for the Derbyshire cricket team and as a publican at both Temple Normanton, near Chesterfield, and Derby. He went back to Newcastle United as coach before the Second World War, but, when I met him in the early 1950s, he was back in Derby in very different roles.

At that time, he was employed, with his former Rams clubmate George Collin, as a fireman at the Rolls-Royce works. He was also running a small general store on Cockpit Hill, a site opposite the bus station since swallowed up by a modern shopping centre, with the help of his wife who was the daughter of Jack Frettingham, a former Forest and Gillingham player. For a while he had been attached to the Derbyshire FA as a coach, working with Frank Broome, then a current Derby County player, Bill Corkhill, a Notts County half-back, and Tom Peacock, a former Forest forward, in giving instruction to schoolmasters and pupils in various parts of the county, but he had since made that work more of a hobby, restricting it to private classes.

Early in 1954, he was appointed team manager of Belper Town in the Central Alliance, but in the following March, while still on the Rolls-Royce pay roll and having his store to run, he was released to return to the Heanor club. Their 'more attractive offer' gave him wider scope because they ran three teams, and also provided the opportunity he welcomed to work with a smaller committee. That, however, did not avoid a rapid development of differences that led to his being given a month's notice before the end of the year. Yet, within days 'an amicable settlement' was announced and Bedford was told to carry on with a contract which ran for two more years.

With such a diversity of interests, he had fewer opportunities than he would have liked to revisit the Baseball Ground. I last saw him there at the Rams' final match of the 1974–75 season, when he was among the past Derby players who paraded on the pitch as part of the club's celebration of their second First Division title in four seasons (after having gone without one in the previous 72 since the League's formation). Harry Bedford died in Derby just over a year later, aged 76.

It was to accommodate the reinstatement of Jack Bowers at centre-forward that Harry Bedford was switched to inside-right on October 11th, 1930, for a home game in which both players scored as Cup-holders Arsenal, hitherto unbeaten leaders of the First Division, were defeated 4–2 after conceding three goals in the first 22 minutes. Bedford had first stepped aside, to inside-left, when, on the strength of scoring 27 goals in 13 appearances for the reserves, Bowers had been given his first senior chance against Bolton Wanderers on February 2nd, 1929. They shared the Rams' scoring in a 2–1 home victory that day, when Bowers, 21 later that month, earned this praise in a local newspaper:

> He tackled his job with invigorating freshness, took up position like an old hand, and distributed with discretion. He could always be designated dangerous, with foot or head…

Jack Bowers, the fearless centre-forward who was twice the First Division's leading scorer and raised the Rams record for League and Cup goals in a season to 43 in 1932–33.

(Derby Evening Telegraph)

Prophetic words! But despite that accolade, and despite following up his encouraging debut with a hat-trick in a 5–1 win at Portsmouth the next Saturday, Bowers was soon returned to the reserves for more grooming. With Bedford still one of the League's most free-scoring centre-forwards, enjoying his best Derby seasons with 30 goals in 1928–29, and 31 in 1929–30 (including Cup-ties), the wiry lad from Lincolnshire was playing only his tenth first-team game for the Rams when he was brought back for that game against Arsenal, their tenth fixture of the 1930–31 season. That, though, was the big turning point of his career. Goals in all but one of the first six matches of that recall established him as a constant choice. It became abundantly clear that Derby had unearthed one of the sharpest scorers in their history when he went on to crack the club's individual record for one season with 37 League goals in only 33 games, plus two more in a shock third-round FA Cup failure away to Exeter City, a modest mid-table side in the Third Division's Southern Section.

That overall total of 39 also took him well ahead of the previous best by a Derby player for all matches in a season—the 32 in 1908–09 by 'Snobby' Bentley who, in 1909–10, had set the old League record of 30 equalled by Bedford in 1929–30. Not until the 1956–57 season was Bowers's League best of 37 equalled, and then it was not in the First Division, but down in the Third North, that Ilkeston miner Ray Straw did so in spearheading Derby's escape from that lowly sphere at the second attempt.

Three times in his record-breaking first season as a Rams regular Jack Bowers netted four goals in a match. The first of those feats coincided with Bedford's farewell appearance, all scored in the second-half recovery from an interval deficit in the 6–2 beating of the Chelsea visitors whose forward line included two of Scotland's famous 1928 'Wembley Wizards'—Alex Jackson and that great little man Hughie Gallacher, who features in the next chapter as an exceptional addition to George Jobey's sensational signings.

It was Portsmouth, in another 5–1 pounding, this time at Derby, who bore the brunt of the second of the four-goal sprees by Bowers during a rich vein of form in which he also did the hat-trick against Sheffield United and Grimsby Town in scoring 15 times in six successive games. The third to be four-timed, in the Rams' last home match, were relegation-bound Manchester United, whose 6–1 thrashing left Derby expecting a higher final placing than sixth. They slipped to that position by losing their remaining three fixtures—two to clubs above them, Sheffield Wednesday and Huddersfield; the final one against the other going down, Leeds United.

Fearlessly flinging himself among the flying boots to satisfy his thirst for goals, Bowers broke his own club record with 43 in 1932–33, when his 35 in the League put him at the top of the First Division list which he again headed with 34 (plus three in the Cup) the following season. Sammy Crooks was instrumental in a good many of the centre-forward's goals as, with one of his favourite moves, the winger cut in quickly after a dash down the touchline and lobbed the ball over the opposing centre-half. This gave Bowers a shooting chance before he could be tackled, and when he saw this ploy developing he knew just what position to take up.

Hat-tricks in consecutive convincing wins against Leeds and Stoke early in the the 1933–34 campaign, when Bowers scored all but one of Derby's 11 goals in their first six matches, led to his first representative selection for the inter-League encounter with the Irish at Preston on October 4th, 1933. The side was captained by Crooks, the not-so-tall Rams' right-winger, who later said that he often smiled to himself when he thought back to that 'red letter day for me' explaining:

> As I ran out leading the team with the ball tucked underneath my arm I felt that I must be staggering under its weight, especially when I glanced at those following.
>
> Immediately behind me came four or five six-footers including, Jimmy Allen, Jack Bowers, George Beeson and Tommy Grosvenor. The selectors must have noticed this rather odd parade. At any rate, I was never appointed captain again!

Another Bowers hat-trick, against Birmingham, on the Saturday after that midweek 4–0 victory for the Football League in which he scored twice (Cliff Bastin, of Arsenal, and Crooks got the other goals) was his third in four games for Derby over 22 days. It was followed a week later by the Derby dreadnought's debut for England in Belfast, where he was yet again on target in a 3–0 defeat of Ireland. Eric Brook and Tom Grosvenor were the other scorers, in this team:

> **Hibbs** (Birmingham); **Goodall** (Huddersfield Town), **Hapgood** (Arsenal); **Strange** (Sheffield Wednesday), **Allen** (Portsmouth), **Copping** (Leeds United); **Crooks** (Derby County), **Grosvenor** (Birmingham), **Bowers** (Derby County), **Bastin** (Arsenal), **Brook** (Manchester City).

No changes were made for the following month's match with Wales at Newcastle, but Bowers's failure to score in a 2–1 defeat cost him his place against France at Tottenham three weeks later. The man who took over, George Camsell, of Middlesbrough, netted twice in a 4–1 victory, yet he was back playing for his club, goalless in defeat at Sunderland, when Scotland paid their biennial visit to Wembley on April 14th, 1934. Bowers, having supplied a typically dynamic reminder of his powers the week before with another four-goal blast, despite not being fully fit, in a 4–3 thriller against Tottenham, again led the England line. Also there, making his international debut between Bowers and Sammy Crooks, was Raich Carter, a future Derby captain.

Bowers scored one of the three goals to which the Scots had no answer, only to be overlooked for the ensuing tour games in Budapest and Prague. In fact, he never did get back. The player preferred to him, Fred Tilson, scored in both of England's 2–1 defeats by Hungary and Czechoslovakia, and when the Manchester City centre-forward had to drop out through injury, after getting two more goals in the 4–0 win over Wales in Cardiff, Bowers was himself out of action (more about that shortly). To fill the vacancy, the selectors turned first to George Hunt, of Tottenham, but he also reported unfit. So, Ted Drake, the courageous Bowers-type raider Arsenal had recently signed from Southampton, was awarded his first cap for what became notoriously known as the 'Battle of Highbury' against Italy on November 14th, 1934.

Drake's inclusion brought the number of Arsenal players in that England team up to a record seven.[2] Five were originally selected: goalkeeper Frank Moss, full-back

---

2. On February 5th, 1936, Arsenal had six players in the England team against Wales at Wolverhampton: Male, Hapgood, Jack Crayston, Bowden, Drake and Bastin. Jack Barker

Four Rams in England Trial Team

Although three is the greatest number of Derby County players to be capped together for England, four of them lined up in the following England side against The Rest in the international trial at Portsmouth in March, 1933:

Sagar (Everton); **Cooper** (Derby County), **Blenkinsop** (Sheffield Wednesday); **Britton** (Everton), **Barker**, **Keen**; **Crooks** (all Derby County), **Grosvenor** (Birmingham), **Coleman** (Arsenal), **Carter** (Sunderland), **Bastin** (Arsenal).

England, for whom Bastin scored, lost 5–1 to this Rest team: **Moss**; **Male**, **Hapgood** (all Arsenal); **Strange** (Sheffield Wednesday), **White** (Everton), **Copping** (Leeds United); **Hulme** (Arsenal), **Starling** (Sheffield Wednesday), **Hunt** (Tottenham Hotspur), **Pickering** (Sheffield United), **Arnold** (Fulham).

The Rest's scorers were Hulme (2), Hunt (2) and Pickering.

The team selected to meet Scotland in Glasgow on April 1st, 1933 included Cooper and Blenkinsop as the full-backs, and six members of The Rest side, Strange and the complete forward line. The three brought in who did not play in the trial were **Hibbs** (Birmingham) in goal, and **Hart** (Leeds United) and Derbyshire-born **Weaver** (Newcastle United) alongside Strange in the half-back line. Scotland won with two goals from McGrory (Celtic) to one by Hunt.

Eddie Hapgood, wing-half Wilf Copping, and forwards Ray Bowden and Cliff Bastin. The sixth was the Gunners' other full-back, George Male, who made his international debut as deputy for Derby's injured Tommy Cooper, from whom Hapgood took over the captaincy he was to hold, with just one brief break, for more than eight years. To complete Arsenal's monopoly for a match played on their own ground, the Highbury club's trainer, Tom Whittaker, was in charge of the England side, and their manager, George Allison, broadcast the running commentary.

One of the four 'outsiders' among the players was Jack Barker, who had made the first of what were to be ten successive appearances for England in the game with Wales. The other non-Arsenal men were Cliff Britton, of Everton, who played on the Derby man's right in the half-back line; Stanley Matthews, the Stoke winger who had displaced Crooks in Cardiff on sharing his England debut day with Barker; and Eric Brook, the Manchester City outside-left.

and Sammy Crooks also played in that match, which Wales won 2–1. Arsenal also contributed six players (Male, Hapgood, Crayston, Copping, Bowden and Bastin) when England again lost by 2–1, to Austria in Vienna, the following May. Before the 1934 game against Italy at Highbury, Barker, who also played in the Vienna match, said to the Manchester City left-winger, Eric Brook: 'You've got to take your hat off to these Arsenal players. If one of us was to drop out, another Arsenal man would step in!'

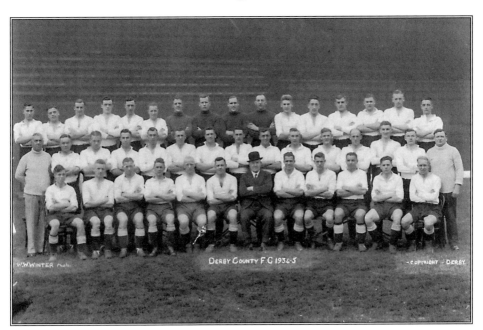

The Derby players who reported for the 1934–35 season. *Back row (left to right):* Ted Roberts, Nicholson, Donald Bird, Dave Bell, Ted Udall, Alan Hughes, Tom Pearson, Webster, Jack Kirby, Vincent Blore, George Hannah, Ralph Hann, Jack Webb, H. Wright, Arnold Robinson, John Philbin. *Middle row:* Dave Willis (trainer), G. Lowe, Keith Hague, Sid Reid, George Collin, Jack Nicholas, Jack Barker, Jack Bowers, Freddie Jessop, Ossie Bowden, Jock Rafferty, Billy Carr, David Halford, Jimmy Hagan, Bill Bromage (assistant trainer). *Front row:* Lisle, Jimmy Randall, Reg Stockill, Sammy Crooks, Tommy Cooper, Peter Ramage, George Jobey (manager), 'Dally' Duncan, Arthur Groves, Arthur Dobbs, Syd Wileman, Ike Keen.
(W.W. Winter)

There was a supercharged start to that clash with the Italians. Inside the first minute, goalkeeper Ceresoli magnificently saved a penalty taken by Brook, but the same player beat him twice within 12 minutes of the kick-off—first with a header from a Matthews cross, then, two minutes later, with a ferocious free kick from just outside the penalty area. After that the Italians went beserk, starting a rough-house that put Hapgood and Brook in hospital, and left Bastin, Bowden and Drake also requiring treatment. Cheers for the second goal had barely died down when Hapgood was assisted off with a broken nose, after having an elbow deliberately smashed into his face. He returned, temporarily patched up by Whittaker, to find that the Italians had also been reduced to ten men by an injury to their captain, Monti, who had broken a small bone in stubbing a toe into the turf. And, to make the Italians' tempers even hotter, they had fallen further behind to a goal by Drake.

Copping, the stubble-chinned former Leeds wing-half, and Barker revelled with some solid shoulder-charging in the rough going that left Brook the other main casualty, with an injured elbow that had to be strapped, but much-provoked England needed every bit of self-control and determination to hold on for a 3–2 victory as the Italians stepped up their frenzied efforts after the interval. Meazza scored two fine goals in as many minutes midway through the second half, and it took an agile save by Moss to deny him an equalising third.

Afterwards, an explanation for the visitors' over-zealous tactics, which caused one reporter's account to be labelled 'By Our War Correspondent', came when it was learned that the Italian dictator, Mussolini, had offered his team big inducements to win: £150 and an Alfa-Romeo car per man, plus, most important of all, exemption from annual military service.

The injury that removed Jack Bowers from the international reckoning, to which he was confined by such worthy rivals, besides Tilson and Drake, as Bob Gurney (Sunderland), W.G. Richardson (West Bromwich Albion), George Camsell (Middlesbrough) and Freddie Steele (Stoke City), occurred on the very day, September 29th, 1934, that Jack Barker was away in Wales playing his first game for England. A week after registering another of his hat-tricks in a 4–1 win at Sunderland, Bowers seriously damaged a knee when he collided with the railings at the Osmaston end of the Baseball Ground during a match with Tottenham Hotspur. It was not until April that he reappeared and played just two more first-team games that season.

The Rams sent Spurs home empty-handed with a couple of goals from Reg Stockill, but the margin might well have been wider than 2–1 if Bowers had still been on the field to take the penalty Stockill missed. The hard-shooting centre-forward never failed with a spot kick in a League match for the Rams, though he nearly did so in a home game with Blackburn. Goalkeeper Billy Gormlie parried his penalty, but he followed up to score from the rebound.

From the time he established himself in Derby's first team shortly before Harry Bedford's departure, until that costly tumble against Tottenham, Bowers missed no more than seven matches out of 183 (only one in each of his first two full seasons) and scored 152 goals. For four successive seasons he was the club's leading scorer, with totals of 39, 26, 43 and 37. Not bad going for somebody who had started out as a full-back, shown some promise as an inside-forward with an Appleby works team, and joined Scunthorpe as a winger before settling down in the centre of the attack. His recovery from the injury was so protracted, however, that subsequently he made only 37 more senior appearances for the Rams—though with a highly respectable bag of 23 goals.

For almost half of his games in the 1935–36 season Bowers was in the Reserves,[3] or the Young Rams as the local evening newspaper used to call them—heedless of the fact that there were usually quite a few second-teamers who were flattered by such disregard of their advanced age in the footballing sense. At that lower level, Bowers, entering his 29th year, tucked away 29 goals, a total mainly responsible for Derby County's first Central League title. He scored the last two in his 16th second-team game of that season, in the 5–0 win against Everton Reserves that clinched the championship

---

3. Those who played most frequently in the Reserves' title-winning team of 1935–36 were Ken Scattergood (41 games), Dave Bell (38), Syd Wileman (32), Ralph Hann (31), Jack Summers and Jack Webb (30 each), Jimmy Boyd (28), David Halford (25) and Jimmy Hagan and Ted Roberts (22 each).

on the final day in front of a record Baseball Ground crowd for a reserve match of 10,260. This was how the top two finished:

	P	W	D	L	F	A	Pts
Derby County Reserves	42	26	4	12	97	66	56
Newcastle United Reserves	42	22	9	11	105	62	53

Six years earlier, the Rams' Reserves, with a team bolstered by Nicholas, Ramage and Bowers, had missed the Central League title just on goal average behind Aston Villa Reserves. Both had won 27 and drawn six of their 42 games in 1929–30, but Villa had edged home with goals figures of 127–72 against 116–74.

The Derby line-up that made certain of finishing first in 1936 was: Scattergood; Webb, Collin; Bell, Hann, Jessop; Boyd, Roberts, Bowers, Ramage, Halford. Everton's side included Billy Cook, the Irish international full-back who had been a Cup winner in both Scotland (with Celtic) and England, and the experienced left-wing pair of Willie Miller and Jackie Coulter. Cook and Miller, a new signing from Partick Thistle, had begun that season by helping Everton to a 4–0 home First Division victory over Derby County, but Coulter had been out of the first team since breaking a leg while playing for Northern Ireland against Wales at Wrexham the previous season.

The three other goals for the 'Young Rams' in their defeat of Everton's second string were scored by David Halford, nicknamed 'Spider' because he was so tall and slim, with long arms and legs, that it was playfully suggested by Hughie Gallacher that he should get out of the communal bath first, before it started to drain, in case he was washed away down the plughole.

The young David Halford…and as he is today, at 84 the oldest surviving former Derby County player.

At a time when the York area was particularly rich in young footballing talent, Halford played in the same York Boys team as Reg Stockill. They also both played—but not together—for Yorkshire and England Boys, then for Scarborough. In one schools match, Stockill scored seven goals for Yorkshire against North-East Derbyshire. It was from Scarborough that Halford moved to Derby in December, 1932, after being spotted playing for England Boys against Scotland Boys at Hillsborough.

As deputy to Duncan, 'Spider's' first-team opportunities were restricted to nine, and the last of them, in a 4–0 home win over Sunderland on the Saturday before his hat-trick against Everton Reserves, was the only occasion on which he and Stockill played together in the Rams' League side. That, too, was a memorable day for him, for he shared the scoring with Stockill, who netted twice, and Gallacher. He also got the goal that set the Rams on their way to revenge for their 1928 Cup defeat by Nottingham Forest, by the same 2–0 scoreline, in a fourth-round tie that attracted the biggest Baseball Ground gate of the Jobey era (37,830), but in the 1936 close season, a few months before his 21st birthday, he was allowed to leave for Bolton Wanderers.

Two seasons later he went to Oldham Athletic, then, after the outbreak of war in 1939, guested for Ipswich Town before going off to battle with the Irish Guards. He took part in the landing at Anzio, in Italy, where he was severely wounded in the legs. After his recovery, he was sent to fight in Germany, but was again a casualty, suffering serious chest injuries. The damage done by those horrific experiences put an end to any hope of continuing his footballing career when peace returned, but this remarkable and most likeable character has since proved himself to be one of life's great survivors.

Halford kept in touch with soccer by doing some coaching in his spare time from his new employment in the insurance business, in which he rose to be an assistant manager in York. In retirement, he recently returned to the Derby district, and, in his eighties (he was born on October 19th, 1915), became the oldest surviving former Derby County player.

Celebrations of Derby County's Central League title triumph on May 2nd, 1936, were slightly dampened when news came through that the club's First Division season had concluded that afternoon with a 6–0 trouncing at Brentford, where Scottish international centre-forward Dave McCulloch booked a future passage to the Baseball Ground by getting four of the goals. The Rams still finished runners-up (to Sunderland), and that, plus the reserves' success, contributed to a prosperous year for Derbyshire sport as Chesterfield gained promotion to the Second Division as Third North champions, and the county's cricket team ended the summer at the top of their Championship table.

From the beginning of season 1936–37 Jack Bowers was back as undisputed first-choice leader of Derby County's attack, and in their opening home game he performed the astounding feat with which his name will always be primarily associated. Manchester United, newly returned to the First Division after a five-year stint in the Second, were the visitors for the first time since their four-goal mauling by Bowers in 1931. With the game just over an hour old, nothing seemed further from reality than a repeat of that onslaught as United coasted 4–1 ahead, yet that is exactly what happened.

The game began well for Derby with an early gift goal for Sammy Crooks, whose shot, following a Duncan corner kick, trickled just over the line through the legs of Welsh international goalkeeper Roy John. Inside-right Wassall quickly equalised, however, and Ralph Hann (deputising at centre-half for Jack Barker, who had a poisoned foot) was given a right run-around as Bowers's opposite number, Tom Bamford, another capped by Wales, hurried to a hat-trick with goals in the 24th, 28th and 51st minutes.

Then came the staggering transformation. With 26 minutes to go Bowers dived in headlong to cut the deficit with a characteristically courageous header. Soon afterwards, United's left-back, Hugh McLenahan, injured an ankle and moved to outside-left, causing a reshuffle that enabled Crooks to find the freedom to inspire one of the most dramatic comebacks in Derby County's history. From a centre by the right-winger, Bowers struck his second goal with his left foot in the 68th minute, after John had punched the ball out towards him. Three minutes later, Bowers brought the scores level by completing his hat-trick with another header, this time aided by a cross from Duncan on the opposite flank. Then, 11 minutes from the end, he drove home the winner as he again found space against a disorganised defence—his fourth goal in only 15 minutes. Derby were then so dominant that United, doomed to an immediate descent for another Division Two season, were relieved not to lose by more than 5–4.

It was the fifth time Bowers had scored so many goals in a match, an achievement most closely approached for the Rams by Alf Bentley and Harry Bedford, who both

Dave McCulloch, whose four goals in
Brentford's 6–0 defeat of the Rams 'booked'
his passage to Derby.

managed it on three occasions. An unexpected development, less than three months later, denied Bowers the chance of also adding to the 11 times he had notched three goals in a game for Derby—a number one ahead of Bedford's County tally, and second only to the 18 of Steve Bloomer, who had just the one four-goal spree in the League, in addition to his Rams record of six in the record-equalling 9–0 defeat of Wolves in 1899, to supplement his England efforts of four and five against Wales.

The unexpected development, of November 20th, 1936, was the transfer of Bowers to Leicester City. From seemingly being settled in the side, but rising 29, he was suddenly surplus to requirements when Welsh international Dai Astley, who had turned 27 earlier that month, arrived from Aston Villa. Astley made his Derby debut at inside-right the previous Saturday against his first League club, Charlton Athletic, at the Valley, where the Rams, beaten 2–0, failed to score for the first time that season despite fielding an all-international forward line (Crooks, Astley, Bowers, Napier, Duncan).

For the next weekend's match, won 3–1 at home against Grimsby, Astley was moved to centre-forward, from where he scored twice, and Stockill, who obtained Derby's other goal, was restored as partner for Crooks. Bowers was chosen to play for the reserves, but, on the Friday a party of Leicester directors visited the Baseball Ground and, after lengthy negotiations, they completed the signing of Derby's discarded leader, for a fee of about £6, 000, in time for him to play for City at Swansea the following day. It proved a most sound investment. Leicester ended that season as champions of the Second Division, and the individual scoring list was headed by their new centre-forward with 33 of their 89 goals.

There was to be no happy ending to the Filbert Street story for Bowers, however. After only two more seasons Leicester were back where he had joined them—in the Second Division. They finished 1938–39 at the foot of Division One with only nine wins from their 42 matches. On the eve of the following season, which the war was to bring to an abrupt halt, he had the satisfaction of scoring twice against his old club in Leicester's 6–4 win in a Jubilee Fund match at Derby, but a year later, in September, 1940, he was one of a dozen Leicester players whose suspension was announced by the Football Association after an inquiry into the club's affairs had left a Commission 'satisfied by the evidence that breaches of the FA and Football League rules had been committed'.

In the case of Bowers—and also that of Sep Smith, a fellow former England player—the ban lasted for a year, after which, along with Peter Ramage, he reappeared at the Baseball Ground on Christmas Day, 1941, in the first match Derby County played on resuming their activities during the war. Playing for the Rams against an RAF XI, in a game arranged in aid of the Mayor of Derby's War Fund, he scored their goal in a 3–1 defeat, in this team: Allsop; Parr, Pallett; Hann, Nicholas, Musson; Crooks, Powell, Bowers, Ramage, Duncan.

Bowers took part in all but one of the eight fixtures Derby fulfilled that season, scoring five other goals, then also guested for Notts County and Nottingham Forest. On Boxing Day, 1942, he again scored against the Rams, but this time on the losing side. Notts County were beaten 3–2 on his last playing appearance at the Baseball Ground, their other goal coming from George Antonio, a Stoke forward who was a stop-gap signing by Derby in the first post-war season.

In September, 1945, Bowers was taken back onto Derby County's staff as assistant trainer—originally to Dave Willis, and then to Jack Poole. In November, 1953, he was reunited with two of his former Derby clubmates as Jack Barker was appointed manager in succession to Stuart McMillan, and Ralph Hann was brought in as the next head trainer under whom Bowers worked. Barker made Hann responsible for the fitness of the players, putting him in overall control of a revised training programme in which emphasis was placed on team-work and ball games, as they were divided into four groups under the respective supervision of Hann, Bowers, Poole and Johnny McIntyre.

Hann, another of George Jobey's acquisitions from the fertile North-East, hailed from Whitburn Colliery, a mining village between Sunderland and South Shields. This was also the birthplace of the brothers Smith (Bill and Jackie, who played for Portsmouth, and Sep of Leicester City) and Seed (Jimmy, who managed Orient and Charlton after playing for Sunderland, Tottenham, Sheffield Wednesday and England, and Angus Seed, best-known as manager of Barnsley). After Sunderland had allowed his amateur registration to lapse, Hann turned professional with Newcastle United, whose manager, Andy Cunningham,[4] was grooming him as wing-half understudy to Derbyshire-born

Ralph Hann, who was with Derby as both player and head trainer.
(Derby Evening Telegraph)

4. Cunningham had the distinction as a player of becoming the oldest Football League debutant when he entered Newcastle's First Division side two days past his 38th birthday on February 2nd, 1929. He played inside-right alongside Hughie Gallacher, who scored in a 1–1 draw at Leicester.

Sam Weaver when, in March, 1932, Jobey snapped him up with Duncan Hutchison,[5] a former Dunfermline and Dundee United utility forward, at a joint fee of about £3,000. The negotiations were opened during one of the intervals at a theatre show which Newcastle officials were attending with their Cup team in that year of United's controversial Wembley win against Arsenal.

A year went by before Hann made his First Division debut in a home game with Chelsea which the Rams lost to a goal scored by another former Newcastle player, the renowned Hughie Gallacher who was to be a County clubmate, and that was Hann's only senior opportunity for more than a year. With Derby's wing-half positions firmly in the hands of Jack Nicholas and Ike Keen (another signing from Newcastle), he had to wait six seasons for a regular place in the first team. In the meantime, he demonstrated his versatility in nearly 80 games by capably filling vacancies at inside-right, centre-half and both wing-half positions before Nicholas's move to right-back at last enabled him to establish himself as an ever-present at right-half in the final full pre-war season of 1938–39.

To offset the memory of Hann's unhappy afternoon as Barker's stand-in against Manchester United's Tom Bamford, it is only fair also to recall one of his outstanding centre-half displays, given when Jack Bowers delivered another of his four-goal broadsides—the one against Tottenham. On that day, April 7th, 1934, Hann completely overshadowed Arthur Rowe, the Spurs pivot who was in the international running, in subduing George Hunt, the former Chesterfield centre-forward who, like Rowe, had played for England the previous year.

When I asked Hann which of his 155[6] senior games for Derby he remembered best, he plumped for an away League match with Manchester City in the autumn of 1934. The Rams won with a late goal by Crooks, but the most memorable event of that day at Maine Road was the introduction of the players and directors of both clubs to the Duke of York, later King George VI, before the kick-off. A photograph of the Duke shaking hands with 'Dally' Duncan hung in Hann's home.

After being among more than 20 Derby County players, past, current and future, who guested for Notts County while the Rams were inactive early in the 1939–45 war, Hann made intermittent appearances for Derby before football returned to its normal peacetime format, the last of them in a League South home defeat by Birmingham City shortly before Christmas in 1945. Towards the end of his long stay on the Baseball Ground playing staff he had charge of the club's third team, then, in September, 1946, he left for Crystal Palace, for whom he played in one Third Division South game before concentrating on his duties as trainer.

---

5. Hutchison joined Newcastle in August, 1929, after helping Dundee United to win the Scottish Second Division championship. He made 46 first-team appearances for Newcastle, scoring 21 goals, and 30 appearances for Derby (four goals) before joining Hull City in July, 1934. After 39 games and eight goals for Hull, he returned to Dundee United in June, 1935, and later became a director of the Tannadice club.

6. That total includes the war years. Hann played for the Rams in 115 First Division games, plus two of the three fixtures they fulfilled at the beginning of the aborted season of 1939–40. He also appeared in five FA Cup-ties.

About a year later, he was appointed Luton Town's trainer-masseur, linking up again with 'Dally' Duncan. It was a move he might never have made but for the post-war housing shortage, for his failure to find a home in the London area meant that he had to take lodgings near Selhurst Park while his wife, whose work as a nurse had encouraged him to qualify as a masseur, continued to live in Derby. That was obviously an unsatisfactory arrangement, so when the manager's job became vacant at Luton he decided to apply for it. Although unsuccessful as that post went to Duncan, who was already at Kenilworth Road as player-coach, he became the Town's trainer instead, having been invited to seek that appointment when he contacted his old clubmate to congratulate him.

For some six years Hann was happy as a Hatter, widely regarded as one of the best trainers in the country, but he admitted to a deep-down 'hankering for Derby', and therefore had no hesitation in accepting the offer that came to team up behind the scenes at the Baseball Ground with another former County colleague, Jack Barker. Sadly, it did not turn out to be a fruitful reunion. The new regime, launched with such optimism, was unable to guide the Rams off the slippery slope down which they had already plummeted out of the First Division. Barker lasted only 16 disillusioning months as manager before pre-empting a sacking by resigning at a board meeting just over a week before his contract was due to expire at the end of April, 1955. With two games left that season, and with Derby doomed to drop into the Third North wilderness for the first time, he gave cynics the chance to taunt him with the cruel gibe that he had at least kept his word in undertaking to get the club he called his 'first love' out of the Second Division in which he had rejoined them.

In truth, he had taken on what many a more accomplished manager would have found unfathomable in giving up his work as a Rolls-Royce assistant jet engine tester, and scouting for the County in his spare time, to shoulder the unenviable task laid down by an ailing Stuart McMillan. Unfortunately, he provided a glaring example of excellence on the field not automatically guaranteeing the same high standard off it. His track record between his retirement as a player and his Rams recall was not exactly encouraging: fewer than eight months as Bradford City's manager, five months as Dundalk's trainer-coach in Ireland, less than two months as Oldham Athletic's trainer.

As a player, he remained the most resolute of attacking centre-halves right up to the last Saturday before war was declared in September, 1939, despite being troubled periodically by arthritis stemming from the ankle injury he had suffered at Burnden Park, Bolton, in his unlucky 13th match of the 1930–31 season. At a time when the stopper central defender, as most notably represented by Herbie Roberts, was spawned by the change in the offside law, even some of Barker's rearguard colleagues thought he was too keen to get on the offensive. Rams supporters, however, revelled in his long, raking passes out to wingers Crooks and Duncan which paved the way to the centres on which Bowers and his successors thrived throughout the Thirties.

George Jobey's whole style of play, in fact, was geared to attack, and although many of the club's defenders during his reign were individually sound, it could reasonably be argued that he might well have put some major silverware in the Baseball Ground trophy cabinet if a less adventurous policy had been adopted. On a seasonal average, Derby County conceded only seven fewer goals than they scored (72 to just more than 79) over the 13 seasons in which he managed them in the First Division.

With more defensive security, and a consequent consistency at critical periods, the Rams' record, impressive though it still was, could certainly have been more in keeping with the exceptional talent reflected in the portraits of all their international players that then lined the walls of their boardroom. On the other hand, they would not have been so entertaining, nor so deservedly held the reputation of being one of the most attractive teams in the country.

Barker's bold methods undoubtedly prevented him from extending an international career that ended as it had begun, against Wales in Cardiff. After giving way to Bernard Joy, the Casuals amateur who later won a League Championship medal with Arsenal, for the second match of England's 1936 close-season tour (lost by 3–2 to Belgium in Brussels) he played his 11th and final game for his country in another defeat, by 2–1, in the Principality. For the third time, England's team that day, October 17th, 1936, included three Derby County men, the others being Crooks and Keen.

The selectors' preference for a more defensive-minded centre-half led them to exclude Barker in favour of such stolid stoppers as Everton's Charlie Gee and Huddersfield's Alf Young, who was a former colleague of Crooks at Durham. That their rivalry caused no animosity was clearly shown when Barker, while still the man in possession of the England place, sent Young a letter of congratulation on his being chosen for a Football League XI in 1935. A leading sports writer of the day described it as 'one of the finest sporting gestures I have ever known'.

Jack Barker, a success as Derby's captain, but not on his return as manager.
(Topical Times)

With Barker's ankle problem becoming more troublesome, his enforced absence from late September until early February contributed towards Derby's decline in the 1937–38 season, when there were some serious relegation worries before they struggled to safety in 13th place—but only four points above the pair who went down. Ralph Hann was the chief deputy at that time, but in the following season Barker, again prone to injury, almost equally shared Derby's centre-half position with Worksop-born Leslie ('Big Bill') Bailey, a six-footer signed from Bradford soon after the Rams won a third-round FA Cup-tie at Park Avenue at the beginning of 1937.

The lanky Bailey was then in his early twenties, nearly ten years younger than Barker, but, although he was a hard enough trier, his lack of pace made him look cumbersome by comparison, and the County's captain was back in his familiar place for the only three matches possible before Prime Minister Neville Chamberlain's fateful broadcast to the nation on the morning of Sunday, September 3rd, 1939. Just before the war, Bailey gave up professional soccer to join the Nottingham City Police, but after it was over he returned to the game and spent several seasons as player-coach at Llandudno.

Jack Barker played in a home friendly[7] with Leeds United before Derby County's temporary closedown at the end of the war's first month, and after making a few guest

---

Confusion Over a Clean Thumbnail

In his book *Football Is My Business*, Tommy Lawton, the England centre-forward then with Everton, recalled the day during the Second World War when Jack Barker was detailed to take their Army platoon in a course of exercises, but absent-mindedly caused himself an embarrassing problem. This was how Lawton remembered it:

> *Determined not to give us a chance of ribbing him, which was certain to happen should he make a mistake, Jack, as soon as he had finished his lunch, memorised the various exercises and then noted the numbered order of them in ink on his thumb-nail. But in an absent-minded moment before the parade he quite forgot about his decorated thumb-nail, and, in washing his hands, completely lost the sequence.*
>
> *Imagine his horror when, with the platoon lined up expectantly, he surreptitiously glanced down…at a perfectly clean slate, or, should I say, nail. An urgent whispered 'What do I do now?' was met by a heartless silence, followed by 'A fine set of mates you are', before he blurted out the first order he could think of!*

---

7. This match was arranged to test the Derby public's reaction to wartime football. The size of the crowd was limited to 8,000 in accordance with Home Office regulations, but only 1,805 turned up. As a result, the Rams were out of pocket on the fixture, and they decided that it would be unwise to carry on at the risk of incurring further losses when

appearances for Notts County he turned out for the Rams for the last time when they narrowly defeated an Army XI in a match in aid of the Derby Civil Defence Benevolent Fund at the Baseball Ground on May 2nd, 1942. During the war he became a sergeant-major instructor in the Army Physical Training Corps, but his suspect left ankle eventually caused him to be discharged, and he was warned against strenuous exercise for at least two years.

That enforced lay-off was up at the start of 1946, but, although he promptly did some training at the Baseball Ground, and the ankle stood up to a gruelling test in a local match, he had no intention of trying to make a comeback. Quite apart from the worry that he might break down again, he was then nearly 39, and, in any case, Derby had come up with a new centre-half, Leon Leuty, who was one of the finest of the war-time finds.

A few years later there was the intriguing prospect of another Jack Barker pressing his centre-half claims at the Baseball Ground. In September, 1949, Barker's son was signed as an amateur, and his promising form in the Colts led to his turning professional shortly after his 17th birthday the following August, while serving an apprenticeship as an electrician at Denaby Colliery. At almost 6ft and near 12st, he was well built for the job, but it was not to be. He left at the end of the 1951–52 season, and was also released after a trial with Mansfield Town, then managed by George Jobey. He next spent two seasons with Brush Sports, a Loughborough works team for which 'Chick' Musson, a Derby wing-half in more than 300 matches, was player-manager until his untimely death from leukaemia in 1955 at the age of only 34. After that, young Barker was with Burton Albion at the same time as John Poppitt, a former Derby and QPR full-back.

The son of Jack Bowers did make it into League football, and with Derby County too. John Bowers joined the Rams from Derby Corinthians early in 1957, and after making an isolated League debut at Huddersfield on his 20th birthday, November 14th, 1959, he got back into the Second Division side for an extended run at outside-left that ended only when he badly injured an ankle during a home win over Coventry City, in which he scored, in the opening weeks of the 1964–65 season. He was unable to regain his best form on his recovery, but played in 68 League and Cup games, scoring 20 goals, before going to Notts County, where, unfortunately, his first-team appearances could be counted on one hand.

It was only a few years after that, in July, 1970, that Jack Bowers Senior died at Lichfield at the age of 62. Jack Barker Senior lived on until early 1982, but he had to battle against severe illness in his later years. He took over a public house in Nottingham after his return to the Rams as team manager and coach had ended so bleakly, but he and his wife Anne soon went back to live in Derby. They celebrated their golden wedding anniversary there only a couple of months before his death, in Derbyshire Royal Infirmary, a few weeks short of his 75th birthday.

---

they already had a bank overdraft of more than £30,000—especially as they would have had difficulty in fielding attractive teams because of the number of their key players who had been called up into the Forces. It was not until Christmas Day, 1941 that they started up again.

CHAPTER 9

The Wee Scottish Giant

Jobey claims the headlines by signing Hughie Gallacher from Chelsea – Airdrie runners-up in each of Gallacher's last three seasons with them – His move to Newcastle gives Geordie fans ideal Christmas present – Captains Newcastle to League title and breaks their scoring record – A tragic end

WHEN THE JACK BOWERS GOAL MACHINE came off the rails in that 1934 game against Tottenham, George Jobey commandeered the sporting headlines with his choice of player to fill the gap left by his free-scoring centre-forward's long-term injury.

As has already been noted, Derby's manager was unashamedly ruthless in unloading even key players once they had passed their 30th birthday, but to meet the emergency caused by the loss of Bowers he invested £2,750 in one approaching his 32nd. Hughie Gallacher, however, was somebody very out of the ordinary. Despite being 5ft 5½ in small, he was one of the greatest goalscoring attack leaders of all time, freely acknowledged as being among the cleverest forwards the game has ever produced. An uncanny dribbler and magnificent shot, he was still capable, though past his peak, of destroying the staunchest of defences when he went to Derby.

There was no doubting Gallacher's footballing pedigree. But there was a but—and a big one at that. Against his many attributes, he had a reputation as a truculent trouble-maker, and was frequently at odds with authority both in and outside the game. Several times he was ordered off the field and suspended. In his private life there was an early divorce, the airing of his chaotic affairs in the bankruptcy court, and a weakness for drink. On one overseas tour he was accused of being drunk and disorderly on the field, but was exonerated when an official investigation accepted his explanation that he had washed out his mouth with whisky and water because it was a very hot day!

Gallacher's financial troubles, aggravated by his costly divorce proceedings, caused him to run up debts which Derby County had to agree to meet in order to sign him. This contributed towards the bringing down of George Jobey when the unofficial payments the Rams made to land so many of their stars during his seasons in charge led to the FA-League inquiry that imposed a fine on the club, and cast out members of their board along with the manager.

Hugh Kilpatrick Gallacher was born at Bellshill, to the north-west of Motherwell, in Lanarkshire, on February 2nd, 1903. From kicking a ball around in the street outside his home, he played in schools football with Alex James (they both attended Bellshill Academy) before teaming up with Bellshill Athletic, a junior side, shortly after the First World War. Having decided to concentrate on football, instead of pursuing his original aim to become a professional boxer, he soon made favourable headlines when he moved to Queen of the South and began banging in the goals that earned him selection for the national junior team. However, there were also unpalatable, and tragic headlines, with the swift breakdown of the Protestant-Catholic marriage he entered into at the age of 17, and the death of a son who was less than 12 months old.

His own life then came under threat as he was rushed to hospital with double pneumonia, but, having made a full recovery, he really started to make his mark after his transfer to Airdrieonians in May, 1921. In each of the last three of his four full seasons with the Broomfield Park club they were runners-up for the Scottish League First

Hughie Gallacher, scorer of five goals at Blackburn
in his sixth game for Derby.
(Derby Evening Telegraph)

Division title (they were second yet again at the end of the season in which he left) and, in 1924 he not only helped Airdrie to win the Scottish Cup for the first—and still only —time, beating Hibernian 2–0 in the final, but also made the first of his 20 full international appearances in a defeat of Northern Ireland by the same margin at Celtic Park in Glasgow.

There could have been more caps but for, in particular, the arrival on the scene of one Jimmy McGrory, scorer of over 400 Scottish League goals for Celtic and some 550 in all. Other rivals to wee Hughie for the centre-forward position in the Scotland side included Jimmy Fleming (Rangers), Barney Battles (Hearts), Benny Yorston (Aberdeen and later Sunderland), Neil Dewar (Third Lanark, later Manchester United and Sheffield Wednesday), Willie McFadyen (Motherwell and Huddersfield Town), Jimmy Smith (Rangers) and one of his successors at Derby, Dave McCulloch, then of Hearts. An impressive list.

As Gallacher's goals for Airdrie approached three figures, so he increasingly became the object of envious eyes from south of the border, and after he had scored twice for a victorious Scotland side in his first game against England Newcastle United paid the biggest fee then received by a Scottish club, £6, 500, to win the race for his signature in December, 1925.

What a Christmas present that was for the Geordie fans! An instant success, with two goals in a home 3–3 draw with Everton on his debut, this nimble son of a ploughman rapidly reaped the reward of adulation, becoming a folk hero such as Tyneside had never before seen. With the ability to keep the ball under immaculate control amazingly close to his feet, he found it just as easy to irritate defenders in the English First Division, by foiling their attempts to knock him off the ball, as he had those in Scotland. Although he could easily be stung into retaliation, the one big weakness of his game, he was well able to look after himself when opponents singled him out for the rough treatment that added fuel to his fiery nature. Niggling nudges and sly taps, provocative taunts— Gallacher was never slow to resort to any of them to enable him to exploit his extraordinary natural footballing talent.

Four goals against Bolton, three against both Liverpool and Manchester City, heightened the hero-worship of the wee wizard, and he scored more times than he played, 25 to 22, in that first season with Newcastle. Appointed captain, he proceeded to lead United to their first League Championship since their golden era of three titles in five years during the first decade of the 20th century, piling up a club record 36 goals (plus three in the Cup) in 38 matches as they topped the 1926–27 table by five points from Huddersfield Town, champions in each of the previous three seasons. Pace and poise gave him the openings to cash in on the strength of his shot, but he was also remarkably effective in the air for such a small man.

The goals continued to flow—79 of them over the next three seasons— for an aggregate of 143 in 174 games for Newcastle. In the last of those seasons, also his last on Tyneside, he further endeared himself to the St James's Park faithful by declining a chance to play for Scotland to assist United in a struggle against relegation, a fate they only just averted one point clear of the drop in 19th place. While his country was losing without him on Sammy Crooks's day of England debut glory at Wembley, he was helping to prise a precious point out of Arsenal.

Revered as he was as he strolled around Newcastle smartly tailored, opening garden parties and patronising other social functions, trouble was never far away. On one occasion he got involved in a brawl and was bound over in court to keep the peace. On another, he lost his temper after a defeat suffered despite his two goals in a top-of-the-table clash with Huddersfield, and incurred a two-month suspension for pushing Bert Fogg, one of the most respected referees of those days, into the bath.

In May, 1930, to the consternation of his host of North-East admirers, Gallacher left Tyneside as Newcastle yielded to the temptation of a £10,000 offer from Chelsea after there had been a suggestion that he might go to Sunderland. By one of those freaks of the fixture list, the London club just happened to be the first visitors to Gallowgate the following season, and such was the high regard in which the dynamic Scot was held that United's record crowd of more than 68,000 packed in, with thousands more locked out, for a Wednesday evening match the home side won with a solitary goal from right-winger Cape. Gallacher, who not surprisingly looked back on it as the most touching and memorable highlight of his career, again failed to score when Newcastle drew the return encounter, but he did the hat-trick in a 4–1 Chelsea win when his former club next visited Stamford Bridge the following Easter.

Strangely, that was the only time he obtained as many as three goals in a game for the Londoners, whereas he had done so no fewer than a dozen times for Newcastle, including three lots of four. Even so, he maintained a high scoring rate with 81 goals in 144 matches for Chelsea, and, as in his United years, he was their leading marksman in each of the seasons he spent with them. As a lover of the London night life, he also continued to make the undesirable kind of news, reputedly still having a drink problem and again appearing in court after being involved in a fight in a café.

It was therefore with some misgivings that many Derby County supporters greeted Gallacher's addition to George Jobey's growing list of international stars at the Baseball Ground in November, 1934. At first there was much scepticism when rumours began to circulate that this was the man the Derby manager was after. For one thing, it seemed improbable that Chelsea would agree to part; for another, it did not seem possible that the Rams would be able to meet the anticipated fee demanded even if he were made available.

Both those supposed barriers were swept away by Jobey's successful negotiations for another of his cut-price bargains, but then other uncertainties crept in, and the balding little Scot's stormy behaviour, on the field and off, was not the only reason for such reservations. Some feared he would not fit into the Rams' attack. Others argued that he was past his best, and questioned the wisdom of signing a player nearing the end of his career. But he proved all the doubters wrong, especially those who expected him to be a disruptive influence. Of all the managers under whom he played, Jobey was the one who kept him most under control. In nearly two years with Derby County he scarcely put a foot wrong under the eagle eyes of the club's dictatorial manager, and he repaid the trust placed in him with the remarkable ratio of 40 goals in only 55 games.

It took him no more than six minutes to score the first of those goals, in a 1–1 home draw with Birmingham when he made his debut on November 10th, 1934. He chased after a Ramage pass which the visiting defenders thought was going to run behind for a goal kick, and hit the ball past Harry Hibbs, at the Osmaston end, from an acute angle near the by-line. The equaliser came before half-time from Billy Guest, a nippy winger who was later with Blackburn when they regained First Division status and played for them at Wembley in a war-time cup final.

Four weeks after his debut goal, Gallacher got two more in the 9–3 drubbing of West Bromwich Albion at the Baseball Ground. A week later he did all Derby's scoring in their 5–2 win at Blackburn, where the first of his five was his 300th in Scottish and English League football. Reg Stockill, who had followed Syd Wileman[1] as stand-in for Bowers before Gallacher's arrival, was unlucky not to join the Scot on the scoresheet on reverting to partner Crooks, who also went close to making the victory even bigger.

The 1935–36 group. *Back row (left to right):* H. Wright, Jimmy Hagan, John Philbin, G. Lowe, Tom Pearson, Lisle, Ted Roberts, Jack Summers, Syd Wileman, McDougall.
Second row: Dave Willis (trainer), David Halford, 'Dally' Duncan, Jimmy Boyd, Jack Nicholas, Arthur Groves, Jack Kirby, George Hannah, Sid Reid, Ken Scattergood, Bill Bromage (assistant trainer). *Seated:* Reg Stockill, Sammy Crooks, Donald Bird, Jack Barker, Jack Bowers, George Collin, Ike Keen, Dave Bell, Jack Webb, Ralph Hann, Keith Hague.
On ground: Hughie Gallacher, Peter Ramage, Ted Udall, Charlie Napier, Freddie Jessop.
(W. W. Winter)

---

1. Wileman joined Derby from Gresley Rovers in April, 1931, but played in only 11 first-team games, scoring one goal, before moving to Port Vale in June, 1938.

Goalkeeper, Cliff Binns, who had let in five at Everton in Rovers' previous match, was knocked out by one terrific shot from Sammy.

Not since Jimmy Moore's five against Crystal Palace on Christmas Day, 1922, had a Rams player netted so many in one match. It was Gallacher's first five in English soccer, but the fourth of his career, if his version of how many he scored in Scotland's 7–3 defeat of Northern Ireland in Belfast early in 1929 is included. Some sources have limited him to four goals in that game, but he claimed that 'several newspapers mistakenly credited Alex James with one of my scoring efforts'.

One of Gallacher's other, irrefutable, five-goal flurries made him fear for his life on a visit to Belfast four years earlier. A note containing a death threat was sent into the Scottish League team's dressing room during the half-time interval of the match in which his trickery brought him his five in succession, three of them inside 15 minutes, in a 7–3 demolition of the Irish League. He treated the threat lightheartedly as he continued to tease the exasperated opposition in the second half, but he was compelled to take a very different view when a bullet struck a nearby wall as he later walked through the city on his way to visit friends. Whether or not it was intended for him, amid those Troubles of the Twenties, no one will ever know, but he got away from that spot as fast as he could, and did not venture out again until it was time to go home. Shocked as he was, he could not refrain from observing that 'it seems I haven't managed to teach the Irish how to shoot straight!'

Gallacher, whose other five-goal feat was achieved for Airdrie in a Scottish League match with Clyde in 1923, ended his first season with Derby as easily their top scorer, getting twice as many goals as the next highest, Sammy Crooks, in totalling two dozen in 30 games—including a hat-trick in an away victory against Grimsby. Crooks commented:

> Hughie played so well that season that I am certain we should have won the First Division championship but for Reg Stockill being seriously injured at a vital stage. The decision to buy Gallacher was a masterly stroke of business. In view of the fact that gates were falling, the Rams had to secure a centre-forward who could draw the crowds when Jack Bowers needed a cartilage operation. Gallacher, the most talked-of player of his day, was just the man for the job. Everybody got a shock when Chelsea decided to release him, and they got a bigger one still when the fee was announced. A number of clubs would have paid twice as much if they had thought that Chelsea could have been persuaded to part with him.

Chelsea did not take long to spend most of the money they received for Gallacher, who was the first of the big signings they made on scrambling back into the First Division after several near-misses. They twice finished third, and once fourth, before making it in second place—and then only because Oldham lost at Barnsley on the final day when they themselves were beaten at Bury. Within weeks of parting with the talented but troublesome Scot they secured another international as replacement by paying out £2,000 for James ('Joe') Bambrick, scorer of 94 goals in one season for Linfield, and of six for Northern Ireland in a Belfast game against Wales. Though laughingly low by current standards, no expense was spared as the Stamford Bridge club strove to compete with the mighty achievements of their London rivals Arsenal, yet they merely succeeded in making themselves the butt of music-hall comedians as they only twice finished in the top half of the table in the 1930s despite their collection of capped men.

Ironically, even before they splashed out on Gallacher they already had on their books a centre-forward who cost them no more than the £10 signing-on fee, but who was also to see off Bambrick besides meeting the challenge of another costly import, Joe Payne (scorer of ten goals when Luton first fielded him at the head of their attack, against Bristol Rovers). This was George Mills, who followed Payne into the England team and did the hat-trick on his debut in the 1937 Belfast game against Northern Ireland. Further irony lay in the fact that another inexpensive signing who became an international did much to help preserve Chelsea's hard-won status during those years of frustration. He was goalkeeper Vic Woodley, whose recall from non-League oblivion, to gain a Cup-winner's medal with Derby County in 1946, was something any writer of schoolboy fiction would have been proud to have thought up.

In 1934–35, when Woodley was having to contend with his only pre-war rival for a place in Chelsea's team—John Jackson, the Scottish international whose transfer from Partick Thistle required another deep dip into the bank account—the injury to Stockill was not the only reason why Derby County slipped out of the title reckoning despite Hughie Gallacher's goals. No club aspiring to be champions could afford to drop as many points at home as Derby did—18 of them, from seven defeats and four draws. The damage done by that fallibility as they finished 13 points off the pace in sixth place was underlined by their contrasting knack of rising to the occasion on their travels, at the most unexpected times. Sunderland, Manchester City, Preston and Grimsby all lost their unbeaten home records to the Rams, who also won away to Leicester, Liverpool and Arsenal as well as at Blackburn on the afternoon of Gallacher's nap hand. Not surprisingly, they became looked upon as that season's shock side.

It was ironic that Derby's home form should falter just as they improved an away record which, three seasons earlier, had reached one of its lowest points and had only slightly improved in the two intervening ones. In 1931–32 when their final 15th placing was the lowest of George Jobey's time at Derby, they did not gain their first away point until mid-December (at Liverpool) and they went right through to April before registering their only victory on an opponent's ground (at Bolton). The heaviest of their 15 away defeats was suffered at Huddersfield, where Dave Mangnall, later manager of a QPR Third Division championship side, scored five of the six goals they conceded without reply. Whereas in that season and the next two Derby lost only seven League games out of the 63 at home, their number of away defeats in the First Division over that period totalled 38.

The victory at Highbury that crowned the Rams' away revival in 1934–35, gained by a Ramage goal near half-time on the last day, made them the only club to do the double that season over Arsenal, who were champions for the third year in succession. It was a distinction Derby were again to have when the Gunners claimed their first post-war title in 1947–48. Furthermore, both the 1935 FA Cup finalists were soundly beaten at the Baseball Ground, for Sheffield Wednesday lost there by 4–0 a month before winning at Wembley against West Bromwich Albion, who had let in nine goals at Derby.

Another interesting feature of Derby's away match with Arsenal that season was that it marked the League debut for the Highbury club of a young full-back who played for the Rams during the 1939–45 war while a Squadron Leader in the RAF. That was the only First Division appearance Reg Trim made for Arsenal, whom he joined from Bournemouth, but he turned out in more than 60 war-time games for Derby, originally as a guest from Nottingham Forest. He then left for Swindon Town with goalkeeper Frank Boulton, the unfortunate former Arsenal clubmate whose injury gave Vic Woodley his fairy-tale opportunity to be a Cup winner at Wembley.

There was an additional aspect of Derby's game at Highbury in the May of 1935 that tarnished their well-deserved eighth away success of the season. At the final whistle, sections of the home crowd, their disappointment in defeat inflamed by what they saw as some over-robust tackling by the visitors, invaded the pitch and demonstrated unpleasantly around the entrance to the tunnel through which the players made their way back to the dressing rooms. More boos broke out as the motor coach carrying the County team drove off with an escort of mounted police. 'Such ill-feeling was hardly warranted' according to one account.

Hughie Gallacher's second, and final, season with Derby County was the one they ended with a 6–0 battering at Brentford, but also as runners-up, on goal average from Huddersfield, eight points behind Sunderland's champions. Although he could have wished for a happier exit, Gallacher did have the satisfaction of again being the club's leading scorer, getting 15 goals in 24 League games and scoring another at the start of a Cup run that came unstuck in the comprehensive sixth-round defeat at Fulham in which the hapless Ted Udall suffered one of his shoulder injuries.

Progress as far as the last eight in that 1935–36 campaign looked extremely unlikely after only just over half-an-hour's play in the third-round tie with Dartford at the Baseball Ground, for the non-League visitors were then two goals ahead. Gallacher's goal began a recovery that was completed by Crooks and the Rams' latest Scottish international capture, Charlie Napier, the summer signing from Celtic who the previous April helped to beat England on the day 'Dally' Duncan was a two-goal matchwinner and Hughie Gallacher last played for his country. That match at Hampden Park was the one in which Gallacher was in direct opposition to his new Derby team-mate Jack Barker, who from that experience and their other clashes at club level always rated him the most difficult-to-hold centre-forward he ever came across.

Charles Edward Napier, a stylist nicknamed 'Happy Feet' because he was always on the go, very fast off the mark in electrifying dashes befitting a former electrician, was one of seven capped players in Derby's team when he made his debut for the club on the first day of the 1935–36 season. The others were Reid, Barker, Keen, Crooks, Gallacher and Duncan. Sid Reid, a skilful young full-back from Belfast Distillery, played three times for Northern Ireland during more than six years with the Rams, but was kept in the Baseball Ground background by the consistent George Collin. That first match for Napier, which Derby lost 4–0 at Everton, despite their strength on paper, was also the last of only 16 in the First Division for Reid before he moved to Reading.

Napier did well at half-back and on either wing after joining Celtic from Maryhill Hibernian in 1929, but inside-left was generally considered to be his best position. Initially, however, George Jobey had different ideas, and Napier occupied all four other positions in the forward line of the contemporary 2-3-5 formation before he played at inside-left for Derby in their last two away games of his first season. Both were lost heavily, a 4–1 reverse against Grimsby preceding the collapse at Brentford, but most of his appearances over the greater part of the next two seasons were made much more successfully in the

Sid Reid, an Irish international but
only a reserve at Derby.
(Derby Evening Telegraph)

Charlie Napier, a Scottish international
known as 'Happy Feet'.
(Derby Evening Telegraph)

partnership with Duncan he first formed for Scotland against Wales at Aberdeen in November, 1934. They did the Scots' scoring in their 3–2 win in that Pittodrie international, Napier netting twice. Dai Astley, then still with Villa, got one of the Wales goals.

Napier played the last two of his five games for Scotland while with Derby County, again scoring as Duncan's partner in a 3–1 victory in Belfast alongside Dave McCulloch, who was also on target, and then helping towards a 1–1 draw with Austria in Vienna. He had 26 goals to his credit in 88 matches for the Rams when he took the well-worn trail from the Baseball Ground to Hillsborough in March, 1938, to fill the gap in Wednesday's forward line left by the transfer to Arsenal of George Drury, formerly of Heanor Town and later of West Bromwich and Watford.

The Sheffield club were going through one of the worst periods in their distinguished history at the time Napier joined them. Relegated from the First Division at the end of the previous season, having only narrowly escaped the year before, they were in danger of sinking even lower, but just managed to wriggle clear. Napier missed only one match for Wednesday during the season in which they were just pipped for the second promotion spot by their United neighbours in the last pre-war spring the following May. 'Happy Feet' scored the goal that beat Tottenham at Hillsborough in their final game, only for

United to edge one point ahead in the final table by thrashing Spurs 6–1 when they completed their own programme at Bramall Lane a week later. Jimmy Hagan, a Derby cast-off who features prominently in a subsequent chapter, did the hat-trick.

Wednesday won just one of the three fixtures they fulfilled in the aborted 1939–40 season, Napier scoring twice in a home win over Barnsley. Discounting those games, he totalled ten goals in 56 League and Cup appearances for the Owls, then had completely contrasting experiences when he played for the club twice more during the war. In the first of those matches, in April, 1940, he netted all three of Wednesday's goals in a League North Cup home win against Leeds United—though that was not enough to give them victory on aggregate over the two legs. On the second occasion, in a League North game with Grimsby at Hillsborough in the autumn of 1943, he was involved in an incident that caused him to be banned by the FA.

The suspension was at first imposed *sine die*, but later lifted, and in September, 1945, Napier, whose brother George was a defender with Kilmarnock and Cowdenbeath, re-entered Scottish football with Falkirk, the club their father served as secretary. A year later he moved to Stenhousemuir, where he concluded his senior playing career in 1948, before, like Arthur Groves, linking up again with 'Dally' Duncan, who was then Luton's manager, by becoming the Bedfordshire club's scout in Scotland.

Crocked by Crooks

Hughie Gallacher paid dearly for being too enthusiastic when Derby County, fighting hard for top place in the First Division, met Manchester City at the Baseball Ground on the first Saturday of November in 1935.

With the scoresheet still blank, 'Dally' Duncan forced a corner early in the second half. Sensing a good chance to break the deadlock, Gallacher shouted to Crooks: 'Come on, get stuck in, Sammy'. This is how the little right-winger recalled what happened next:

> As the ball came across, I dashed in at full speed, took a terrific leap, and shut my eyes. I crashed into another player and we both finished at the back of the net. That player was Hughie Gallacher, and he was absent for the next eight weeks with a shoulder injury caused by me.

Despite his injury, Gallacher managed not only to play on in that match but also to score in the 3–0 victory which lifted Derby to first place. That, however, was the season in which they had to be content to end as runners-up, eight points behind Sunderland.

By that time, Hughie Gallacher was back in the North-East, also retired from playing and having recently lost the distinction of being the player on whom most money had been spent in aggregate fees. This had been gained with further moves from Derby to Notts County for £2,000 in September, 1936, then to Grimsby Town for £1,000 in January, 1938, and on to Gateshead for £500 in June, 1938. His total of £22,750 in transfer fees remained the record until the end of 1946, when another of the Rams' forward favourites, Irish international Peter Doherty, completed £26, 500-worth of moves that took him from Blackpool to Huddersfield by way of Maine Road, Manchester, and the Baseball Ground. The mind boggles to think what that pair would be priced at on current rates.

After leaving Derby, Gallacher maintained his scoring momentum with 32 goals in 45 Third South games for Notts County, hitting hat-tricks against Northampton Town and Bristol Rovers. He managed only three in 12 First Division appearances for Grimsby, then scored 18 in 31 matches for mid-table Gateshead in the Third North. He bowed out when war came with the grand career total of 463 goals in 624 games. Of those goals, 23 were scored for Scotland, four of them in the 7–3 victory in Belfast in 1929. In another match with the Irish, at Ibrox in 1926, he was on target three times; he also did the hat-trick against the Welsh at Rangers' ground in 1928, and in a Scottish trial at Tynecastle in 1925.

If there was one aspect of Gallacher's shooting abilities on which he had particular reason to pride himself, it was in the taking of penalties. So much so that he caused quite a kerfuffle when he failed with one for Notts County against Aldershot in 1937. Only once before had he muffed a spot kick—and that had been 13 years earlier, while with Airdrie. In view of that imposing record it was surprising that he was not automatically relied upon for Derby's penalties, but he took on that job only after Stockill had made a costly miss in a 2–1 home defeat by Liverpool.

It was a former Newcastle team-mate who signed Gallacher for Grimsby. Charlie Spencer, a stopper centre-half of England rank then in his first season as manager at Blundell Park, turned to him as cover for the club's record-scoring Welsh cap, Pat Glover, as the Mariners struggled against relegation under the weight of a casualty list that also pressured him into taking on Irish international winger Jackie Coulter from Everton. Glover, grabber of 180 League goals for Grimsby through the Thirties, missed most of that 1937–38 season because of injury, but he was back in place of Gallacher for the last three matches—the middle one at Derby—from which they gathered maximum points to scramble to safety in one of the most desperate of finishes.

When the last day dawned, six clubs were at the foot of the table with 36 points. Four of them won—Stoke and Grimsby both by 2–0 at home, against Liverpool and Chelsea respectively, Portsmouth by 4–0 against Leeds, also at home, and Birmingham by 4–1 at Leicester. The two others lost and therefore went down. Manchester City, champions the previous season, were beaten by an only goal at Huddersfield, West Bromwich by 4–1 at Middlesbrough. As when they won the title, the Manchester club were the highest scorers in the division, and 13 of their 80 goals were rammed into Derby County's net— six at Maine Road, seven at the Baseball Ground. Peter Doherty, eight years later to be a Cup winner with the Rams, scored twice on both occasions.

Even after leaving League football, Hughie Gallacher was still never far away from attracting unpleasant publicity, and it all came to a terrible climax in the most tragic of circumstances. He first tried to keep in touch with soccer by occasionally playing for veteran teams, but after accepting an invitation to comment on Newcastle matches in a local paper he was banned from St James's Park because he was considered too critical. Years before this, his journalistic efforts had been cut short when the sensational nature of a newspaper column bearing his name had incurred a fine by the Football Association, with whom he now again came into conflict for refereeing a charity game without their approval.

After that he turned from football to working with mining machinery, then as a machinist in a chemical factory. Such employment was not new to him. Back in the 1914–18 war he had done vital work as a coalminer and in a munitions factory. His private life, however, descended into turmoil, the downward spiral accentuated by the heavy drinking to which he increasingly resorted after losing his second wife through illness. It all came to its awful end on June 11th, 1957, the day before he was due to appear in court at Gateshead, accused of assaulting, ill-treating and neglecting his 14-year-old son Matthew.

A day earlier, Gallacher, who had two other sons—Hugh, then 21 and newly demobilised from the RAF, and Tommy, 19, who was in the RAF on National Service—gave his last interview to a *Daily Mail* reporter he called to his council-house home at Gateshead. Gallacher told him:

> My life is over. I don't think I'll be going to court. It's no good fighting this. Drink has been my downfall. I'm going away. I can't tell you where, but I've had a good life and there's no point in staying here. Since my wife died it has been an unhappy home. I came home drunk and had a fight with my sons. I didn't know what I was doing. I admit I hit my son with an ornament. I overstepped the mark. I have never hit him before.

Two hours before he met his death, Gallacher called on the youngest son he was accused of ill-treating, who had left to live with an aunt (Mrs Dorothy Armstrong, Hughie's sister-in-law) since the NSPCC had begun their prosecution. He told the boy 'Mattie, look after your Aunt Dolly. She's been a good pal to you'.

An hour later, Gallacher chanced to meet another relative, the wife of a nephew, while she was out shopping. He told her, 'I'm going to have a slow walk down there'. She thought he meant that he was going to the factory where he worked, but she was dreadfully wrong.

He was on his way to the fatefully-named Dead Man's Crossing at Low Fell on the main London to Edinburgh railway line. Two train spotters, a boy and his sister, saw him pace an iron footbridge as the express from York, bound for the Scottish capital, sounded through the trees. The time was eight minutes past midday. As the train approached, the youngsters watched him cross the footbridge and run down the embankment. Out of their sight, he threw himself in front of the speeding locomotive and, 54 years and five months after it had begun, the turbulent life of this wayward genius was snuffed out in the most horrifying manner.

The news of Gallacher's suicide spread shock waves far wider than through just the world of soccer. For all his faults, this colourful and controversial character, though diminutive in stature, stood tall among the outstanding personalities of his day. Even those who so strongly disapproved of his often regrettable behaviour could not fail to recognise his brilliance. He will always have a high place in football's Hall of Fame.

CHAPTER 10

A Clutch of Goalkeepers

Derbyshire-born goalkeepers – Patience pays for Ernald Scattergood – Promotion won with lowest goals-against total – Depressing debut for Ken Scattergood – Methven subterfuge lands Lawrence – Olney sets Rams record – Wilkes repays Jobey's faith – Kirby foils Sunderland – Injury blow for Boulton

O F THE FOUR GOALKEEPERS on whom George Jobey mainly relied throughout his 14 full seasons as Derby County's manager, Jack Kirby, from the village of Overseal near Swadlincote, was the only addition to the list of locally-born players in that position for which the club were so noted into the fifth decade of their existence.

From the time of the Football League's formation in 1888, no Rams team was without an established goalkeeper from within the county until early in 1922, when the man between the sticks Jobey inherited, Ben Olney, a Londoner raised in Birmingham, became the first choice he was to remain until the last Saturday of September, 1927. Three of the five regulars in the Derby team before Olney arrived played for England: John Wilks Robinson, Harry Mart Maskrey and Ernald Oak Scattergood.

Ernald Scattergood, the only ever-present in Derby's 1911–12 promotion team. His son Ken (who is in the 1935–36 group photograph in the previous chapter) had an unhappier time at Derby.
(Derby Evening Telegraph)

Scattergood, who was the Rams' only ever-present player when they won the Second Division championship in 1911–12 with the club's lowest goals-against total of 28 (he kept a clean sheet in 21 of their 38 matches), could have wished for better than being beaten three times in his only game for England, even though he finished on the winning side by the odd goal of seven against Wales in Bristol. Any disappointment he may have felt, however, was as nothing compared with what his son Kenneth had to endure when he made his League debut for Derby County at Goodison Park on Christmas Day, 1936. The Rams' second Scattergood had the depressing experience of having to pick the ball out of the net on seven occasions, with not even one goal scored in reply.

There was some excuse for such a crushing defeat—by the very club against which Derby had also suffered their heaviest-ever 11–2 reverse in an 1890 FA Cup-tie—for the chastened visitors finished the game with only eight sound men. They did well to concede just the one goal before the interval, as Jack Barker had to go off with a head injury after ten minutes' play and Dai Astley, who damaged a knee, was a passenger on the wing for most of the match. Then Sammy Crooks, reduced to a hobble by a pulled muscle, joined the casualties as Everton ran riot in the second half. Jimmy Cunliffe did the hat-trick, and 'Dixie' Dean and Alex Stevenson both scored twice. Three days later, Derby had the satisfaction of winning the return game 3–1 with a hat-trick of their own, scored by Astley. It was the first of three by the Welshman in seven matches.

Ken Scattergood, although having to withstand further fusillades from Preston (2–5), Arsenal (5–4), Brentford (2–6) and Manchester City (0–5) before giving way to Jack Kirby after a very hectic couple of months, at least had the consolation of knowing that his nightmare start was less horrendous than that inflicted upon another new goalkeeper nearly three years before. In January, 1934, Steve Milton was in the Halifax goal for the first time when they were thrashed 13–0 by Stockport County. The closest anyone else came to that record blitz on a debut, was in 1951, when a young Crewe Alexandra 'keeper named Murray let in 11 against Lincoln.

The end for Ken Scattergood as Derby County's first-team goalkeeper came after he had played in the club's first seven matches of 1937–38, the only season of George Jobey's reign in which there were real fears for their First Division future. In two of those seven matches Scattergood had to do a lot more back-bending, and one was even more torrid than the grilling Everton had given him. His former club, Stoke City, who also knocked the Rams out of the FA Cup in that season's third round, ran up the biggest score against Derby since the 8–0 defeat at Sunderland on the opening day of 1894–95 in thrashing them 8–1 at the Victoria Ground. Freddie Steele, the England centre-forward who later preceded George Jobey in charge at Mansfield, scored five times— just as he had against West Bromwich Albion earlier in the year.

Ken Scattergood, who had been signed from Stoke after short spells with Wolves and Bristol City, survived that slaughter back in the Potteries—but for only another fortnight. Out he went after a 6–1 slump in the next away match, against Manchester City and his early release became inevitable as, handicapped by injuries, he faded out of the reckoning after letting in 62 goals in 25 senior games. With only two wins in their first dozen games that season, the County slumped to 21st place in the table, but they picked up to finish 13th, if only four points above the relegated pair, Manchester City and West Bromwich, in the hectic scramble to which reference has already been made.

Whereas the Baseball Ground was the last League stop for the Bradford-born Ken Scattergood, his father returned to the First Division in leaving a Rams team with which he had dropped back into the Second for what was to be the last normal season for four years following the outbreak of the 1914–18 war. In moving to Bradford—not to Valley Parade as Harry Maskrey had done, but to Park Avenue—after falling only eight short of 200 appearances for Derby, the senior Scattergood joined a club that had just reached the top section for the first time. He helped to maintain a mid-table position in each of his first two seasons with them, which were separated by the war in which he survived being gassed, and Tom Maley, who was then Bradford's manager, regarded him as one of his soundest investments.

Ernald Scattergood emphasised the accuracy of that assessment when Derby's climb back to Division One at the first attempt gave him the opportunity to revisit the Baseball Ground. His superb display salvaged a point in a scoreless draw, and he was again in prime form when the Rams lost at Park Avenue in Harry Storer's debut match. Adept as he was at preventing goals, he had to give up his sideline of scoring them. With Derby County he had been entrusted with taking penalties, converting three, but at Bradford he handed the job over to somebody else after only just managing to get back to his own goal following his first failure after four successes. His goals tally altogether numbered eight, the other coming after he had moved into the outfield on being injured during Bradford's Boxing Day game against Clapton Orient in 1921.

In contrast to more recent times—during which Alex Stepney, of Manchester United provided the best-remembered example—goalkeepers then were more likely to be given the chance to get a bit of their own back by taking penalties. Arnold Birch set the record for a goalkeeper in one season, scoring with five spot kicks for Chesterfield in the Third North of 1923–24.

Despite their encouraging start to life in the League's upper echelon, Bradford were unable to stay at that level beyond a third season. They ended 1920–21 at the foot of the First Division, and down they went, along with Derby County. Worse still, the Yorkshire club sank straight through Division Two to the Third North, and, after a near-miss as runners-up to Nelson in 1923, five more years went by before they managed another promotion.[1] By then, Ernald Scattergood, who, like Maskrey, had joined the Rams from Ripley Athletic, was back near his roots, having finally left the League for Alfreton Town. In the three seasons before he joined them, Alfreton were runners-up, and then twice champions in the Central Alliance, and they were just embarking upon a switch to the Midland League.

They made a fairly successful start there, but had a poor season financially in 1926–27 and resigned membership. For an area which had produced so many outstanding players, the disbandment of the club that had arisen in 1921 in the wake of the one for which other former Derby County men (notably George Davis and 'Snobby' Bentley) had played, came as a severe blow, and brought down a most inappropriate curtain

---

1. Bradford stayed in the Second Division from 1928 until 1950, when they returned to Division Three North. In 1958 they dropped into the new Fourth Division, and although they won promotion in 1961 they went down again in 1963. Seven years later they lost their place in the League to Cambridge United.

on Ernald Scattergood's career. Not until more than 30 years later, in 1959, did a new Alfreton Town come onto the scene, following the merger of the Alfreton Miners' Welfare and Alfreton United clubs.

Strictly speaking George Harold Lawrence, next in line after Scattergood Senior as Derby County's goalkeeper, was not among the club's Derbyshire-born occupiers of that position, but he hailed from only just down the road, at Basford, and played for Ilkeston Primitives and Ilkeston United in the Notts and Derbyshire League before joining the Rams in May, 1910. He was first brought to the attention of Jimmy Methven while playing for Ilkeston against Ripley Town towards the end of the previous season. Derby's manager was suitably impressed, but, cagey as usual, he resorted to some subterfuge to complete the signing. This was how he explained it:

> If I had approached the Ilkeston people for his transfer, no doubt they would have opened their mouths pretty wide. As it was getting towards the end of the season, I thought it best not to bother them. To get a word with Lawrence, without the Ilkeston folks knowing, was impossible, as I was generally shadowed by one or another of the Ilkeston committeemen. So I asked a friend of mine, who was one of Derby County's oldest supporters, Harry Ellison, who was commonly known as 'Inky' in the Ripley district, to tell Lawrence not to sign any forms until I saw him at the finish of the season. Ellison always declared that he was the man who got Lawrence for Derby.

Lawrence duly refused to re-sign for Ilkeston, but Methven was not alone in seeking his services, and the Derby manager had to make a hasty journey to Ilkeston to clinch the deal. Even then, there was a last-minute hitch to overcome, for in his hurry he forgot to take the necessary forms. Astute as ever, he produced an old Amateur League form and held his hand over the printed matter while Lawrence signed. The legal papers were completed the next day.

After all that, Lawrence was allowed only intermittent chances in Derby's first team during the following four seasons, due to Ernald Scattergood's determination to hang onto the position for which he himself had been made to wait behind Harry Maskrey. Methven had to ward off several transfer requests from his impatient reserve before Scattergood's exit, in October, 1914, finally allowing Lawrence to play for the rest of a season he ended with a Second Division championship medal. Lawrence played in just over a dozen of the club's war-time and Midland Victory League games, but he resumed as first choice for most of the difficult first three seasons after the war, including another relegation in the abysmal campaign of 1920–21, before he had to stand down when Ben Olney's claims became too strong to ignore.

Although reduced to infrequent senior appearances—the 145th and last of them in a 3–3 home draw with Fulham, was the only one he made in the 1923–24 season—Lawrence was well into his 15th year with the club by the time he moved to Bristol City in September, 1924. Then aged 35, he was valued by the Rams at £500, but successfully appealed for a reduction of the fee to £100. About a year later he was transferred to Lincoln City, then completed his career back where he had started, with Ilkeston United.

With Jimmy Kidd having long left for Fleetwood, the unenviable task of understudying Ben Olney after Lawrence fell first to Derby-born Walter Fox, formerly of the towns

Harry Wilkes jumps to it, with George Collin *(left, behind net)* and Jack Barker at the ready.
(Derby Evening Telegraph)

Matlock and Alfreton, and then to William Cowell, an ex-England schoolboy international who was one of Cecil Potter's signings from Hartlepools United. In common with Olney's other deputy before Lawrence left—Ernest Hoffman, a North-Easterner who played a couple of times for Tottenham during the First World War and later assisted Ashington and Darlington—these understudies were allowed just one first-team match apiece, and those at widely-spaced intervals as dependable Ben made the last 213 of his record number of 240 League and Cup appearances by a County keeper before finally going off to play for Aston Villa…and England.

The man Holborn-born Olney eventually had to make way for was Harry Theodore Wilkes, who hailed from Sedgley, a district of Dudley in the West Midlands. He, too, might have played for Villa, to whom he was recommended by their former England forward Harry Hampton, who is still the highest scorer in their history. Hampton, who also played in Wilkes's first match for the Birmingham and District League club Wellington (now Telford) Town, was readily impressed, but not Villa. Fortunately for Wilkes, George Jobey did not make the mistake of sharing the Aston club's view that he was too small, and he repaid the Derby manager's faith by getting within 20 of Olney's total of games for the Rams before being transferred to Sheffield United.

Wilkes had to wait some seven months after his signing for his first League chance, but when it came he took it in such accomplished style that Jobey quickly realised he could afford to part with the experienced Olney. The change of goalkeeper was made after nine goals had been leaked in successive away games in which Harry Bedford had done all the County's scoring, in defeats by 4–3 at Newcastle and 5–2 at Liverpool. With only one win being gained in the first six matches of the season, and that only narrowly at home to Leicester City, Wilkes was brought in for the visit of Arsenal. He acquitted himself so well in a 4–0 victory—in which, strangely, Bedford was the only Derby forward not to score—that he earned this commendation from one critic:

> His handling of the ball was very clean, he cleared quickly when that was practicable, and altogether he made a splendid impression. In addition, he had the distinction of helping the Rams to finish a match without conceding a goal for first time since the opening of the season.

From that day, Wilkes was the man firmly in possession for the better part of five and a half seasons, an unflurried, agile performer with a sound positional sense, yet, despite the advantage of large hands, not a goalkeeper by original choice. In his youth, he was a fair, but not outstanding, inside-forward with his local Congregational side, having previously played in that position in schoolboy and scouts soccer, until one Saturday the regular goalkeeper failed to turn up and he was persuaded to take his place. He took to the switch so successfully that he never returned to the attack, maintaining form that soon caught Wellington's attention.

Derby County's deputy goalkeeper on the first dozen occasions Wilkes was unavailable was Jack Hampton, who was also signed by George Jobey after playing for Wellington Town—but first for Wolverhampton Wanderers. He completed half a century of first-team games for Wolves before Jobey signed him again, for the Rams, but in 1930 he was released to Preston North End, later going to Dundalk, as the player who was to be Wilkes's successor began to press his claims. This was Jack Kirby, the former South Derbyshire Boys goalkeeper from Newhall United, but although he eventually made good he at first had an even leaner time of it than Hampton.

After taking over from Hampton, while Wilkes was still out with a knee injury, for the last two matches of 1929–30 (and conceding six goals in the second of them, at Storer-stirred Burnley) Kirby had only two more opportunities in each of the next two seasons (including the 5–1 home beating by Bedford-inspired Newcastle). He then had to continue as second choice until halfway through the following season before finally getting in to stay on the last day of 1932 after the Rams had run into a sticky patch, during which they had given George Jobey one of his worst days by losing 6–1 at Liverpool after leading, and then let in four goals in each of their games against Sheffield United, Wolves and Blackpool. Kirby's recall began promisingly with a 5–1 home win over Leeds United, but it was not immediately a happy new year for him. He encouraged anticipation of a return for Wilkes by making several glaring mistakes before suddenly striking such a rich vein of his best form that he ended the season generally regarded as one of the most improved members of the team.

Making full use of his height of over 6ft, he especially excelled with his clean and safe catching of high balls, and the strength of his goal kicking was also a decided asset. Never was his worth more recognised than in the epic sixth-round FA Cup replay at

Sunderland, which he described to me as 'undoubtedly my most memorable match'. Modestly, he refrained from even hinting at the magnificent contribution he made to the Rams' extra-time victory, which he ensured by choking the Rokerites' roars of 'Goal!' in the dying seconds with a stupendous save from Bert Davis that killed off Sunderland's last hopes of forcing a second replay. And that was but one of the many times he came to the rescue in that quarter-final. The *Derby Evening Telegraph* reported:

> Kirby held the ball in almost miraculous fashion. He was here, there and everywhere, making cat-like springs across the goal to prevent some really fine efforts from finding the net.

After Kirby's heroics in that match of March, 1933, Harry Wilkes was kept in the Derby background for another year until his move to Sheffield, where he spent 15 frustrating months in what he called 'a goalkeeper's graveyard' before joining Rhyl Athletic for a reunion with Tommy Davison, then the Welsh club's player-manager. About a year later, in 1936, he returned to live in the Derby area, at Chaddesden, where, after spending

Jack Kirby *(left)* is congratulated by Harry Hibbs,
Birmingham's England goalkeeper, on being chosen for the
international trial match of March, 1936.

one season guarding Heanor Town's net, he concentrated on running a fish and chip shop with his Derby-born wife, Effie. He kept a keen interest in Derby County until his death near his 77th birthday in 1984.

Just as Wilkes was missed by Aston Villa, so Jack Kirby was by Wolves, who were interested enough to give him a trial, but not enough to retain him. Again, George Jobey, who, in Harry's estimation 'could spot a footballer a mile away' was quick to take advantage—no doubt influenced by the fact that in Kirby's last season in Burton Association football his Newhall team conceded only seven goals. In his first full season guarding Derby's net, 1933–34, Kirby missed only two matches as they finished fourth in Division One, and in 1935–36, when they were second, he played in all their 42 League games and four Cup-ties. While at his peak he had the misfortune to find his way into the England team blocked by Harry Hibbs (Birmingham), Frank Moss (Arsenal), Ted Sagar (Everton) and Harry Holdcroft (Preston), so he had to be satisfied with selection in this Possibles team against the Probables in the international trial at Old Trafford, in March, 1936:

> **Kirby** (Derby County); **Griffiths** (Manchester United), **Stuart** (Middlesbrough); **Stoker** (Birmingham), **Vose** (Manchester United), **Smith, S.** (Leicester City); **Birkett** (Middlesbrough), **Eastham** (Bolton Wanderers), **Cheetham** (QPR), **Goulden** (West Ham United), **Cunliffe** (Middlesbrough).

The Probables line-up was:

> **Holdcroft** (Preston North End); **Rochford** (Portsmouth), **Barkas** (Manchester City); **Willingham**, **Young** (both Huddersfield Town), **Cockroft** (West Ham United); **Matthews** (Stoke City), **Carter** (Sunderland), **Richardson, W.G.** (West Bromwich Albion), **Dawes** (Crystal Palace), **Hobbis** (Charlton Athletic).

Frank Boulton, Derby's regular goalkeeper in the last pre-war season, but kept out of the first post-war FA Cup Final by injury after helping the Rams to reach the quarter-finals.

(Derby Evening Telegraph)

For a couple of seasons, Kirby's deputy at Derby was Vincent Blore, from Uttoxeter, who filled in the rest of his pre-war years with West Ham, Crystal Palace and Exeter City. Kirby then found stronger competition coming from Ken Scattergood and Harry Wright, before his own departure, in August, 1938, coincided with the arrival from Arsenal of Frank Boulton, who became Jobey's fourth main goalkeeper as the automatic choice for what was to be the last League season for seven years. Despite losing weight through suffering from malaria and dysentery while serving overseas with the RAF during the war, Boulton came back to play in the first six of Derby's games on their way to Cup glory at Wembley in 1946. Then, along with Sammy Crooks and full-back Jack Parr, he had the rotten luck to miss the chance of a winner's medal because of injury. Instead of being able to carry on from where he had left off in the top flight with the Rams in 1939, at only just turned 22, he then had to play out his last League days in the Third Division, with Swindon Town, after football had at last restored to been its peacetime pattern.

With the inclusion of his limited war-time appearances, Boulton still fell 16 short of adding his name to the list of goalkeepers who completed a century of senior matches for Derby—an exclusive band Jack Kirby comfortably joined by getting to within nine of a second century before becoming Folkestone Town's player-manager in the Southern League. Others on that Kent club's staff for the ensuing 1938–39 season included Trevor Jones, a full-back who had helped Walsall to their shock Cup victory over mighty Arsenal in 1933, and Harry Ashley, a forward who had been with Derby County but without reaching the first team.

The coming of the war led to a homecoming for Kirby. He brought his family back to Derby where he lived until his untimely death, at the age of only 49 in June 1960, and obtained employment in the British Celanese process works at Spondon. Among other ex-professional footballers who also worked there, apart from George Collin and Arthur Groves, were Alf Bennett, who used to keep goal for Nottingham Forest, and Cyril Quinn, a former Blackpool winger.

In the early war years, Kirby continued his goalkeeping with a local side, Markeaton Rangers, and linked up with some of his old County clubmates to play friendly matches against Services sides before the Rams officially got back into action, but then, on doctor's advice, he reluctantly had to retire from playing because of heart trouble.

Harry Wright, who cost £2,500 from Aldershot, shared Derby's last line of defence with Kirby from the time Ken Scattergood was jettisoned until the last three games of the disappointing 1937–38 season, and he was the unfortunate fellow in the firing line as Manchester City went one better than the roasting they had given Scattergood at Maine Road when they visited Derby for the return fixture. City repeated the 7–1 margin of their win at the Baseball Ground when they were hosts to West Bromwich some weeks later, yet down to the Second Division the reigning champions went, with Albion despite also scoring six against Leeds United in their next, and last, home match.

That seven-goal spree at Derby by the Manchester club, who had put five past Ken Scattergood in the corresponding fixture the previous season, resulted in the last recall for Jack Kirby. It was short-lived, but although Harry Wright then got back in favour he had to give way for the last three games of that season to Frank Boulton's immediate predecessor, Frank King, who fleetingly found even less scope at Derby than he had been granted by the consistently efficient Ted Sagar at Everton. King, a former Blyth

Spartan, was beaten six times as Derby picked up only one point out of the six at stake when he played. His contract was cancelled the following autumn, shortly after Boulton's arrival.

Harry Wright stayed on as Boulton's rarely-needed deputy until shortly before the war, when he moved to Chelmsford City. After the war, he had a varied career as trainer and coach, both in England, with Walsall, Luton Town and Everton, and abroad, in Norway and the Lebanon.

Born at Tottenham, he played for Harwich and Parkeston before entering League football with Charlton Athletic in tragic circumstances. The man from whom he temporarily took over at the Valley, his namesake, Alex Wright, died after a bathing accident at Torquay, fatally damaging his spine when he dived into shallow water. Not long afterwards an out-of-work miner named Sam Bartram came down from the North-East to make Charlton's goalkeeping position his exclusive domain for some 20 years.

CHAPTER 11

A Sheffield 'Steal'

*Hagan makes memorable debut at 17 – Hat-trick helps
to clinch promotion for Sheffield United – Profitable
link-up with Lawton – England score eight goals
against Wales and Scotland in successive matches –
Hagan bows out back at the Baseball Ground –
Friction at Peterborough – Leads West Bromwich to
two League Cup finals but stirs up a players' strike –
Success at Benfica before more trouble*

A MID THE GALAXY OF FORWARD TALENT George Jobey accumulated for Derby County, there was reason for one big regret—that a gem such as Jimmy Hagan, who cost nothing more than the £10 signing-on fee, should have been allowed to get away. At £2,500, he became one of Sheffield United's most celebrated players, twice helping them to promotion to the First Division in almost 20 years at Bramall Lane, and becoming a key member of England's free-scoring attack during the 1939–45 war.

The trouble as far as Derby County were concerned was that Jimmy Hagan and their dictatorial manager did not see eye to eye. Right from the start they were at loggerheads. Hagan, a schoolboy international whose father, Alf, had been an inside-forward with Newcastle, Cardiff, and Tranmere, was first signed as an amateur by Liverpool just after his 14th birthday in January, 1932, but some difficulty over the amount of wages to be paid to a boy of his age resulted in his return to Tyneside and put Jobey hot on his trail. Readily recognising Hagan's potential after watching him in a junior match while on one of his scouting missions back in the Newcastle area, the Rams' manager made what he presumed would be uncomplicated overtures—only to run straight into difficulties when he decided that it would be in the youngster's best interests for him to take a job in Derby, as an apprentice motor mechanic, until he was old enough to become a full-time professional.

Hagan promptly made it plain that he had very different ideas. Interested only in playing football, he scorned the threat that he would not be signed unless he complied. This rankled with Jobey, who was accustomed to having his word obeyed without question, but, at the same time, he was anxious not to miss an exceptional emerging talent, and he had to climb down to lure this obstinate lad to the Baseball Ground. There was no stipulation about a temporary job outside football when Hagan did sign amateur forms for Derby County in May, 1933, although, as one of the most junior members of the staff at the age of 15, he first had the unappealing task of weeding the pitch.

Having turned professional on reaching 17 in January, 1935, Hagan continued to be carefully coached in being confined to the Colts and an occasional Central League game and he was kept waiting until the club's last League match of that year, at home to Everton, for his entry into the First Division. It was a debut well worth waiting for. He made it on the right wing as that season's fourth deputy[1] for the injured Crooks, and this is what the reporter in the local evening paper had to say about him:

> Any review of Derby County's last match of the year must in fairness open with a tribute to Hagan, who, at the age of 17, made his first appearance in League football—and made a pronounced success of it, too. Outside-right is not the normal position of this gifted young player, but his natural aptitude for the game enabled him to make an excellent debut in nerve-testing circumstances. He showed confidence and craft in beating his man, and he skilfully varied his service of passes from the wing.

It was largely due to Hagan's efforts that Derby forced a 3–3 draw with Everton after being behind for most of the match. Jimmy ('Nat') Cunliffe headed the visitors in front in the fifth minute from a centre by Albert Geldard, who made it 2–0 on the half-hour

Jimmy Hagan, the star who got away.

---

1. The others were Jimmy Boyd, Charlie Napier and Jack Summers. Chorlton-born Summers, signed from Leicester City, was a member of Derby's Central League championship side in 1935–36, but he played only twice in the first team before moving to Southampton.

by beating two men to net the best goal of the game. Then came the Hagan-inspired comeback. The fledgling forward created the openings from which Ike Keen and Peter Ramage brought the scores level again with headers in the first ten minutes of the second half. It was against the run of play when Everton regained the lead through Stan Bentham 18 minutes from time, but Freddie Jessop saved a point from the penalty spot two minutes later.

Splendidly though he had started, Hagan's second opportunity in the League side was delayed for a few weeks. With Crooks fit again, and making a scoring return in a win at Bolton, the youngster returned in his usual inside-forward position as the England winger's partner in the absence of Charlie Napier, and he made another excellent impression with an unduly thoughtful and intelligent display for one of his tender years in a home victory over Sheffield Wednesday. One reporter, anonymous as most of them were in those days, felt moved to observe that it was 'a pity that a regular place cannot be found for him in the Rams' First Division line-up'.

For most of the rest of that 1935–36 season, however, and also for sizeable stretches of the next two, Hagan was kept in the background. He had only 30 First Division matches behind him (seven on the right wing, the others at inside-right) when George Jobey made what many came to regard as his biggest mistake over a player in letting him leave for Sheffield United in November, 1938. The longest run Hagan was permitted in Derby's League team was nine games alongside Crooks in the spring of 1938, following Napier's exit to the other side of Yorkshire's steel city. That was at a difficult period, for the Rams were slipping to a finish in the bottom half of the table for only the second time in 11 seasons as their goals tally dipped 30 below the 96 of 1936–37 that had equalled the club's record for a First Division season set in 1927–28.

How ironic it was, when Sammy Crooks was envying 'Dally' Duncan in decrying his lack of a settled partner, that Derby County dispensed with a player who was hardly given a fair chance to parade skills which made him an international player with another club in whose colours he was the star well into a second decade. In the first volume of his splendidly researched *Sheffield Football, A History*, my friend Keith Farnsworth, a former Sports Editor of the *Sheffield Telegraph*, observes that 'few players in United's entire history, and probably none in the past half-century, have been more idolised by supporters'. Yet George Jobey saw fit to let Hagan go, so leaving himself open to suggestions that he had been influenced by his personal feelings of animosity, arising from their clash of wills, in making this debatable decision which led him to further expensive ventures into the transfer market.

Hagan's marvellous ball control, pinpoint passing and penchant for scoring spectacular goals thrived on the stability of being an automatic choice with Sheffield United. The popularity in which he basked at Bramall Lane was assured from the last day of the 1938–39 season on which he did the hat-trick in the defeat of Tottenham Hotspur that inched the Blades ahead of their Wednesday neighbours and clinched promotion to the First Division as runners-up to Blackburn Rovers.

Came the war, and Army service in the Physical Training Corps enabled Hagan to hone his skills in the company of some of the country's top players, not only as one of Aldershot's star guests, but also in the Army and England teams. He struck up a particularly profitable understanding at all three of those levels with Tommy Lawton, the spearhead of Everton's League champions in the last pre-war season. Lawton had good cause to be grateful for the unobtrusive support he received from the Sheffield schemer he called 'the master craftsman'. As the England centre-forward was quick to acknowledge, Hagan's intelligent springing of an attempted offside trap engineered the six goals Lawton scored for Aldershot in one game against Luton Town—'and every one was made in different fashion' Tommy recalled.

For the Army, Hagan gave one of his finest displays, scoring twice, in a 3–1 defeat of a strong Football Association side, but, without doubt, the war-time match he looked back upon with the greatest pleasure was that in which England provided a classic example of teamwork in trouncing Scotland 8–0 at Maine Road, Manchester. These were the teams that day, October 16th, 1943:

ENGLAND: **Swift** (Manchester City); **Scott** (Arsenal), **Hardwick** (Middlesbrough); **Britton** (Everton), **Cullis** (Wolverhampton Wanderers), **Mercer** (Everton); **Matthews** (Stoke City), **Carter** (Sunderland), **Lawton** (Everton), **Hagan** (Sheffield United), **Compton, D.** (Arsenal).

SCOTLAND: **Crozier** (Brentford); **Carabine** (Third Lanark), **Miller** (Hearts); **Little**, **Young** (both Glasgow Rangers), **Campbell** (Morton); **Waddell** (Rangers), **Gillick** (Everton), **Linwood** (St Mirren), **Walker** (Hearts), **Deakin** (St Mirren).

This was the second successive match in which England piled up eight goals and, as on the previous occasion, against Wales at Wembley a few weeks earlier, Hagan scored two of them. He opened the floodgates in the swamping of the Scots after a quarter of an hour, smartly pouncing on a back-heel from Lawton, and he got his second shortly before Stanley Matthews brought the house down by rounding things off with a spectacular solo effort. In between, Lawton collected four goals—one of them in a 10-minute hat-trick, while sitting on the ground with his back to goal. Raich Carter obtained the other, but also failed with a penalty. Only the week before Carter had played his first game for Derby County, scoring three of their five goals as a guest against Birmingham.

In the heavy defeat of Wales—who like Birmingham against the Rams replied three times—the England attack was led not by Lawton but by Don Welsh, of Charlton Athletic, who did the hat-trick but then had the mortification of missing the match with the Scots. Welsh was also England's centre-forward, scoring all their four goals against his namesakes in Nottingham, when Hagan made the first of his 14 war-time international appearances in April, 1941, but it was alongside Lawton that the Derby discard showed to most advantage—and mainly at the Scots' expense. They shared the scoring against them at both Wembley and in Glasgow in 1942, though England lost their away game by 5–4 despite another Lawton hat-trick, and they were responsible for half the six goals (two for Hagan) when Scotland were again well beaten at Wembley early in 1944, in their next meeting after the Manchester avalanche.

Hagan also played for England in two of their Victory internationals in 1946, but both were lost. Jimmy Delaney, recently signed by Manchester United from Celtic, scored a last-minute winner for Scotland at Hampden Park, and Hagan's 13th goal for his country came too late to avoid a shock 2–1 defeat by France in Paris. With Carter, by then with Derby, and Middlesbrough's Wilf Mannion filling the inside-forward positions for England when the normal peacetime programme was resumed, and Stan

Mortensen, of Blackpool, taking over from where Carter had to leave off, Jimmy Hagan —for all his superb form when caps were not awarded—had only one opportunity to play in a full international match.

It came in Copenhagen, in September, 1948, when, in his 31st year, his hopes of a late flourish at the top foundered in a dismal England display that was a complete contrast to the high point he had helped to attain in the Manchester mauling of the Scots. A scoreless draw with the amateurs of Denmark unleashed unanimous criticism, especially of the attack's shortcomings, even though Lawton had a goal controversially disallowed and two shots from Len Shackleton, Sunderland's 'Clown Prince', were kicked off the goal-line.

In addition to his muted performance that day, Hagan's chances of further caps were nullified not only by his age but also because Sheffield United were on their way back to the Second Division. But he still had some 250 League games with the Blades left in him, taking him to a total of just over 380 with Cup-ties included, and, in successive years at the beginning of the Fifties, he was in FA parties on tours of Canada (where his colleagues included two Derby County players, Tim Ward and Bert Mozley) and Australia. Although not normally a prolific marksman, he scored eight goals in a 17–0 defeat of Tasmania. The most he ever obtained in a League season was 16, plus one in the Cup, on two occasions—the second of them in 1952–53 when United gained promotion as Second Division champions—and he had an aggregate of nearly 130,[2] counting the seven he scored for Derby.

Though prolonged, Hagan's career at Sheffield was not without unrest and, indeed, there were several times when it was almost abbreviated. Among his fellow professionals he was noted for his dry sense of humour, but the stubborn streak George Jobey had encountered brought him into conflict with United as they prepared for the first post-war season of 1946–47 fresh from winning the transitional League North title with very little help from Hagan (due to his Army service, he played fewer than 50 games for United during the war years). Anxious to safeguard his future, he started studying to be an architect and surveyor before deciding to re-sign after missing the first few matches.

All was sweetness and light again as, under his inspiring influence, United finished that season in the First Division's top six, and reached the Cup quarter-finals before losing to Newcastle with about 60,000 packed into Bramall Lane. Then the Blades went into a decline that two years later resulted in another relegation, and soon afterwards Hagan was not only relieved of the captaincy, at his own request, but also dropped for the first time. Though reinstated, he had his appearances restricted by injury when promotion at the first attempt was foiled in 1950 in the most galling manner—by the Wednesday on goal average.

It was around this time that rumours about his impending departure began to circulate. Charlton Athletic were reported to have made an unsuccessful bid; Oldham were said to have wanted him as player-manager. There was even talk of a move to Hillsborough for a fee near the then-record £35,000 which Wednesday soon afterwards paid Notts County for Jackie Sewell.

---

2. Hagan also scored 100 or so goals during the war, nearly 80 of them for Aldershot.

Hagan, however, was to stay for another eight seasons. In the last of them, 1957–58, when approaching his 40th birthday, he appropriately played his last League game[3] back at the Baseball Ground—as a late replacement for 'flu victim Tommy Hoyland, but on the losing side. During the intervening period he had resisted two more attempts to tempt him away from Bramall Lane, rejecting a player-manager offer Mansfield Town made after parting with Stan Mercer, George Jobey's successor there, and refusing to join Rotherham after another Mercer (his old England mate Joe, who had become Sheffield United's manager) had been willing to negotiate an exchange deal involving another inside-forward, Frank Meadows.

Hagan leads out Sheffield United.

---

3. That match with Derby, who won 2–0, was played on September 14th, 1957. Hagan last turned out for Sheffield United in his testimonial match, under the Bramall Lane floodlights on March 10th, 1958, nearly two months after his 40th birthday.

When Hagan did leave, in August, 1958 (shortly before Joe Mercer also left, to manage Aston Villa) it was as Peterborough United's third managerial choice in succession to one of Mercer's ex-Arsenal clubmates, George Swindin, who had returned to take over the reins at Highbury. Peterborough, then of the Midland League, first unsuccessfully approached Jimmy Dickinson, the veteran Portsmouth wing-half, and Jimmy Scoular, the former Pompey player who was with Newcastle.

Difficult as he could be at times, through being so independently-minded, there was only one blot on Hagan's long service with Sheffield United—a sending-off against Swansea. His dismissal from the field, a few days before Christmas during his second promotion season with the Blades, was for retaliation under extreme provocation. It came five minutes from the end of a match in which he had tormented the visitors with his brilliant promptings, and two minutes after he had joined in the scoring to seal a 7–1 triumph. The FA Disciplinary Commission took his previous unblemished record into account, limiting his punishment to a severe caution.

Though Hagan's playing days were largely free from trouble, his passion for perfection in fitness and discipline made his life as a manager anything but serene. 'The Posh'— a long-standing nickname Peterborough had embellished with some notable Cup exploits—were admitted to the new Fourth Division of the Football League, to the exclusion of Gateshead, in 1960, and straightaway Hagan guided them to the title with a record total of 134 goals. Soon afterwards, however, he complained of being 'messed about' in having to sign 'under pressure' a new contract which contained some clauses he did not like, and, although he kept Peterborough near the top of the Third Division, he was sacked in October, 1962 following mounting friction within the club that led seven of his players to demand a transfer.

At his next club, West Bromwich Albion, matters became even worse—and not solely because he had the alarming experience of being in his car when it ran backwards down an 80ft embankment near the club's practice ground and fell into a canal from which he was rescued in the nick of time. The monotony of his rigorous training methods unsettled the whole first team, and they went on strike when he forbade them to wear track-suit bottoms in the 1966 freeze-up. Undaunted after the resolving of that rebellion, he proceeded to pilot Albion to two successive League Cup finals. They won the first, beating West Ham 5–3 over two legs, but lost the second, 2–3 to Third Division Queen's Park Rangers after being two goals up, when the competition was uplifted to a one-match finale at Wembley in 1967. Another dismissal quickly followed, arising from differences with the West Bromwich directors, but he had built up a reputation as a bargain spotter, and most of his signings were in the Albion sides that won the FA Cup in 1968, defeating Everton after extra time, and again reached the League Cup Final in 1970, losing to Manchester City—also after an extra half-hour. Recognition of his team-building ability came from a most unexpected quarter—he himself admitted to being very surprised—while he was running a driving school near Birmingham after doing some scouting for Manchester City. The call came, in March, 1970, from Benfica, who had just missed winning the Portuguese championship for a fourth consecutive year (and for a 12th time in all) in finishing runners-up to Lisbon's other big club, Sporting.

His appointment, at the then sky-high annual salary of £10,000, was a disappointment to supporters who knew little, or nothing, about him, and had been expecting the job to go the famous former Hungarian centre-forward Nandor Hidegkuti. However,

Hagan overcame that early coolness, and also some disagreements behind the scenes when the side got off to a poor start, to claim the league title again in each of the three seasons he spent at the Estadio da Luz (Stadium of Light). Indeed, in 1972, Benfica completed the league and cup double, for the fifth time.

It was also in 1972, on October 25th, a date which has gone down as one of the truly great occasions in Derby County's history, that Hagan revisited the Baseball Ground and saw his Benfica team comprehensively beaten 3–0 in the second round of the European Cup—a competition in which the Portuguese club had five times reached the final, winning the trophy twice in succession at the beginning of the Sixties after Real Madrid had monopolised it for the first five years. Then, in front of a Lisbon crowd of 75,000, the Rams, fortified by the defiance of goalkeeper Colin Boulton, magnificently held onto that advantage in a scoreless second leg on their way to a semi-final with the Italian giant Juventus.[4]

Hagan's break with Benfica came in September, 1973, only a few months after they had landed their third title treble in 11 years. Once more he was at odds with his associates, an argument arising over the selection of players for the testimonial match for the club's African star, Eusebio, the Mozambican formally known as Ferreira da Silva. Hagan would have liked to have returned to England, but his subsequent employment took him to Kuwait, as a coach, and then back to Portugal, where he stayed in retirement after ending his managerial careeer with spells at Sporting Lisbon and Oporto.[5] Among the men he followed in that role at Oporto was Tommy Docherty, the former Scotland wing-half whose many clubs as a manager included Derby County.

---

4. Derby were controversially beaten 3–1 by Juventus in Italy, then were held goalless in the second leg after Alan Hinton, usually so reliable from the spot, had missed a penalty and Roger Davies had been ordered off. In the final, Juventus lost 1–0 in Belgrade to Ajax, of Amsterdam, who won the trophy for the third successive year.
5. Hagan, who was born at Washington, County Durham, on January 21st, 1918, died only a few weeks after his 80th birthday, on February 27th, 1998.

CHAPTER 12

Forward Stars from Aston Villa

Astley starts with scoring spurt – All-capped attacks at Charlton – First Division scoring record equalled – Capped with four League clubs – Dix, the 'Boy Wonder' – Youngest scorer, at 15, in the League – Barred by League from leaving Bristol Rovers – Short-lived move to Blackburn

AT THE TIME JIMMY HAGAN LEFT DERBY late in 1938, the inside-forwards keeping him out of the Rams' League side were Dai Astley and Ronnie Dix, both signed from Aston Villa for an outlay of around £5,000 apiece.

Astley arrived first, in November, 1936; Dix followed in February, 1937. Astley came as a seasoned international, having made his debut for Wales in a 3–2 victory against Northern Ireland at Wrexham in April, 1931, while with Charlton Athletic, and twice helped Wales to win the British Championship in successive seasons, 1932–34 as a Villa player. Dix gained his one England cap after joining Derby, scoring in a 4–0 win over Norway, at Newcastle in November, 1938.

David John Astley was born at Dowlais, an industrial area of Mid-Glamorgan, in November, 1909, and worked as a miner before becoming a professional footballer shortly after leaving the Dowlais Welfare team for neighbouring Merthyr in 1927. Of slim build, standing 6 ft and weighing about 11 st, he looked too frail to make a success of his move to Charlton early in 1928, but he showed no lack of stamina in helping them to the Third Division South championship in the following season. His impressive form, if in defeat, at Villa Park in the second replay of a third-round FA Cup-tie against West Bromwich early in 1931 encouraged Aston Villa to snap him up a few months later during the close season.

Though there were some complaints about his work-rate, he commanded a regular place because of his sharp finishing, and in just over 170 Cup and League games for the Claret and Blues he netted exactly 100 goals, with 33 in 1933–34 the biggest of his double-figure hauls in four consecutive seasons. That total included his best bag in one match for Villa, four in a 7–2 Cup defeat of Sunderland.

Such scoring consistency was bound to attract envious glances from other clubs, and Charlton, Bolton and Manchester United were at the head of the queue when Villa regretfully agreed to his request for a change of scene after they and Blackburn Rovers had both been relegated from the First Division for the first time in their history at the end of the 1935–36 season. A Villa team that again had Astley as top scorer, and which also included two other future members of Derby County's attack, Ronnie Dix and Frank Broome, ended three points from safety despite the splashing out of more than £35,000, an extravagant amount for those days, on seven players in the desperate attempt to beat the drop. Only 13 League wins were gained, and, of the 110 goals conceded 56 were leaked at home—seven of them (from eight shots) by Arsenal's Ted Drake.

When it became known that Astley was set to leave Villa Park, it was generally anticipated that he would return to Charlton, where one of his clubmates would have been his brother-in-law Bert Turner,[1] the defender who was to put his name in the record books by scoring for both sides in one minute during the 1946 FA Cup Final against Derby County. Astley, however, had an aversion to retracing his steps, and when the Athletic failed with their approach for that reason George Jobey was quick to jump the queue to get him. Attracted by the abundant international company in which he would be at the Baseball Ground, the wiry Welshman unhesitatingly signed,

Dai Astley who scored three hat-tricks among
his 29 goals in his first 30 games for Derby.
(Derby Evening Telegraph)

---

1. Astley and Turner were the uncles of Trevor Edwards, a full-back who played for Charlton and Wales after the war.

and it was therefore not for Charlton, but against them, that he played at the Valley two days later, making his debut for Derby there on November 14th, 1936, in the first-ever match between the clubs.

As recalled earlier, Jack Bowers made his last League appearance for the Rams in that game before leaving for Leicester, at the head of an all-capped attack as Astley came in at inside-right to the exclusion of Hagan. Two years afterwards, almost to the very day, Astley was again in a complete international forward line for Derby at Charlton, again as partner for Sammy Crooks, with Dave McCulloch at centre-forward, and Ronnie Dix in Charlie Napier's former place at inside-left alongside 'Dally' Duncan, but on that occasion he was the one about to be transferred. Ten games later he was reluctantly on his way to Blackpool, at a profit to the Rams of about £3,000.

Despite the formidable-looking front five Derby fielded in those matches at Charlton, they were beaten both times without scoring. The visit to the Valley on Astley's debut day was the Rams' 15th game of the 1936–37 season, and the first of them in which they failed to find the net. It was a far from auspicious start for Astley, but also a very deceptive one. Switched to succeed Bowers as leader of the line, he then embarked upon the most plentiful phase of his career. It began in his first home game, with a brace of goals against Grimsby which helped his new club to their first win at the Baseball Ground in two months, and also included a purple patch of 16 goals in nine consecutive matches, in only one of which he drew a blank. This was that sequence, with Cup-ties in italics:

December 28	H	3–1	Everton	Astley 3	
January 2	A	2–2	Manchester U	Astley, Ramage	
9	H	3–2	Sheffield Wed	Napier, Ramage, Astley	
16	*A*	*4–0*	*Bradford*	*Napier, Astley, Duncan, Stockill*	
23	A	2–5	Preston NE	Stockill 2	
30	*H*	*3–0*	*Brentford*	*Astley 3*	
February 3	H	5–4	Arsenal	Astley 3, Stockill 2	
6	A	2–6	Brentford	Astley 2	
13	H	3–0	Bolton W	Astley 2, Napier	

Astley might well have had four goals in the Cup-tie against Brentford, for Duncan was a most unexpected choice ahead of the newcomer to take the penalty kick with which he failed in the opening minutes. The three hat-tricks, two of them in five days, were registered against three of the best centre-halves then in the business: Charlie Gee, of Everton (against whom Astley overshadowed the mighty William Ralph Dean as the Rams extracted revenge for their 7–0 Christmas Day eclipse at Goodison); Jimmy James, captain of Brentford; and Herbie Roberts, the celebrated Arsenal stopper. Gee and Roberts had both played for England, the Everton man as recently as the previous month.

Frank Boulton, destined for Derby, was Arsenal's hard-pressed goalkeeper in the second match that season in which the Rams nicked the odd goal of nine in a Baseball Ground thriller (the first one was transformed by that four-goal blast by Bowers against Manchester United). Among Arsenal's four were a Bastin penalty and an own goal by full-back Jack Howe, another of George Jobey's North-East recruits. Susceptible as

Derby were in defence, too frequently for comfort as emphasised by the concession of 15 goals in three successive League games, they were no slouches as scorers themselves, mainly through the sharpness of their new Welsh spearhead, and in getting to within four goals of a League total of 100 they were only one short of breaking their record for a First Division season. In ending with a 3–1 setback at Wolverhampton, they were also only one point short of equalling their highest tally of 21 from away games, achieved in 1934–35, but their full total of 49 assured them of a top-six finish for the fourth successive year.

Dai Astley's goal in the last-day defeat at Molineux took him to 25 in 27 League games for Derby, and with four more in the Cup, plus his five for Villa before his transfer, he raised his personal best for one season to 34. He was unable to maintain such a high striking rate as the Rams slumped to 13th in 1937–38, but he was again their highest scorer, with 17 in his ever-present 42 appearances—all but six of them at centre-forward —and he left in January, 1939, with the very respectable total of 49 in 98 games.

With Blackpool, he had time for only 20 League games before war intervened, playing in both inside-forward positions as well as centre-forward, and scoring half-a-dozen goals, but his selection for Wales against France in Paris in May, 1939, when he scored in a 2–1 defeat, gave him the distinction of winning full caps while with four League clubs. Previously he played in one international match as a Charlton player, nine when with Villa, and two with Derby, for a total of 13 to add to his four appearances in other Welsh fixtures and the international honours he had gained as a schoolboy. The final call from his country came early in the war, against England.

Only a few months before entering his 31st year, Astley broke off his Blackpool connection after completing the 1939–40 season with the Seasiders in the hastily-arranged North-West Regional League and League War Cup. His last game for them, on May 25th, 1940, was a home quarter-final in the cup competition, but Newcastle denied him a scoring farewell, and Blackpool the victory, by winning 2–0. After the war, he played briefly in French football, then coached in Iran, Italy, Sweden and Persia. In the late Fifties he was back in Derby, working for the Prestige Group. He died in 1989—in November, the month of his 80th birthday.

Ronnie Dix, Derby County's other star signing from Aston Villa during the 1936–37 season, had been the most famous schoolboy footballer in England ten years before he joined the Rams—the 'Boy Wonder' who graduated from that level with another outstanding forward whose path was to lead to the Baseball Ground, one Horatio Stratton Carter from Sunderland.

The stocky, fair-haired Dix, who was born in Bristol, in September, 1912, and died there in April, 1998, at the age of 85, packed a tremendous shot for a schoolboy. His scoring feats for his South Street School in the Bedminster district of Bristol earned him a place in the Bristol Boys team at the astonishingly early age of 10. At 13 he captained the side, and one year later, on April 23rd, 1927, he skippered the England team against Wales at Bristol Rovers' Eastville ground, in the first schools international match to be staged in his home city.

A crowd of nearly 9,000 saw England coast to a 6–2 victory, and Dix, ably abetted by Carter, struck four of their goals—two in each half and the first of them a trademark blockbuster in only the fourth minute. The scoring was suitably completed by Carter, the smallest and cleverest player afield.

In that vintage year for English schools soccer, the other members of the winning team included Alex Scott, a goalkeeper who went on to play for Burnley, Wolves and Crewe, George Mason, the centre-half who became one of Harry Storer's best signings for Coventry City, and Albert Geldard, a winger who gained an FA Cup-winner's medal at the end of his first season with Everton. The best-known of the Welsh players were Willie Evans, who made his name as a winger with Tottenham, Bill Whatley, a full-back who also played for Spurs, and Leslie Boulter, an inside-forward with Charlton and Brentford.

A few days before leaving school, Dix also played against Scotland Boys at Hampden Park, where he was denied a goal in unusual circumstances in England's 2–1 defeat. In those days a second crossbar was nailed below the one used for senior games, and the referee disagreed with those who thought a shot from Dix had gone in by ruling that the ball had passed between the two crossbars. As a result, nets were attached to the lower bar in subsequent matches to avoid any controversy.

Ronnie Dix, the 'Boy Wonder' who was the League's youngest scorer at 15.
(Derby Evening Telegraph)

Despite the fact that Dix had been such a marked success in schools' soccer, and even though Ashton Gate, the home of Bristol City where he had been treated for injuries, was nearest to where he lived, the only approach he received from a Football League club when his schooldays were over was made by Bristol Rovers. Maybe City shared the view of some, even at Eastville, who felt that he was too heavily built for a youngster of his medium height. At any rate, they neglected to rival Rovers for his signature, and although he did eventually get to play for them it was not until the early years of the 1939–45 war—and then only as a guest while on Tottenham's books.

The approach from Bristol Rovers was made by one of their directors, Percy Chapman, a woollen merchant at whose offices Dix worked after signing amateur forms. Young Ronnie had reached that stage of his soccer career without any coaching, and he found precious little of it in those early days with Rovers. He recalled.

> I went training at Eastville on Tuesdays and Thursdays. The training consisted mainly of lapping in spikes, or road work around the neighbouring district of Stapleton. We had a practice game, but there was little in the way of tactical talks, or even a get-together. We were given some instructions in the dressing room just before a match, but that was all.

Dix went straight into the Eastville club's reserve team, making his debut at Exeter in a match that featured two other youngsters who rose to First Division stardom. On his own side, also playing his first game for the club, there was fellow Bristolian Cliff Britton, a wing-half who was as frail as Dix was sturdy—'terribly thin' in the words of Bert Williams, then Rovers' trainer with the reserves—but whose cultured style served Everton so splendidly through the Thirties, and who formed one of England's finest middle lines with Stan Cullis, the Wolves captain, and his Goodison clubmate Joe Mercer. The opposing line-up contained a third newcomer—Cliff 'Boy' Bastin, the scoring winger who, with Arsenal, was to win every major football honour then available while still a teenager.

In Bristol Rovers' public practice match on the eve of the 1927–28 season, Ronald William Dix emphasised the power of his shooting by blasting a hat-trick past Jesse Whatley, a goalkeeper reliable and fit enough to make 246 consecutive appearances for Rovers in the League—a record at that time. Early the following year, on February 25th, 1928, Dix was given his first chance to join Whatley in the club's Third Division South team, at home to Charlton Athletic, at the age of 15 years and 173 days.

Albert Geldard became the youngest Football League debutant when he played for Bradford Park Avenue in a Second Division match with Millwall at 15 years, 156 days on September 16th, 1929, but Dix has kept a niche for himself in the record books as the youngest scorer in a League game. He was 15 years and 180 days old when he opened his account on his second appearance, again at Eastville, in a 3–0 defeat of Norwich City on March 3rd, 1928. In fact, he was unlucky not to get that first goal in his first game the previous Saturday, when Rovers won 2–1, for he beat goalkeeper Albert Lindon, the 16 st Charlton player-manager who was later Arsenal's chief scout, only for left-back Edwin Herod to clear off the line.

Dix's historic goal against Norwich was also a mighty close thing. He obtained it 20 minutes from time, when his typically terrific shot bounced down off the underside of the crossbar and City players protested unsuccessfully that the ball had not crossed the line. He was given just two more League games that season, then was recalled by the Rovers' new manager, David McLean, a former Scotland centre-forward who had been a prolific scorer with the Wednesday, for an away FA Cup-tie with Clapton Orient. On a pitch that was a sea of mud, Orient went ahead with a twice-taken penalty, but Rovers had the chance to equalise when they, too, were awarded a spot kick. What happened next provided a clear insight into Ronnie Dix's phlegmatic character. This was how he remembered it:

> Somebody said 'You take it', so I stepped up and hit it—but the ball struck the bar and we lost. I never gave it a second thought. I never let football worry me at any time, and I remember Jack Barker, at Derby County, telling me 'You'd be twice the player if you really bothered'.

The report in one newspaper questioned the wisdom of not calling upon a more experienced player to take the kick, but nobody blamed Dix for missing. They would have been wasting their time if they had, just as fans at his other clubs were wasting their time when they shouted to show their displeasure with him because he was inclined to strut rather aristocratically about the field. He took not the slightest notice of them and merely got on with the game.

After two years of first-team football with Bristol Rovers, Dix and Britton were targets for several clubs higher up the League scale. Following the replacement of manager McLean by the flamboyant Captain Albert Prince-Cox, a former League referee, Rovers engaged a trainer named Billy Barr who recommended a centre-forward, Arthur Attwood, who was then with Everton. Attwood duly turned up at Eastville, giving rise to strong rumours that, in return, the Goodison club were to have first claim on Britton and Dix when they became available. The rumours proved true. Everton put in their bid for the pair, at £1,500 each, in the summer of 1931, but although Britton made the move, Rovers had to abandon the Dix part of the deal when, on belatedly informing him of his involvement, they discovered that he did not want to go.

Despite his clearly stated preference to stay with Rovers, Dix still found himself being sought by a number of First Division clubs, with Aston Villa leading the way, but the League placed an embargo on any proposed transfer until they had carried out an investigation. This left them 'satisfied that Bristol Rovers have been unwilling to carry out their obligation to Everton under their agreement' and they accepted that the reason was the player's wish not to leave Bristol. Consequently, the League's secretary was instructed to notify all clubs that a transfer for Dix would not be accepted until he said that he wanted one, and until agreement to his move from Eastville was put in writing by both Rovers and Everton. The Bristol club had to pay Everton's costs, plus those of the inquiry, because they had not officially notified Dix of the Everton option and had refused to honour it.

Dix thus remained with the Rovers for another season, but in May, 1932, a worsening financial situation at Eastville made a parting inevitable as he was foremost among the playing assets that had to be realised. It was then that Derby County first tried to sign him, but, like Villa, they had to wait their turn. Chelsea also failed in their quest for Dix, having to be satisfied with taking one of the other players on offer, winger Eric Oakton, a speedy, no-frills Yorkshireman who was a Stamford Bridge regular for two seasons before joining Nottingham Forest. Instead, Dix remained a Rover, moving to

Blackburn for £3,000 in May, 1932, the month before half-back Cliff Bryant,[2] another Bristol-born schoolboy international, also left Bristol Rovers to rejoin him at Ewood Park. Everton's chairman, Will Cuff, said his club would not stand in the way of Dix's transfer, though there were certain conditions attached to the deal that he would not divulge.

Just under a year later, Dix revisited Eastville with another former Bristol Rovers player, Frank Britton, Cliff's younger brother, for a midweek friendly which Blackburn[3] won 5–1. Britton, who was later with Oldham and Worcester City, upstaged his more publicised companion by scoring four of the goals. Around that time Blackburn also had on their books a centre-forward, Ernie Thompson, who had played for Bristol City and Bath City. He, like those signings from Bristol Rovers, was recommended to the Lancashire club by Ted Davis, a former goalkeeper who was then Bath's manager and later became Arsenal's scout in the West Country.

Dix did not score when he made his Blackburn debut alongside Thompson in a 2–2 home draw with Chelsea, whose team included two other future Derby players, Vic Woodley and Hughie Gallacher, and his former Eastville colleague, Oakton, but he ended the 1932–33 campaign as his new club's joint second highest scorer in the League with outside-left Arthur Cunliffe, on 14 goals, three behind Thompson. For most of that season Dix formed a productive partnership with right-winger Jack Bruton, one of Sammy Crooks's international predecessors, in an attack that up to Christmas usually had another Ram-to-be, Arthur Groves, in the other inside-forward berth, but he also made a few appearances as partner for Cunliffe, whose penetrative raiding earned him his two games on England's left wing, against Ireland and Wales, that winter.

To the considerable dismay of Blackburn fans, the season had barely ended when quite a surprise was sprung on both Dix and Cunliffe. Manager Arthur Barritt, successor to the legendary Bob Crompton, called them to his office and told them: 'I'm sorry to have to let you go, but Aston Villa have made a big offer for the pair of you, and we can't refuse it'. So, still only 20, Dix departed with the 24-year-old Cunliffe at a combined cost of £8,500. Cunliffe moved again, to Middlesbrough, midway through Villa's relegation season of 1935–36, but Dix stayed on to reach 104 games and 30 goals for his third League club before he, too, was restored to Division One by his transfer to Derby on February 10th, 1937.

For the Rams, Dix shared the main scoring responsibility first with Astley, and then McCulloch, his 16 goals putting him level, as an ever-present, with the big Scot in 1938–39 and taking him to 35 in 96 League and Cup matches for Derby before his close-season move to Tottenham. His one call-up by England came the week after he had twice hammered the ball past one of Scotland's better goalkeepers, Bobby Brown, in

---

2. After leaving Bristol Rovers, Clifford Samuel Bryant played in only four League games and one Cup-tie for Blackburn. In May, 1936, he moved to Wrexham, but was limited to eight League appearances in his one season with the Welsh club.

3. On the following evening, April 6th, 1933, Blackburn, who were on their way to a First Division match at Portsmouth, played another friendly with Bath City, but they did not take it so seriously and lost 2–1 in gathering darkness. They also fitted in a tour of the Cheddar area, and after such a busy week it was perhaps not surprising that they were beaten 2–0 at Fratton Park.

the Football League's 3–1 defeat of the Scottish League at Wolverhampton—a game at which he renewed acquaintance with his former Bristol Rovers manager Davie McLean, then manager of Hearts and a member of the Scottish selection committee.

The first three appearances Dix made for Spurs in the Second Division were wiped out by the war-enforced abortion of the 1939–40 League programme. He went on to complete that season with them in the emergency League South, in which they topped their group, and the League Cup, in which they were beaten over two legs by Crystal Palace in the first round.

After that came his guest appearances for Bristol City, and also Chester, before he was among the many servicemen posted to Blackpool. There he had the chance to partner Stanley Matthews in what the Stoke winger, who later signed for the Seasiders, considered to be the best club team for which he had played—the Blackpool side that defeated Sheffield Wednesday in the 1943 League North Cup Final, by 4–3 over two legs, and beat Arsenal, winners of the South Cup, by 4–2 at Stamford Bridge. That team (Blackpool's own players except where indicated) was:

> **Savage** (Queen of the South); **Pope** (Hearts), **S. Jones/Hubbick** (Bolton); **Farrow, Hayward, Johnston**; **Matthews** (Stoke), **Dix** (Tottenham), **Dodds, Finan, Burbanks** (Sunderland).

Sam Jones, an Irish international who had joined Blackpool at about the same time as Peter Doherty, gave way to Harry Hubbick after the 2–2 first leg against Wednesday. Goalkeeper Reg Savage guested for Derby County later in the war—as did Fred Tapping one of Dix's other right-wing partners at Blackpool. George Farrow was among Raich Carter's team-mates with Sunderland Boys.

Dix, whose best scoring feats for the Lancashire club were five goals against Bury and four against Tranmere, was on the mark in the Arsenal play-off, and also when Blackpool again reached the League North final the following year. They lost that one, however, by 5–4 on aggregate to Aston Villa after winning the first leg 2–1. Dix later did the rounds as a guest with Bradford, Liverpool, Wrexham and York City before returning to Tottenham for the last transitional season of 1945–46. Including war-time games, his number of appearances for Spurs increased to 96, in which he scored 20 goals, before he went into the Third Division South with Reading, newly under the management of ex-Gunner Ted Drake in November, 1947.

Dix's 13 goals in 44 matches for the Berkshire club took him to career totals of more than 130 in nearly 450 games before a knee injury compelled him to hang up his boots in 1949. After that, he helped his wife to run a children's wear shop back in Bristol, at Bedminster, and he maintained an active interest in sport as an accomplished cricketer and golfer. He was a member of Long Ashton Golf Club for about 50 years.

One of the cricket teams for which he played was that run by the *Bristol Evening World*, for which he reported on local soccer matches. Though then well into middle age and bulky around the midriff, he very rarely failed to make a useful contribution with either bat or ball—and quite often with both. I had the pleasure of being in the same team, for, although I worked for the rival *Bristol Evening Post*, I received invitations to play from the *World*'s sports editor, George Baker, an old friend who became a valued colleague with the *Post* after the *Evening World* had been closed down.

So Ronnie Dix, capped by England as a footballer, could say that he played cricket for the World. It was a claim which, even if misleading, I was content to share.

CHAPTER 13

The Title That Got Away

Derby top the First Division for 15 weeks, then slip to sixth, in final pre-war season – Jobey breaks Rams' transfer record to sign McCulloch – Revival with Hearts earns first Scottish cap – Five-goal return against Mansfield – Beaten by weight problem after war-time scoring sprees – Management at Waterford and Alloa after enjoyable years with Bath City

FOR THE 15 WEEKS FROM OCTOBER 22nd, 1938, to February 4th, 1939, Derby County sat proudly at the top of the First Division. Then three successive home defeats diverted them into a slump to a final sixth place, with only three wins and two draws to set against nine defeats in their last 14 matches. It was one of the most disappointing and disturbing turnabouts of form in their long history, a far from fitting end to George Jobey's distinguished managerial reign.

The season began uneventfully for the Rams, with a 2–2 home draw with Wolves owing much to an own goal by the visitors' captain, Stan Cullis, and anxious 1–0 wins over Huddersfield and Aston Villa being followed by a 3–0 defeat in the return game against the Yorkshire club at Leeds Road, but there was only one other reverse, at Birmingham, and again by 3–0, in their next seven matches. All but one of those, a 1–1 away draw with Grimsby, were won, two of them in particularly impressive fashion, by 2–1 against Arsenal, the reigning champions, at Highbury (Reg Stockill again scored against his old club) and by 5–0 at home to Stoke City.

It was on the Saturday after the setback at St Andrew's that the Rams hoisted themselves into first place in the table with another big victory, by 5–1 at the Baseball Ground. Their opponents were Manchester United, who, in contrast to the heights they were to scale in the second half of the 20th century, were then striving to secure a foothold in the First Division after a yo-yo existence of two promotions and one relegation in the past three seasons.

On October 21st, 1938, the day before that match with the Old Trafford club, George Jobey made the most audacious of his many bold ventures into the transfer market by breaking Derby County's transfer record to add David McCulloch to the illustrious Bedford–Bowers–Gallacher–Astley parade of centre-forwards who graced the club's attack during his years as manager. The £9,500 handed over to Brentford for the burly Scottish international remained the highest fee ever paid by the Rams for a player until

An all-international attack. Sammy Crooks (England), Dai Astley (Wales), Dave McCulloch (Scotland), Ronnie Dix (England) and 'Dally' Duncan (Scotland) face the camera before the First Division match at Chelsea on October 29th, 1938. Derby won 2–0 with goals from Dix and Astley.
(Hulton Getty)

they raised the British record to £15,500 in taking another famous Scot, Billy Steel, from Greenock Morton in June, 1947.

The story of how Dave McCulloch became a Derby player provides yet another example of Jobey's resourcefulness. During the previous few weeks, Brentford had been searching for a new half-back, and only days before the Rams' manager completed the deal it was believed that McCulloch would be exchanged for Jack Percival, a Manchester City wing-half. That proposal fell through, however, when the Griffin Park club's directors, naturally reluctant to release such a big-name free scorer, asked for a big fee in addition to the suggested player swap. Wolverhampton Wanderers, although then already possessing a sharp-shooting centre-forward in Dennis Westcott, were the next to try to tempt Brentford to make a profit on McCulloch, but on hearing of their interest Jobey went hot foot to London and beat them to him.

With Dai Astley switched to inside-right, from where Ronnie Dix moved to partner 'Dally' Duncan after Charlie Napier's departure, the centre-forward position had been in urgent need of strengthening if a serious challenge were to be made for the championship. At the start of the season, the leadership of the attack was entrusted to Harry Travis, a well-built Mancunian who had been given a free transfer by each of his first four League clubs, Manchester City, Oldham Athletic, Accrington Stanley and Leeds United. He gained first-team experience with only one of those clubs, scoring one goal in four games for Accrington in 1933–34, before topping Bradford City's scoring list with 15 goals in two dozen matches in 1935–36. Travis, whose younger brother Don made good in a second spell with Oldham in the mid-Fifties after also including Accrington among his collection of clubs, did well enough at Valley Parade to encourage George Jobey to pay just over £800 for him in February, 1937, but, game trier though he was, he failed to measure up to First Division standards, and in the month after McCulloch's arrival he was on the move again, to Tranmere Rovers.

McCulloch himself did not look like making the grade in the early stages of his career. He failed to come up to expectations in two seasons with Third Lanark after catching their attention with Shotts United, a junior side near his Hamilton birthplace, and in 1934 they allowed him to join Hearts. That change was the making of him. Showing rapid improvement, he scored 38 goals in 35 League games in his first season at Tynecastle, and the reward of his first international cap[1] came in the 3–2 win over Wales at Aberdeen. This was the game in which Napier, then of Celtic, and Duncan did Scotland's scoring, and Astley obtained one of the losers' goals.

Such startling progress by McCulloch was not lost on Brentford as they embarked upon their first season in Division One, having advanced from the Third South with two promotions as champions in three years. Towards the end of 1935 they persuaded Hearts to part with him by making an offer of about £6, 000. McCulloch did not let them down. He was their leading scorer as they finished in the top six in each of the three seasons he spent with them, and he made Derby County well aware of the punch he packed by getting half of the dozen goals the Rams conceded on their first two League visits to Griffin Park—four in 37 minutes in the 6–0 win on the last day of the 1935–36 season, two in a 6–2 victory the following February.

With the Rams, he got off to a mouth-watering start by scoring the second and fifth goals in the beating of Manchester United (besides playing a big part in the three others), and nine more in their next dozen matches up to the end of 1938. That, though, was when things began to go wrong for both himself and the club. There had been a warning sign in a 4–1 home defeat by Middlesbrough on a December day when pace-setting Everton had lost at Goodison for what was to be the only time that season—coincidentally by the same score at the hands of Charlton Athletic, the only other side to beat Derby in a run of 13 games from the demolition of United to a 2–1 home success over Aston Villa (Dix and Astley scored against their old club) on the last day of the old year.

In retrospect, however, the turning point was seen as another Baseball Ground setback in the County's first game of the new year. It was inflicted in the third round of the FA Cup, for which they had been favourites, by Everton, from whom they had taken three League points out of four on successive days at Christmas despite conceding

---

1. McCulloch sent the shirt he wore in his first international match to his former schoolmaster at Hamilton, and the boys there were given a day's holiday to celebrate.

a penalty[2] in both games. The margin of that Cup failure was just one goal—scored by left-winger Wally Boyes, who had also been on target as a losing finalist with West Bromwich against Sheffield Wednesday in 1935—but it set the tone for a decline that produced only 11 more points out of the remaining 36 at stake.

The month of January, 1939, was indeed a bleak month for Derby County. During it, they also lost the only two other matches they played, at Sunderland and Stoke, both without scoring, and most unexpectedly dispensed with the services of Dai Astley. Whether or not the Welshman's transfer to Blackpool upset the balance of the team was a moot point, for he had fallen off the goal standard to such an extent since his initial spurt that he had scored only three times in his two dozen games at inside-right for Derby that season, but once off the top of the table the Rams never looked like returning there. Two weeks after his transfer, Astley led the Blackpool attack against Derby at Bloomfield Road and, although he did not score the 2–2 draw enabled Everton, convincing winners that afternoon of the Merseyside derby at Anfield, to regain the leadership they retained to become the last pre-war champions, four points clear of runners-up Wolves.

One of Derby's scorers at Blackpool was Astley's temporary successor, Tom Hinchcliffe, who hailed from Jack Barker country and played for Denaby United before entering League football with Grimsby Town. He appeared to be settling in well with his next club, Huddersfield Town, when his two goals helped to end Everton's unbeaten start to the season, but he lost his place following the arrival of Harry Baird from Manchester United and George Jobey nipped in to sign him within days of seeing Jimmy Hagan off to Sheffield.

Baird, who guested a few times for Derby during the war, gained his one Irish cap soon after his move to Huddersfield, but he found it a most sobering experience. He and the two star forwards on either side of him, Alex Stevenson, of Everton, and Peter Doherty, the human dynamo Manchester City were to lose to the Rams, scarcely got a look-in as Tottenham's Willie Hall monopolised the scoring with five goals out of seven in another big England win in Manchester.

Like Travis, who, after dropping out with a poisoned hand, was unable to regain the place he lost to Reg Stockill for the half-dozen games before McCulloch's arrival, Hinchliffe soon found himself on the sidelines at Derby. His total of League appearances with four clubs fell three short of a half-century, with only six of them for the Rams. Approaching his middle thirties when the war ended, he moved into the Second Division with Nottingham Forest, but played only once in their first team—in a defeat at Barnsley on the day, the last one of August, 1946, when the Football League resumed after seven seasons in limbo.

An especially disturbing feature of Derby County's decline in the second half of their 1938–39 programme was that their three consecutive home defeats immediately after being deposed as leaders were all suffered not against sides challenging strongly for the title that got away from them, but against teams, Brentford, Birmingham and

---

2. Both the penalties, in a 2–2 draw at Goodison and a 2–1 defeat at Derby, were converted by Irish international full-back Billy Cook, who had also scored from the spot in Everton's previous game, a 4–0 home win over Blackpool.

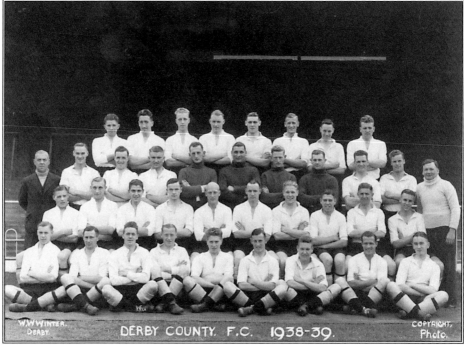

On parade for the start of the 1938–39 season, the last full one of George Jobey's stay with Derby County. *Back row (left to right):* Sullivan, Ralph Hann, George Wilcox, Harry Travis, Smart, Tom Alton, Jack Parr, Jack Nicholas. *Second row:* Dave Willis (trainer), Leslie Bailey, David Bell, Bramley, Frank Boulton, Harry Wright, Wood, Frank King, Jack Barker, Jack Howe, Bill Bromage (assistant trainer). *Seated:* Steve McLachlan, Verdun Jones, Alf Jeffries, Jimmy Hagan, Ronnie Dix, Dai Astley, Tommy Eggleston, 'Chick' Musson, Bradley, Tim Ward. *Front row:* Johnson, Jack Brinton, Sammy Crooks, Reg Stockill, Lisle, Bertie Mee, H Jones, 'Dally' Duncan, Thompson.
(W.W. Winter)

Chelsea, which were struggling to ward off the threat of relegation. And although they won at Fratton Park on Good Friday the Rams lost the Easter Monday return game with Portsmouth, another club in the toils, and they picked up only one point from their last five matches. That point was gleaned at home to Leicester City, who went down with Birmingham, straight after the Baseball Ground failure against Pompey that dashed the Derby players' hopes of sharing in talent money, the payment of which was sanctioned for the first time to those finishing in the top four.

The extent to which the Rams deteriorated is emphasised by this comparison of how they fared that season before and after the end of 1938:

	P	W	D	L	F	A	Pts
Before:	24	15	5	4	46	27	35
After:	18	4	3	11	20	28	11

Dave McCulloch was clearly unfortunate to be caught up in such a marked contrast in form while still endeavouring to establish himself with a new club, but he was not free from criticism for his reduced effectiveness. While with Brentford he was the dashing type, adept at finishing off moves fashioned by his more skilful team-mates, but after his early successful displays for Derby he made the mistake of trying to copy the tip-tap methods of his cultured inside-forwards, Astley and Dix. It was entirely foreign to his natural style, and simply did not work.

The resulting drop in his scoring rate was one of the main reasons for the Rams' poorer results, and it also led to his losing the leadership of Scotland's attack. Discounting one recall against England during the first wartime season, when caps were not awarded, he made the last two of his seven full appearances for his country during his first two months with Derby—in victories over Wales, back at his old Tynecastle stamping ground in Edinburgh, and Hungary, at Ibrox—but he failed to add to his three international goals and was replaced by Preston's nippy little Jimmy Dougall for the Glasgow clash with England the following April. Dougall did score in that last pre-war encounter, giving Scotland a lead they held until some 20 minutes from time, but England hit back to snatch their first Hampden victory for 12 years. Tommy Lawton scored a dramatic last-minute goal after Huddersfield's former Arsenal winger Albert ('Pat') Beasley had celebrated the award of what was to be his only cap by equalising. McCulloch scored two of his three goals for Scotland in a 5–0 defeat of Czechoslovakia at Ibrox in his last international while with Brentford, in August, 1937. The other one was netted the previous October, in a 3–1 win over Northern Ireland in Belfast.

The war denied McCulloch the chance of fully repaying the faith George Jobey had placed in him. He was whisked away on Army service after playing, without scoring, in Derby's three matches before the 1939–40 First Division fixtures had to be abandoned, and he did not reappear in their colours for more than three years. It was quite a comeback. Mansfield Town were the visitors to the Baseball Ground in the War Cup qualifying competition on January 9th, 1943, and big Dave bagged half the goals in a 10–0 victory. In the Third Division club's team there was a much less happy return to Derby for George Hannah, a wing-half who was on the Rams' staff shortly before the war without breaking into the senior side.

Just over a year after that Mansfield massacre, McCulloch ended another absence from Derby's line-up with a hat-trick in a 7–3 home success against Notts County in another War Cup qualifying tie, but after what turned out to be his final games in the First Division he altogether made only 14 appearances for the Rams during the seven seasons before normal service was resumed, totalling 11 goals. He spent most of his wartime football as one of the star guests who boosted teams of modest means to well above their normal strengths, sharing it between Aldershot, Bath City and the Newport-based Welsh club Lovell's Athletic,[3] but, although he gave each of them a fair haul of

---

3. Lovell's Athletic—the successful 'Toffeemen' of war-time football, with guest players who made them a match for most teams in the country—won the Welsh League title in the five peacetime seasons from 1937–38 to 1947–48, but they fell on more difficult times after venturing into the Southern League, from which dwindling crowds caused them to resign at the end of 1958–59. Their chairman, John Lovell, said 'It's simply a question

goals he was only a shadow of his old self when he finally returned to the Derby fold halfway through the League South of the last transitional season of 1945–46. He told me:

> You may recall that when I returned from the Army to Derby County I was carrying about two stone overweight—a modest estimate—and I found this extremely hard to lose.

Consequently, he was too heavy-footed to be a serious challenger for a place in the team that brought the FA Cup back to Derby by winning the first post-war final. In the summer of 1946 he was transferred to Second Division Leicester City along with Tommy Eggleston, a Mitcham-born wing-half who played in a few League South games and the second

Tommy Eggleston, a respected coach and physiotherapist after having his playing career interrupted by the 1939–45 war, during which he was a Petty Officer in the Royal Navy.
(Derby Evening Telegraph)

of economics. Next season the Southern League are extending again and the new set-up will increase our travelling and other costs. Our gates are poor. We'd be happy with 1,000, but we get only about 200. Newport is a rugby stronghold. Our team is mainly amateur. Now we must get out and concentrate on the Welsh League.' It was a far cry from those peak years during the war, but one Lovell's product, centre-half, Harry Clarke, went on to play for Tottenham and England.

leg of the third-round Cup-tie against Luton Town after returning from service as a Petty Officer in the Royal Navy. Neither made his mark with Leicester. Eggleston had his best League playing days with Watford before giving up through injury and becoming an accomplished coach and physiotherapist, both in England and abroad.

McCulloch, still bedevilled by his weight problem, had a transfer request granted after dropping into Leicester's reserve side, and, with no bids forthcoming to keep him in the Football League, he decided to renew his war-time friendship with Arthur Mortimer, chairman of Bath City and the Southern League, by signing for the Somerset club around Christmas-time in 1946. He spent what he called 'three enjoyable years' with Bath, during which his former Derby colleague Vic Woodley was player-manager, but shortly after top-scoring with 49 goals in 1948–49 he was released from his contract to accept an offer to continue playing while also managing Waterford in the League of Ireland. From the off-putting experience, on his debut against Shamrock Rovers, of having two penalty kicks brilliantly saved by Tom Godwin, the goalkeeper who in that same month of September, 1949, moved to Leicester City after also defying England in Eire's shock win at Everton's ground, he prospered with four goals in one match and ended the year as the league's leading scorer. He recalled:

> Waterford were a club with an unusual administration, directed by members of the local junior league, and we could call upon any junior player to turn out for the senior side. They were all amateurs, and after a short time they started to settle down into a promising team. We finished third from the top of the league table. Then we had the Rams over for a tour, which provided a fitting end to a grand season for us. But success brings its penalties, and when I returned from holiday I found that five of our most promising lads had turned professional and had joined other clubs. My second season was spent rebuilding, but we still managed to maintain a respectable position. However, when I was asked to return in the following year, I had to decline. I must say that I made that decision with regret, for the people of Waterford were really wonderful. But there's no future in finding and developing players for more or less the wholesale benefit of other clubs.

Back home he went to Scotland, surprising a good many people by taking over as manager of Alloa Athletic, who had just finished at the foot of Division B of the Scottish League for the second successive season. He was full of optimism after steering them to sixth from the top in 1951–52 and more than halving their debt by the sale of a winger named Pattison to Barnsley, but just a few days before the start of the next season he had a difference of opinion with his directors and resigned.

Turning his back on two decades in senior soccer at the age of 40, he went to work in the Progress Department of the new Rolls-Royce factory at East Kilbride, near Glasgow, which had only recently gone into the production of aero jet engines. When I asked him if he was happy out of football, he replied:

> Most assuredly. I have a fine, interesting job, and on a Saturday I can please myself what I do. Two Scottish clubs have asked me to do some scouting for them, but I feel that up here it's not worth the trouble of giving up one's spare time at the weekend.

CHAPTER 14

Cup of Contrasts in Fortune

*Tim Ward, one of soccer's gentlemen – Freak goal
at Bournemouth – Keen addition to Jobey's North-East
captures – Canadian tour leads Ward to Bansley
after being unfairly discarded by England –
Promotion with Barnsley and Grimsby before unhappy
return to Derby as manager – Howe the first League
footballer to wear contact lenses*

DAVE McCULLOCH, who was in his 68th year when he died back at Hamilton in May, 1979, was one of five regular members of Derby's team in the last pre-war season of 1938–39 who were still with the club when they reached the first post-war FA Cup Final in 1946, but were denied a place in the line-up at Wembley.

The others were Frank Boulton and Sammy Crooks, who were ruled out by injury, Ralph Hann, who dropped out of the reckoning the month before the Rams set out on the Cup trail at Luton, and Tim Ward, who played in the first leg of that third-round tie at Kenilworth Road while on Christmas leave from the British Army of the Rhine, but then had to rejoin his unit and was not demobilised until shortly before the final. He returned to civvy street just in time to join in the big day as a spectator.

Ward, one of soccer's gentlemen, was a part-timer with his home club, Cheltenham Town, when, after having trials with Leicester City, he was signed by George Jobey in April, 1937, on the recommendations former Rams player Frank Keetley made with the backing of another ex-Derby forward, fellow scout Jackie Whitehouse.

For all of £200, Derby's discerning manager acquired the rich dividend of a classy half-back who was later the subject of an unsuccessful £10,000 bid by Arsenal. Ward made up for losing his best years to the war, during which he was slightly wounded in the D-Day landings on the Normandy beaches, by taking his total of League and Cup appearances to 260, rising to the County captaincy, and fully deserving more than the two England caps to which unfortunate circumstances confined him.

Ward scored with his first kick when he was given his trial in Derby's third team, but it was as a stylish creative influence, and not as a marksman, that he built his reputation. In fact, he obtained only five goals for the senior side—and one of those, scored while he was playing as an experimental outside-left, was such a king-size fluke that his captain, Raich Carter, began to berate him for seeming carelessness in the moments before his ballooned effort was transformed into a high-bouncing baffler of a bemused Bournemouth goalkeeper. It was the first of two goals in that game, both scored in the opening five minutes and the second of them one of Carter's hard-hit specials, by which Derby began their defence of the FA Cup with an unconvincing victory at Dean Court in 1947. Charles Mann, who then reported on the Rams for the *Derby Evening Telegraph*, called it 'one of the queerest I can remember' and described it as follows:

> Tim received the ball on the left wing, midway between halfway line and corner flag, and he banged it into the air almost haphazardly in the direction of the Bournemouth goal, wishfully thinking, maybe, that some colleague might get his head to it. The look of incredulity on his face, which changed slowly, first to a grin of delight then to a smirk of amusement, when Bird, the Bournemouth goalkeeper, missed the ball as it bounced high and went over him into the goal would have earned Ward a contract if he could reproduce it in a film test.

Raich Carter was on the opposing side when Ward made his debut for Derby at Sunderland on January 15th, 1938. Deputising for the injured Ike Keen, the 20-year-old newcomer did such a good job of marking the Wearsiders' England forward, despite being in the losing team, that Keen, an experienced international with more than 200 League outings behind him, was unable to regain his place and was soon on his way to Chelmsford City.

After only a few games as the automatic choice he was to remain for the rest of his League days with Derby, Ward, like Sammy Crooks before him, was encouraged to beard the daunting George Jobey in his den and ask to be put on top wages. As with Crooks, the manager, in effect, told him: 'Get out of here. When you have proved to me that you are a real first-team player I'll give you maximum wages.' If that was the forceful put-down to be expected from the Geordie firebrand, it was also typical of him that both received the highest pay possible very soon after plucking up the courage to apply for it—and both stayed at that level for the remainder of their careers with the County. Those two instances of such a reward after a rebuff were the ones that I heard about, though I have not the slightest doubt that there were others.

Ike Keen, whose forenames of Errington Ridley and Liddell made him sound more like a firm of solicitors, was another of Jobey's North-East bargains. As conspicuous as Tommy Cooper with his blond hair, he joined Newcastle United from local football near his Walker-on-Tyne birthplace, but played only once in their League side. That game, in October, 1930, just happened to be against Derby County, and although it was the one in which the Rams ran up five goals at St James's Park, Keen did enough to convince Jobey that he could develop into a regular first-teamer at the Baseball Ground. He was duly signed a couple of months later, and after occasionally deputising for Johnny McIntyre at right-half he settled in as successor to Gavin Malloch on the opposite flank of the middle line during the 1931–32 season.

The first of Keen's four England caps soon followed, in a 4–3 defeat of Austria at Stamford Bridge in which Sammy Crooks was among the scorers. Keen then found his former Newcastle clubmate Sam Weaver ahead of him in the international reckoning, then Wilf Copping (Leeds United and Arsenal), Horace Burrows (Sheffield Wednesday), Jackie Bray (Manchester City) and Walter Alsford (Tottenham Hotspur), before he was

Ike Keen, who was signed by George
Jobey after playing against Derby in
his only League game for Newcastle.
(Derby Evening Telegraph)

Tim Ward, the gentleman
from Cheltenham.
(Derby Evening Telegraph)

recalled for three successive matches late in 1936. Selected along with his Derby team-mates Barker and Crooks against Wales in Cardiff, he was the only Rams player retained after the 2–1 defeat for the following game with the Irish at Stoke, where England won 3–1, but, like the again-recalled Crooks, he was discarded for good after facing Hungary at Highbury, even though the winning margin was increased to 6–2.

Earlier that year, Keen ran into difficulties off the field, ending up in the bankruptcy court after the failure of the business in which he invested his £650 benefit cheque. And, only just over a year after losing his England place, he was also dropped by Derby County as young Ward emerged as the heir-very-apparent. Noted for the fine attacking qualities with which he so constantly delighted Rams' fans behind the Ramage/Napier–Duncan wing, Keen found his less assured defensive attributes being increasingly called into question and was not retained at the end of the 1937–38 season, in which he lost his place after giving Leicester City a winning goal at the Baseball Ground by trying to dribble his way out of trouble close to his own goal-line.

He spent the next season with Chelmsford City before being appointed Hereford United's player-manager shortly before the war, during which he served with the RAF in India. With the return of peace he made unsuccessful attempts to resurrect his playing career with, in quick succession, Lincoln City, Leeds United, Bacup Borough and Hull City, before turning to coaching abroad in places as far afield as Egypt, Hong Kong and Cuba. He was back in England, at Fulham, when he died in July, 1984, aged 73.

Tim Ward made all his pre-war appearances for Derby at left-half, missing only three games out of 66 before the closedown in September, 1939, but, with local product 'Chick' Musson, whose 'Iron Man' image so contradicted his nickname, securing that position in his absence, it was at right-half that Ward played most of his 198 League and Cup matches for the club on his return from the Army. There were occasional excursions for him on the left wing, and one at inside-right when he scored the winner against Fulham after having a shot cleared off the line. He also had a short run at centre-half in an emergency.

For England, he answered another emergency by switching to right-back when Arsenal's Laurie Scott was injured inside the opening half-hour against Wales, at Villa Park, in 1948, but despite being hailed as a big success, even out of position, in the 1–0 victory, he was never chosen for his country again. It was a repeat of the hard-luck story he could tell after winning his first cap the previous year, when, having had to put up with being identified by his second forename, of Victor, in one national newspaper headline which announced him as England's only newcomer, he found the selectors disagreed with one respected reporter who declared that he was 'here to stay' after giving a sound display in a 5–2 defeat of Belgium in Brussels.

Ward's subsequent tour of Canada with an FA party, in company with Derby's right-back Bert Mozley, was something of a consolation prize for those who missed places in England's squad for the 1950 World Cup finals in Rio, but it did bring him to the attention of the man who led him into football management. One of the officials with the tourists, Joe (later Sir Joseph) Richards, Barnsley's chairman and a future League president, was so impressed with Ward's demeanour and ability that he saw him as the ideal successor to Danny Blanchflower when the Irish international left the Yorkshire club for Aston Villa. The deal with Derby was rushed through only five minutes before the March, 1951, midnight deadline for unrestricted transfers that season, and next day Ward helped Barnsley to beat a Notts County side that included his former Derby clubmate Leon Leuty, who had reached Meadow Lane via Bradford in moves that temporarily made him the costliest defender in the British game.

At the end of his first full season at Oakwell, 1951–52, Ward was appointed player-coach of Barnsley's Yorkshire League team. Almost a year later, at the age of 34, he became the youngest manager in the Football League—with Barnsley, after provisionally accepting an offer from Exeter City while Joe Richards and his colleagues dithered over deciding who should fill the vacancy caused by the death of Angus Seed, brother of the then Charlton manager.

It was too late for Ward to avoid Barnsley's relegation from the Second Division, but he took only two seasons to guide them back as Third North champions[1] as Derby

---

1. Barnsley finished Ward's first full season as their manager second to Port Vale. In those days, until the introduction of the Fourth Division for the 1958–59 season, only the champions were promoted from the Southern and Northern sections of the Third Division. In 1954–55, Barnsley ended four points ahead of runners-up Accrington Stanley, who resigned from the League in 1962 and were replaced by Oxford United.

County plunged past them in the opposite direction. Although he could not prevent Barnsley slipping down again, Ward went on to pilot Grimsby Town to promotion before returning to the Baseball Ground as Derby's manager in the summer of 1962.

Like Jack Barker's return, Ward's was not a happy one. His delight at being invited to replace the retired Harry Storer was swiftly dispelled as he was unable to raise the Rams above a very average level in the Second Division while working under severe financial constraints. He made a rod for his own back with several inexpensively successful signings that led his directors to expect him to keep pulling off such coups, though he was allowed one big 'splash'—by Derby's modest standards of those days—when £40,000 was found for the transfer, from Bradford Park Avenue, of Kevin Hector the nimble sharpshooter who repaid that now-insignificant expenditure numerous times over with more than 200 goals and a club record of nearly 600 appearances.

Two England caps, both almost literally as a last-minute substitute, were insulting international recognition for Hector, the favourite Rams fans hailed as 'Zak the King' who was a gem of a legacy Tim Ward left when he was dispensed with to make way for the brashly revolutionary Brian Clough era after what he regarded as the unhappiest five years of his career. Following one final managerial spell at Carlisle which ended after a year of struggle with his resignation in September, 1968, Ward did some scouting for Nottingham Forest before becoming a representative for a concrete-making firm near his Staffordshire home at Barton-under-Needwood.

He retained his links with Derby County, of whose cricket team he was an able and enthusiastic member, by lining up with other former Rams players in charity soccer matches until he was well into the veteran stage. In 1991 he was a popular choice as the first chairman of the club's Former Players' Association, for the formation of which he was the guiding light. Sadly, he was taken ill during the ensuing year, and died in hospital early in 1993, aged 75.

To mix metaphors, the finger of fate might be said to have given Tim Ward the thumbs down when he left the Royal Army Medical Corps too late to be considered for a place in the 1946 FA Cup Final. It was, however, a beckoner of good tidings at that time for one of his pre-war colleagues at the Baseball Ground, John Robert Howe, the North-Easterner Ward followed as Derby's captain. Jack Howe, the club's left-back for most of the three seasons leading up the war, had only recently landed back in Britain from three years with the Cameron Highlanders in West Africa and India when, having had time for just one reserve game, at Chesterfield, he deputised for the injured Leuty in the replayed semi-final against Birmingham City, in front of a record midweek Maine Road crowd of more than 80,000. Though centre-half was a position new to him, he was outstanding in the 4–0 extra-time win that took the Rams to Wembley, but his chance of playing in the final appeared to have gone when Leuty reported fit again.

That, however, was where fortune smiled on him again, at the sad expense of a full-back George Jobey had signed as a junior from the local club Little Eaton St Peter's during the 1937–38 season. Jack Parr, a Rams regular since they had started up again in the third year of the war, was tipped as a coming international before he broke his right arm in a heavy fall near the end of a League South home match with Luton Town only a week after maintaining his ever-present record through the Cup run in that Manchester replay. As the pre-war partner for Jack Nicholas, Howe was the natural replacement. And it was not until the former Hartlepools defender left for Huddersfield

Town in the autumn of 1949 that Parr was able to enjoy an extended spell in the First Division, increasing his League appearances beyond the century mark, before his own departure for a reunion with Sammy Crooks at Shrewsbury.

Jack Howe, yet another Jobey bargain at £750, was one of the best two-footed full-backs of the period. Like Tim Ward, he made his Derby debut against Sunderland, but unlike Ward, in a successful side almost exactly ten years before he went up to collect his unexpected Cup-winner's medal at Wembley. Weakened by the absence of their captain, Alec Hastings, and inside-forwards Raich Carter and Paddy Gallacher, the new champions to whom the Rams finished runners-up compounded their 4–0 defeat at the Baseball Ground on April 25th, 1936, by failing with two penalties. Jimmy Connor fired the first one over the crossbar; Russell, one of the reserves brought in, directed the other straight at a grateful Jack Kirby.

Howe impressed with his clean kicking, and, injuries apart, he made the left-back position his own until war service took him first to Scotland, where he guested for Aberdeen, Falkirk, Hearts and St Mirren, and played for the Scottish League against the British Army, before being posted abroad. His longest pre-war absence from Derby's

Jack Howe, the first League footballer to wear contact lenses.
(Derby Evebing Telegraph)

side was for the last dozen games of 1938–39, during which George Jobey called upon his own Billy Steel, a £1,275 signing from Birmingham (the year before Howe's arrival) who had made the first of more than 100 appearances for Liverpool against Derby County after not missing a match in three seasons with St Johnstone.

Not long after Howe's return from war service, he was found to have an eyesight defect, so the Rams made him the first League footballer to be fitted with contact lenses (price £70). Stuart McMillan, then their manager, explained:

> I noticed that Jack often seemed to lose the ball when going up to head clear. After a chat, I discovered that, while his vision was perfectly normal, it sometimes fogged out when the ball was close to him. He was examined by specialists in Derby and London, tried out all kinds of contact lenses, and went through exhaustive tests. I made him dribble a ball round the field while keeping his head down; stood him under shower baths with water pouring into his eyes; made him stand in the rain and look up at the sky; tested him by having players shoot the ball at him from all angles. Then came the test of a reserve match, which he passed with flying colours.

Howe first wore his lenses in the first team when Chesterfield visited the Baseball Ground for an all-Derbyshire FA Cup-tie in January, 1948, and, again in the words of McMillan, 'he lasted 90 minutes of a fierce Cup battle with perfect vision and without suffering the slightest inconvenience'. The Rams, beginning a run that carried them to their eighth losing semi-final, triumphed 2–0, goalkeeper Billy Townsend keeping a clean sheet by brilliantly saving a penalty taken by veteran full-back George Milburn in the closing minutes.

Thriving on the extension of his first-class career which contact lenses made possible, Jack Howe won the first of his three England caps only a few months later, even though he was then in his early thirties. He gave an immaculate display in an epic 4–0 win over Italy in Turin, but after also helping towards a 6–2 defeat of Northern Ireland in Belfast he was jettisoned following a 3–1 reverse against Scotland at Wembley in which a Derby clubmate, the other Billy Steel, was among the winners' scorers.

Having succeeded Raich Carter in the County captaincy, Howe took his total of League and Cup games for the club to within six of 250 before he obtained the move he sought because he was anxious to return to the North-East. Some months earlier there had been rumours that he would be joining Newcastle in an exchange deal, but Derby had issued a denial, and the only offer he received from that area at the time he became available was that of player-manager with Gateshead in the Northern Section of the Third Division. It was because he wanted to stay in the First Division for as long as possible that he turned down the offer and shelved his hopes of a return home in favour of continuing as a player only at Huddersfield. There he took over as skipper from Eddie Boot, the wing-half who had been signed from Sheffield United, along with ex-Ram Bobby Barclay, just before the 1937 transfer deadline.

At Derby, Howe's cultured style was not always appreciated by spectators who liked to see their full-backs unceremoniously hack the ball long and hard upfield rather than elaborating with it inside their own penalty area. At Huddersfield, on the other hand, it earned him the accolade of being likened to the club's former England full-back Sam Wadsworth, a composed and confident defender noted for his constructive qualities.

Howe was, however, into his 35th year when he moved to Leeds Road, and his first-team appearances petered out in his second season there. Only one of them was against Derby County, who were beaten 2–0, in a match played at Elland Road, Leeds, because a fire, the cause of which was never found, gutted the wooden main grandstand at Huddersfield's ground.

Having had a transfer request rejected after losing his place to Irish international Charlie Gallogly, Howe was eventually released by Huddersfield shortly before the 1951–52 season in which they finally failed to win their annual battle against relegation. He became player-manager of King's Lynn, the Eastern Counties League club from which Derby County had signed a reserve full-back, Norman Rowe, within a few months of Howe's departure from the Baseball Ground. Rowe rejoined King's Lynn after a year with Walsall, but by then, August, 1953, Howe was no longer their manager. Though staying on as a player, he had handed in his resignation, which was accepted with 'great regret', mainly because he had the opportunity of a job with greater security outside the game. He had, however, been disturbed by barracking and, according to the club's chairman, E.A. Warnes, had been subjected to 'malicious gossip and anonymous letters'. The letters criticised his selection of the team which included such experienced players as goalkeeper Percy Hooper, formerly of Tottenham Hotspur, and Cliff Whitelum, a forward previously with Sunderland and Sheffield United, who scored more than 40 goals in Howe's second and final season as player-manager.

As licensee of the Station Hotel, Howe became one of five footballing publicans in the Norfolk town. The others were his successor as player-manager, Paul Todd (at the White Horse), who had been a forward with Doncaster, Blackburn and Hull, Alf Kimber (Railway Tavern), Hooper (Live and Let Live), and 'Taffy' Williams (Duke of Fife), an ex-Northampton forward who was still serving King's Lynn as a committee member after having to give up playing because of cartilage trouble. There was also Dick Everitt, a former King's Lynn centre-forward who ran the Swan at nearby West Lynn.

Early in 1953, Howe was among those flooded out when a high tide overwhelmed the sea defences along the East Coast. Getting on for three years later, he left the Linnets of King's Lynn, first accepting the post of player-manager with Long Sutton United, in Lincolnshire, but soon afterwards joining nearby Wisbech Town. He was over 40 before he completed his playing career there. Eventually he wound up back at Hartlepool, where he died aged 71, in April, 1987.

CHAPTER 15

Stamps, a Battler Against Adversity

Jobey's Wembley legacy – Stamps overcomes adversity and becomes Cup Final hero – Pluck and endurance against Burnley – First repeat of a Bowers feat: four hat-tricks in one season

AND SO, LAST, but not remotely resembling the least, we come to John David Stamps, the fourth member of the last team fielded by George Jobey in the First Division who was in the 'Crown Derby' County line-up that won at Wembley in 1946.

If it had not been for Frank Boulton's injury, Tim Ward's too-late availability, and Dave McCulloch's loss of form, there could have been seven Cup finalists from the side that defeated Aston Villa with a Jack Nicholas penalty on the day before war was declared at the beginning of September, 1939. That team, with the names of the four Wembley winners in bold type, was: Boulton; Wilcox, **Howe**; **Nicholas**, Barker, Ward; Walsh, Redfern, McCulloch, **Stamps**, **Duncan**.

Wilfred Walsh, the stand-in for Crooks, was a £2,000 signing during the last pre-war summer from Arsenal, to whom he graduated out of their Margate nursery. His appearances in each of Derby's three League games at the start of the abandoned 1939–40 season equalled the number he made for the Gunners as Alf Kirchen's deputy in the autumn of 1938, but only one stands to his name in the Rams' records—their first post-war Division One match, at Sunderland, on the last day of August, 1946. Walsh moved to Walsall the following March and was later player-manager of Redditch Town and Hednesford Town.

Jack Stamps, a sturdy Yorkshireman, was one of the most courageous of all Derby's players, a thoroughly genuine and loyal battler in the County's cause to whom the club's fans warmed after not a few of them had considered him too slow and cumbersome to make the grade. His life was studded with adversities which he overcame with the spirit and determination that won him a wealth of admiration.

To begin with, he had to show strong resolve to break into professional football. He progressed from the Rother Valley team to the Yorkshire side in schoolboy soccer, but economic circumstances then forced him to go down the pit near his home in the Thrybergh district of Rotherham. His burning ambition to forsake that job for football surmounted the setbacks of an unsuccessful trial with Huddersfield Town and a free transfer from Mansfield Town. Then, having spent five months with New Brighton alongside former Everton winger Jimmy Stein, he had improved to make George Jobey consider him worth £1, 500 of Derby County's money in March, 1939, shortly after he had left his teens.

Just over a year later, having enlisted in the Royal Artillery when war came, he was wounded in the miraculous escape from Dunkirk. Next, while playing in an Army match, he severed a knee ligament and was told by a specialist that he would never

Jack Stamps, loyal and courageous.
(Derby Evening Telegraph)

kick a ball again. He was to hear similar fateful predictions from other experts at various times, but, although the knee troubled him periodically throughout his career, it was not until some 15 years after that first gloomy prognosis that he did pack up playing. He was then with Burton Albion, the Staffordshire club he joined after becoming a licensee in the brewery town and completing his last Football League season in Division Three South with Shrewsbury Town in 1953–54.

Stuart McMillan had promised him a scouting and coaching job with Derby when he retired as a player, but with the change of manager there was a change of policy. Consequently, in December, 1953, shortly after being recalled for only his second game with the newly-relegated Rams in the Second Division (he was denied a farewell goal, but helped towards 2–1 home win over Leicester City), he decided to accept the invitation from Shrewsbury manager Sammy Crooks that also reunited him with two other former County colleagues, Jimmy Bullions and Jack Parr. Bullions, who had been with Stamps in the Cup-winning team at Wembley, made his way to Shrewsbury by way of Leeds.

After declining Shrewsbury's terms for a second season at Gay Meadow, Stamps also refused the chance to head ex-Rams goalkeeper Ray Middleton's band of Derby old boys at Boston because of the travelling involved. Instead he accepted the more convenient invitation from Burton, whose player-manager, the former Swansea centre-half Reg Weston, had briefly been with Derby County without getting near the first team.

From player only, ever-willing Jack advanced to be Albion's player-coach then, in steady stages, progressed to being a general assistant involved with coaching and scouting, assistant manager after Crooks had moved in to succeed Weston for the club's move up into the Southern League, temporary manager after Crooks's speedy dismissal, and finally the official team manager. His appointment lasted from the first day of March, 1958, until October, 1959, when his final break from an active part in football was forced by Burton's parlous financial situation.

Then it was back to the Baseball Ground for Jack Stamps, as a regular attender at Derby's matches—even when, for the last 23 years of his life, this indomitable character was totally blind. He had a companion who kept him informed of what was happening on the field. His loyalty and service to the Rams were rightly recognised when, in January, 1983, he was made an honorary vice-president of the club. The doctor who attended him during his last illness (he died in November, 1991, the month before his 73rd birthday) told his wife Norah, to whom he had been married for 51 years, that he had never met such a brave man.

That bravery was never better exemplified during his playing days than it was on Easter Monday, 1949, when Burnley were Derby's First Division visitors. In the *Derby Evening Telegraph*, my old friend and colleague Frank Nicklin, later Sports Editor of the *Sun*, wrote:

> Stamps gave an exhibition of pluck and endurance such as has seldom been seen at Derby. In scoring the Rams' first goal [they won 2–0] in the 11th minute with a grand header from Ward's pass, he collided with Cummings [Tommy Cummings, the Burnley centre-half] and slumped in a heap. Three of Stamps's front teeth were torn out by the roots, and his lips were split. He had to be persuaded by his team-mates to leave the field for attention, but to everybody's amazement he returned only seven minutes later.

That goal was one of exactly 100 Jackie Stamps scored for Derby in the League. He got the first two of them when he made his debut on March 18th, 1939, in a 3–1 victory at the Baseball Ground over Charlton Athletic, the club against which he notched another double as the extra-time hero of the FA Cup Final win seven years later.

Those two Wembley goals helped him to a total of 26 in the 29 Cup-ties he added to his 233 First Division games for the Rams. He opened that Cup haul with four of the six goals with which Derby set out at Luton along the path to the final which stretched to ten matches, including a semi-final replay, in that season of two-legged ties up to the last four, but even that achievement did not make his place in the team secure.

Having rarely been available during the war, when, like Tommy Eggleston, he had guested for Southampton, Stamps returned to find Peter Doherty in his former place at inside-left, and Angus Morrison, a young Scot whose 'transfer fee' was a box of cigars,[1] a more serious rival than Dave McCulloch at centre-forward. It was only because Morrison was switched to replace the injured Duncan on the left wing that Stamps played in the first leg of the third-round tie at Kenilworth Road, and he did not manage to establish himself in preference to Morrison at the head of the attack, between Carter and Doherty, until just before Aston Villa were ousted in the quarter-finals.

He went on to render unselfish service in both inside-forward positions as well as at centre-forward. He was even tried as one of Derby's experimental outside-lefts, but that was a one-off, and a definite flop on a day when Jack Howe was also unsuccessfully moved out of position, to left-half, for an away match with Manchester United that plunged the Rams into a sequence of three heavy defeats during which they conceded 13 goals.

The persevering Stamps was seen in a far better light when he equalled his loot of Luton by scoring all Derby's goals in a 4–1 home First Division victory over Blackpool in 1950. Moreover, he might have registered another four-goal feat but for failing to add a penalty to his hat-trick against Bolton on the last day of the 1949–50 season in which he also scored three goals in a 5–3 third-round FA Cup defeat of Manchester City at Maine Road, and in a 5–2 home replay win in the fourth round against Bury.

Those three goals in the 4–0 win over Bolton at the Baseball Ground made Stamps the first player to score four hat-tricks for Derby in one season since Jack Bowers, 16 years earlier. They also took him to his biggest seasonal total of 29, seven of them in the Cup, and he bagged seven more during the visit the Rams paid to the Republic of Ireland that close season at the invitation of Waterford's player-manager, Dave McCulloch.

Yes, Jack Stamps was truly one of Derby County's greats. Loyal and lionhearted, he made a most fitting final major signing for the club by George Jobey.

---

1. The cigars were a gift from Major Reginald Whitehead, an Army officer who spotted Morrison playing for an RAF team and recommended him to Ben Robshaw, his friend on the Derby board.

Appendix One

DERBY COUNTY'S SEASON-BY-SEASON RECORD

Before the formation of the Football League

Season	P	W	D	L	F	A
1884–85	34	14	9	11	75	64
1885–86	36	18	6	12	87	65
1886–87	45	23	7	15	111	76
1887–88	35	20	4	11	82	68

Football League

Division	Season	P	W	D	L	F	A	Pts	Pos
One	1888–89	22	7	2	13	41	60	16	10th
	1889–90	22	9	3	10	43	55	21	7th
	1890–91	22	7	1	14	47	81	15	11th
	1891–92	26	10	4	12	46	52	24	10th
	1892–93	30	9	9	12	52	64	27	13th
	1893–94	30	16	4	10	73	62	36	3rd
	1894–95 [1]	30	7	9	14	45	68	23	15th
	1895–96	30	17	7	6	68	35	41	2nd
	1896–97	30	16	4	10	70	50	36	3rd
	1897–98	30	11	6	13	57	61	28	10th
	1898–99	34	12	11	11	62	57	35	9th
	1899–1900	34	14	8	12	45	43	36	6th
	1900–01	34	12	7	15	55	42	31	12th
	1901–02	34	13	9	12	39	41	35	6th
	1902–03	34	16	3	15	50	47	35	9th
	1903–04	34	9	10	15	58	60	28	14th

1. Won test match to avoid relegation.

Division	Season	P	W	D	L	F	A	Pts	Pos
	1904–05	34	12	8	14	37	48	32	11th
	1905–06	38	14	7	17	39	58	35	15th
	1906–07	38	9	9	20	41	59	27	19th
Two	1907–08	38	21	4	13	77	45	46	6th
	1908–09	38	16	11	11	55	41	43	5th
	1909–10	38	22	9	7	72	47	53	4th
	1910–11	38	17	8	13	73	52	42	6th
One	1911–12	38	23	8	7	74	28	54	1st
	1912–13	38	17	8	13	69	66	42	7th
	1913–14	38	8	11	19	55	71	27	20th
Two	1914–15	38	23	7	8	71	33	53	1st
One	1919–20	42	13	12	17	47	57	38	18th
	1920–21	42	5	16	21	32	58	26	21st
Two	1921–22	42	15	9	18	60	64	39	12th
	1922–23	42	14	11	17	46	50	39	14th
	1923–24	42	21	9	12	75	42	51	3rd
	1924–25	42	22	11	9	71	36	55	3rd
	1925–26	**42**	**25**	**7**	**10**	**77**	**42**	**57**	**2nd**
One	**1926–27**	**42**	**17**	**7**	**18**	**86**	**73**	**41**	**12th**
	1927–28	**42**	**17**	**10**	**15**	**96**	**83**	**44**	**4th**
	1928–29	**42**	**18**	**10**	**14**	**86**	**71**	**46**	**6th**
	1929–30	**42**	**21**	**8**	**13**	**90**	**82**	**50**	**2nd**
	1930–31	**42**	**18**	**10**	**14**	**94**	**79**	**46**	**6th**
	1931–32	**42**	**14**	**10**	**18**	**71**	**75**	**38**	**15th**
	1932–33	**42**	**15**	**14**	**13**	**76**	**69**	**44**	**7th**
	1933–34	**42**	**17**	**11**	**14**	**68**	**54**	**45**	**4th**
	1934–35	**42**	**18**	**9**	**15**	**81**	**66**	**45**	**6th**
	1935–36	**42**	**18**	**12**	**12**	**61**	**52**	**48**	**2nd**
	1936–37	**42**	**21**	**7**	**14**	**96**	**90**	**49**	**4th**
	1937–38	**42**	**15**	**10**	**17**	**66**	**87**	**40**	**13th**
	1938–39	**42**	**19**	**8**	**15**	**66**	**55**	**46**	**6th**
	1939–40 [2]	3	2	0	1	3	3	4	

2. Programme abandoned after outbreak of war.

Seasons under George Jobey's management in bold type

Seasons since the 1939–45 War

Division	Season	P	W	D	L	F	A	Pts	Pos
One	1946–47	42	18	5	19	73	79	41	14th
	1947–48	42	19	12	11	77	57	50	4th
	1948–49	42	22	9	11	74	55	53	3rd
	1949–50	42	17	10	15	69	61	44	11th
	1950–51	42	16	8	18	81	75	40	11th
	1951–52	42	15	7	20	63	80	37	17th
	1952–53	42	11	10	21	59	74	32	22nd
Two	1953–54	42	12	11	19	64	82	35	18th
	1954–55	42	7	9	26	53	82	23	22nd
Three North	1955–56	46	28	7	11	110	55	63	2nd
	1956–57	46	26	11	9	111	53	63	1st
Two	1957–58	42	14	8	20	60	81	36	16th
	1958–59	42	20	8	14	74	71	48	7th
	1959–60	42	14	7	21	61	77	35	18th
	1960–61	42	15	10	17	80	80	40	12th
	1961–62	42	14	11	17	68	75	39	16th
	1962–63	42	12	12	18	61	72	36	18th
	1963–64	42	14	11	17	56	67	39	13th
	1964–65	42	16	11	15	84	79	43	9th
	1965–66	42	16	11	15	71	68	43	8th
	1966–67	42	12	12	18	68	72	36	17th
	1967–68	42	13	10	19	71	78	36	18th
	1968–69	42	26	11	5	65	32	63	1st
One	1969–70	42	22	9	11	64	37	53	4th
	1970–71	42	16	10	16	56	54	42	9th
	1971–72	42	24	10	8	69	33	58	1st
	1972–73	42	19	8	15	56	54	46	7th
	1973–74	42	17	14	11	52	42	48	3rd
	1974–75	42	21	11	10	67	49	53	1st
	1975–76	42	21	11	10	75	58	53	4th
	1976–77	42	9	19	14	50	55	37	15th
	1977–78	42	14	13	15	54	59	41	12th
	1978–79	42	10	11	21	44	71	31	19th
	1979–80	42	11	8	23	47	67	30	21st
Two	1980–81	42	15	15	12	57	52	45	6th
	1981–82	42	12	12	18	53	68	48	16th
	1982–83	42	10	19	13	49	58	49	13th
	1983–84	42	11	9	22	36	72	42	20th
Three	1984–85	46	19	13	14	65	54	70	7th
	1985–86	46	23	15	8	80	41	84	3rd
Two	1986–87	42	25	9	8	64	38	84	1st

Division	Season	P	W	D	L	F	A	Pts	Pos
One	1987–88	40	10	13	17	35	45	43	15th
	1988–89	38	17	7	14	40	38	58	5th
	1989–90	38	13	7	18	43	40	46	16th
	1990–91	38	5	9	24	37	75	24	20th
Two	1991–92[3]	46	23	9	14	69	51	78	3rd
One	1992–93	46	19	9	18	68	57	66	8th
	1993–94[4]	46	20	11	15	73	68	71	6th
	1994–95	46	18	12	16	66	51	66	9th
	1995–96	46	21	16	9	71	51	79	2nd
Premiership	1996–97	38	11	13	14	45	58	46	12th
	1997–98	38	16	7	15	52	49	55	9th
	1998–99	38	13	13	12	40	45	52	8th

3. Lost 4–5 on aggregate (2–4; 2–1) to Blackburn in semi-final play-off, but in Division One for 1992–93 because that is what Division Two became with the formation of the Premiership.
4. Lost 1–2 to Leicester City in play-off final at Wembley.

Note: Three points for a win, instead of two, came into effect from season 1981–82.

Appendix Two

GEORGE JOBEY'S SIGNINGS FOR DERBY COUNTY

KEY: fb full-back; if inside-forward; or outside-right; ch centre-half; cf centre-forward; g goalkeeper; up utility player; wf wing-forward; ol outside-left.

Transfer fees are give where known

Players who became internationals after joining the Rams

	Posn	Club signed from	Date	Fee paid
TOMMY COOPER	fb	Port Vale	March 1926	£2,500
BOBBY BARCLAY	if	Scotswood	Feb 1927	
SAMMY CROOKS	or	Durham City	April 1927	£300
GEORGE STEPHENSON	if	Aston Villa	Nov 1927	£2,000
JACK BARKER	ch	Denaby United	April 1928	£275
JACK BOWERS	cf	Scunthorpe United	May 1928	£150
SID REID	fb	Belfast Distillery	Dec 1929	£1,150
IKE KEEN	wh	Newcastle United	Dec 1930	£150
'DALLY' DUNCAN	ol	Hull City	March 1932	£2,000
JIMMY HAGAN[1]	if		May 1933	
JACK HOWE	fb	Hartlepools United	March 1936	£750
RONNIE DIX	if	Aston Villa	Feb 1937	£4,875
TIM WARD	wh	Cheltenham Town	April 1937	£200

1. Hagan turned professional in January 1935. He was capped with Sheffield United. Barclay also did not play for England until after leaving Derby for Sheffield United.

Other signings (international players in bold type)

	Posn	Club signed from	Date	Fee paid
TOMMY DAVISON	ch	Wolverhampton W	July 1925	
WALTER FOX[2]	g	Alfreton Town	Aug 1925	
HARRY BEDFORD	cf	Blackpool	Sept 1925	£3,000
JACK HART	cf	Mansfield Town	Jan 1926	£400
FREDDIE JESSOP[3]	up	Staveley Works	Jan 1926	
JIMMY GILL ⎫	if			
GEORGIE MEE ⎭	ol	Blackpool	Feb 1926	£3,750
BERT MANN	ol	Griff Colliery	Feb 1926	
MICK O'BRIEN	ch	Hull City	Dec 1926	
TOM ROBINSON	wh	Burton	Dec 1926	
GAVIN MALLOCH	wh	Benburb (Glasgow)	Jan 1927	£150
JACK HOPE	if	Crook Town	Jan 1927	£100
TED NELSON	wh	Crook Town		
WILLIAM ROBSON	fb	Hylton Colliery	Jan 1927	
HARRY WILKES	g	Wellington Town	Feb 1927	£400
DAN KELLY	or	Hamilton Acads	Feb 1927	£300
ARCHIE SCOTT	hb	Airdrieonians	April 1927	£350
JACK WEBB	fb	Southwick	May 1927	
JACK HAMPTON	g	Wolverhampton W	June 1927	
GEORGE COLLIN[4]	fb	Bournemouth	Nov 1927	£1,250
ALFRED WHITE	cf	Spennymoor Utd	Nov 1927	
JACK NICHOLAS	wh/fb		Dec 1927	
TOM RUDDY	cf	Darlington	May 1928	£500
JACK ROBSON	ol	Reading	June 1928	£1,500
PETER RAMAGE	if	Coventry City	Aug 1928	£1,525
JACK KIRBY	g	Newhall United	April 1929	£300
JAMES RANDALL	ol	Bradford City	May	1930
OSWALD BOWDEN	if	Newcastle Utd Swifts	May 1930	
NORMAN ROBSON	if	Preston NE	May 1930	£850
WILF LEWIS	ir	Huddersfield Town	April 1931	£800
SYD WILEMAN	if	Gresley Rovers	April 1931	
ROBERT GREEN[5]	if	Bournemouth	May 1931	
RICHARD NEAL	wf	Blackpool	May 1931	£500
A.H. FABIAN[6]	if		Dec 1931	

2. Fox, who was with Matlock Town before Alfreton, was signed as an amateur in August 1925. He turned professional the following month. He played only once in the League side, deputising in goal for Ben Olney in a 2–0 home win over South Shields on November 21st, 1925.

3. Jessop was signed as a professional in March 1926.

4. The fees paid for Collin were £1,000 to Bournemouth, £250 to West Stanley.

5. Green played only one first-team game for Derby, at the start of season 1931–32, before moving to Manchester United. He was later with Stockport County.

6. Fabian was an amateur who also played for Casuals, Corinthian Casuals and

	Posn	Club signed from	Date	Fee paid
RALPH HANN	up			
DUNCAN HUTCHISON	if	Newcastle United	March 1932	£3,100
DAVID HALFORD	ol	Scarborough	Dec 1932	
ARTHUR GROVES	if	Blackburn Rovers	July 1933	£550
VICTOR BLORE	g	Aston Villa	Aug 1933	
JOHN PHILBIN	if	Washington Colliery	Dec 1933	£150
TED ROBERTS	if/cf	Glapwell Colliery	April 1934	
TED UDALL	fb	Leicester City	May 1934	£800
DAVID BELL	fb	Newcastle United	June 1934	£700
DONALD BIRD	ol	Torquay United	June 1934	£250
REG STOCKILL	if	Arsenal	Sept 1934	£ 2,000
ALAN HUGHES	or	Chesterfield	Sept 1934	
HUGHIE GALLACHER	cf	Chelsea	Nov 1934	£2,750
JIMMY BOYD	or	Newcastle United	May 1935	
JACK SUMMERS	or	Leicester City	May 1935	
CHARLIE NAPIER	if	Glasgow Celtic	June 1935	£3,500
KEN SCATTERGOOD	g	Stoke City	July 1935	£400
'CHICK' MUSSON[7]	wh	Holbrook St Michaels	March 1936	
ALBERT WILSON	ol	Stafford Rangers	May 1936	
GEORGE WILCOX	fb	Denaby United	Oct 1936	
DAI ASTLEY	if/cf	Aston Villa	Nov 1936	£5,250
ALF JEFFRIES	or	Bradford City	Feb 1937	
HARRY TRAVIS	cf	Bradford City	Feb 1937	£825
FRANK KING	g	Everton	May 1937	£200
HARRY WRIGHT	g	Aldershot	Sept 1937	£2,500
VERDUN JONES	if	Aston Villa	Nov 1937	£500
JACK PARR[8]	fb	Little Eaton St Peters	Dec 1937	
JACK BRINTON	ol	Newport County	Jan 1938	£1,000
STEVE McLACHLAN	wh	Dalbeattie	March 1938	
FRANK BOULTON	g	Arsenal	Aug 1938	£1,850
DAVE McCULLOCH	cf	Brentford	Oct 1938	£9,500
LEON LEUTY[9]	ch	Derby Corinthians	1938–39	
TOM HINCHCLIFFE	if	Huddersfield Town	Nov 1938	£1,000
JACK STAMPS	if/cf	New Brighton	Jan 1939	£1,500
WILLIAM STEEL	fb	Birmingham	Feb 1939	£1,275
WILFRED WALSH	or	Arsenal	June 1939	£2,000
WILLIAM REDFERN[10]	if	Luton Town	Aug 1939	

Cambridge United before joining the Rams. He was later with Sutton United and Fulham.

7. Musson became a professional in October 1937.

8. Parr turned professional in March 1938.

9. Leuty did not sign professional forms until after Jobey had left, in May, 1944.

10. In exchange for Reg Stockill.

Appendix Three

TRANSFERS FROM DERBY COUNTY WHILE JOBEY WAS MANAGER

International players in bold type

	Posn	Club joined	Date
JIM MOORE	if	Chesterfield	March 1926
FRANK KEETLEY	f	Doncaster Rovers	June 1926
JOSEPH GOLBY	ch	Halifax Town	July 1926
GEORGE PUMFORD	cf	Walsall	July 1926
WILLIAM COWELL	g	Grimsby Town	Feb 1927
ALBERT FAIRCLOUGH	cf	Gillingham	Feb 1927
ARCHIE RITCHIE	fb	Guildford City	May 1927
GEORGE ROWE	fb	Norwich City	May 1927
EDWARD DONAGHY	wh	Gillingham	July 1927
ENOS BROMAGE	ol	Gillingham	Aug 1927
GEORGE THORNEWELL	or	Blackburn Rovers	Dec 1927
BEN OLNEY	g	Aston Villa	Dec 1927
LIONEL MURPHY[1]	ol	Bolton Wanderers	Jan 1928
BERNARD McLAVERTY	wh	Norwich City	Jan 1928
TOM CRILLY	fb	Crystal Palace	May 1928
JIMMY GILL	if	Crystal Palace	May 1928
HARRY THOMS	ch	Crystal Palace	May 1928
DAN KELLY	or	Torquay United	June 1928
MICK O'BRIEN	ch	Walsall	June 1928
ARTHUR BACON	f	Manchester City	Dec 1928
HARRY STORER	wh/if	Burnley	Feb 1929
JACKIE WHITEHOUSE	if	Sheffield Wednesday	Feb 1929
HAROLD WIGHTMAN	fb/ch	Chesterfield	May 1929
BERT MANN	ol	Grantham	Aug 1929
JACK HOPE	if	Bury	Feb 1930
TOM ROBINSON	wh	Bury	April 1930

1. Part exchange for Albert Picken.

	Posn	Club joined	Date
JACK HAMPTON	g	Preston North End	May 1930
HARRY BEDFORD	cf	Newcastle United	Dec 1930
TOMMY DAVISON	ch	Sheffield Wednesday	Feb 1931
GEORGE STEPHENSON	if	Sheffield Wednesday	Feb 1931
DAVID FEREDAY	or	West Ham United	May 1931
BOBBY BARCLAY	if	Sheffield United	June 1931
ALFRED WHITE	cf	Bournemouth	Oct 1931
JOHNNY McINTYRE	wh	Chesterfield	Dec 1931
GAVIN MALLOCH	wh	Sheffield Wednesday	Dec 1931
TOM RUDDY	cf	Chesterfield	Dec 1931
RICHARD NEAL	wf	Southampton	Feb 1932
JACK ROBSON	ol	Southend United	June 1932
WILF LEWIS	if	Yeovil	July 1932
GEORGIE MEE	ol	Burnley	Sept 1932
NORMAN ROBSON	if	Bradford City	March 1933
WILLIAM ROBSON	fb	West Ham United	May 1933
ROBERT GREEN	if	Manchester United	June 1933
HARRY WILKES	g	Sheffield United	March 1934
DUNCAN HUTCHISON	if	Hull City	July 1934
ARCHIE SCOTT	hb	Brentford	July 1934
ALBERT ALDERMAN	if/wf	Burnley	Aug 1934
TOMMY COOPER	fb	Liverpool	Dec 1934
OSWALD BOWDEN	if	Nottingham Forest	June 1935
ALAN HUGHES	or	Everton	June 1935
VICTOR BLORE	g	West Ham United	July 1935
BILLY CARR	fb	Queen's Park Rangers	Aug 1935
DONALD BIRD	ol	Sheffield United	Dec 1935
ARTHUR GROVES	if	Portsmouth	Jan 1936
JOHN PHILBIN	if	Torquay United	May 1936
GEORGE COLLIN	fb	Sunderland	June 1936
DAVID HALFORD	ol	Bolton Wanderers	June 1936
SID REID	fb	Reading	June 1936
HUGHIE GALLACHER	cf	Notts County	Sept 1936
JACK SUMMERS	or	Southampton	Oct 1936
JACK BOWERS	cf	Leicester City	Nov 1936
JIMMY BOYD	or	Bury	Jan 1937
TED ROBERTS	if/cf	Coventry City	March 1937
JACK WEBB	fb	Newport County	June 1937
PETER RAMAGE	if	Chesterfield	Aug 1937
FREDDIE JESSOP	up	Sheffield United	Dec 1937
CHARLIE NAPIER	if	Sheffield Wednesday	March 1938
IKE KEEN	wh	Chelmsford City	May 1938
SYD WILEMAN	if	Port Vale	June 1938
ALBERT WILSON	ol	Mansfield Town	July 1938

	Posn	Club joined	Date
JACK KIRBY	g	Folkestone Town	Aug 1938
DAVID BELL	fb	Ipswich Town	Oct 1938
JIMMY HAGAN	if	Sheffield United	Nov 1938
HARRY TRAVIS	cf	Tranmere Rovers	Nov 1938
DAI ASTLEY	if/cf	Blackpool	Jan 1939
RONNIE DIX	if	Tottenham Hotspur	June 1939
ALF JEFFRIES	or	Sheffield United	June 1939
HARRY WRIGHT	g	Chelmsford City	June 1939
REG STOCKILL [2]	if	Luton Town	Aug 1939

---

2. In exchange for William Redfern.

Appendix Four

DERBY'S FA CUP RECORD UNDER GEORGE JOBEY'S MANAGEMENT

Season 1925–26

				Opponents	*Derby scorers*	*Att*
3rd round	Jan 9	H	0–0	Portsmouth		18,854
replay	Jan 13	A	1–1	Portsmouth	Bedford	25,761
2nd replay	Jan 18[1]		2–0	Portsmouth	Thornewell, Bromage	11,076
4th round	Jan 30	A	1–4	Southend Utd	Murphy	4,225

1926–27

3rd round	Jan 8	A	6–2	Bradford City	Bedford 4, Whitehouse, Murphy	20,285
4th round	Jan 29	H	0–2	Millwall		25,763

1927–28

3rd round	Jan 14	A	2–1	Millwall	Stephenson, Bedford	38,850
4th round	Jan 28	H	0–0	Nottm Forest		22,594
replay	Feb 1	A	0–2	Nottm Forest		35,625

1928–29

3rd round	Jan 12	H	4–3	Notts County	Bedford 2, Whitehouse 2	21,318
4th round	Jan 26	A	1–1	Blackburn Rov	Bedford	45,410
replay	Jan 30	H	0–3	Blackburn Rov		28,551

---

1. At Filbert Street, Leicester

1929–30

				Opponents	Derby scorers	Att
3rd round	Jan 11	H	5–1	Bristol City	Stephenson 2, Barclay 2, Bedford	22,559
4th round	Jan 25	H	1–1	Bradford	Barclay	26,358
replay	Jan 29	A	1–2	Bradford	Ramage	29,738

1930–31

3rd round	Jan 10	A	2–3	Exeter City	Bowers 2	16,500

1931–32

3rd round	Jan 9	A	4–0	Burnley	Neal 2, Alderman, Crooks	16,694
4th round	Jan 23	H	3–2	Blackburn Rov	Ramage 2, Bowers	30,825
5th round	Feb 13	A	0–3	Manchester C		62,641

1932–33

3rd round	Jan 14	A	6–3	Wolves	Bowers 3, Duncan 2, Crooks	31,288
4th round	Jan 28	A	3–2	Southend Utd	Bowers 2, A.H. Fabian	15,188
5th round	Feb 18	H	2–0	Aldershot	Bowers 2	30,048
6th round	Mar 4	H	4–4	Sunderland	Duncan 2, Ramage, Bowers	34,218
replay	Mar 8	A	1–0[2]	Sunderland	Ramage	75,118[3]
semi-final	Mar 18[4]		2–3	Manchester C	A H Fabian, Crooks	51,961

1933–34

3rd round	Jan 13	A	1–1	Bristol City	Nicholas	34,283
~~replay~~	~~Jan 17~~	~~H~~	~~1–0~~	~~Bristol City~~	~~Bowers~~	~~24,213~~
4th round	Jan 27	H	3–0	Wolves	Bowers 2, Crooks	37,727
5th round	Feb 17	A	0–1	Arsenal		66,903

---

2. After extra time
3. Ground record
4. At Leeds Road, Huddersfield

1934–35

				Opponents	Derby scorers	Att
3rd round	Jan 12	A	1–0	York City	Crooks	13,612
4th round	Jan 26	H	3–0	Swansea Tn	Duncan, Groves, Gallacher	28,207
5th round	Feb 16	A	1–3	Everton	Crooks	62,230

1935–36

3rd round	Jan 11	H	3–2	Dartford	Gallacher, Crooks, Napier	27,809
4th round	Jan 25	H	2–0	Nottm Forest	Halford, Bowers	37,830
5th round	Feb 15	A	1–0	Bradford City	Bowers	33,937
6th round	Feb 29	A	0–3	Fulham		37,151

1936–37

3rd round	Jan 16	A	4–0	Bradford	Napier, Astley, Duncan, Stockill	21,155
4th round	Jan 30	H	3–0	Brentford	Astley 3	27,376
5th round	Feb 20	A	1–2	Millwall	Keen	48,672[5]

1937–38

3rd round	Jan 8	H	1–2	Stoke City	Nicholas (pen)	28,788

1938–39

3rd round	Jan 7	H	0–1	Everton		22,237

5. Ground record

Appendix Five

MEMORABLE MATCHES DURING GEORGE JOBEY'S REIGN

FA Cup

January 29th, 1927   *Fourth round: Derby County 0, Millwall 2*

Derby County: Olney; Carr, Crilly; McIntyre, Thoms, Plackett; Thornewell, Whitehouse, Bedford, Storer, Murphy.

Millwall: Lansdale; Fort, Hill; Amos, W. Bryant, Graham; Chance, Gomm, Parker, Phillips, Black.

Scorers: Plackett (og), Phillips (pen).

Attendance: 25,763

One of the big surprises of that season's competition. Third Division Millwall followed up their 3–1 third-round win over Huddersfield Town, who had been League champions for the past three years and were on their way to finishing as runners-up for two consecutive seasons, by dashing Derby hopes that had been raised by a 6–2 away win over Bradford City in the third round. Millwall went on to knock out Middlesbrough, that season's Second Division champions, by 3–2, and lost to Southampton, by 2–0, in the quarter-finals only after a replay. In their previous Cup meetings with Millwall, Derby had won by 3–0 in a 1903 semi-final and by 5–0 in the first round at the Baseball Ground on January 15th, 1910. They also defeated them, by 2–1 in the third round at Millwall, on January 14th, 1928, but lost to them again, also by 2–1, in a fifth-round match at the Den on February 20th, 1937.

February 18th, 1933   *Fifth round: Derby County 2, Aldershot 0*

Derby County:	Kirby; Cooper, Collin; Nicholas, Barker, Keen; Crooks, Jessop, Bowers, Ramage, Duncan.
Aldershot:	Robb; Wade, McDougall; Gerrard, Middleton, Lawson; Proud, White, Gamble, Lane, Fishlock.
Scorer:	Bowers 2.
Attendance:	30,048

Aldershot, who were in their first season in the Southern Section of the Third Division, were described in the Derby evening paper as 'the most gallant losers seen at the Baseball Ground for many a long day' after this heroic display. With former Scottish international goalkeeper Willie Robb and his full-backs the star performers, they kept the scoresheet blank until a blinding snowstorm swept the ground shortly after half-time. Then, despite facing the blizzard, Bowers opened the scoring in the 72nd minute and five minutes later he again beat the overworked Robb, who had one of the longest playing careers in top-class British football from August 1912, when he began with Birmingham, until May 1939, when he retired at the age of 44. His other clubs included Glasgow Rangers (with whom he did not miss a league game in five successive seasons in four of which he won a championship medal) Hibernian and, finally, Guildford City, whom he helped to win the Southern League title. He first played for Aldershot before they joined the Football League, and their first Third Division game in August 1932 was his first in the League in England since he had been with Birmingham in 1915.

March 4th, 1933   *Sixth round: Derby County 4, Sunderland 4*

Derby County:	Kirby; Cooper, Collin; Nicholas, Barker, Keen; Crooks, Jessop, Bowers, Ramage, Duncan.
Sunderland:	Thorpe; Murray, Shaw; Thomson, McDougall, Edgar; Davis, Gallacher, Gurney, Carter, Connor.
Scorers:	Duncan 2, Ramage, Bowers (Derby); Connor, Davis, Gurney 2 (Sunderland).
Attendance:	34,218 (record).

March 8th, 1933   *Replay: Sunderland 0, Derby County 1 (after extra time)*

Sunderland:	Unchanged.
Derby County:	A.H. Fabian for Jessop. Otherwise unchanged.
Scorer:	Ramage.
Attendance:	75,118 (record).

March 18th, 1933   *Semi-final: Derby County 2, Manchester City 3*

Derby County:	Kirby; Cooper, Collin; Nicholas, Barker, Keen; Crooks, A.H. Fabian, Bowers, Ramage, Duncan.
Manchester City:	Langford; Cann, Dale; Busby, Cowan, Bray; Toseland, Herd, Tilson, McMullan, Brook.
Scorers:	Fabian, Crooks (Derby); Toseland, Tilson, McMullan (Manchester City). At Leeds Road, Huddersfield.
Attendance:	51,961

February 17th, 1934   *Fifth round: Arsenal 1, Derby County 0*

Arsenal:	Moss; Male, Hapgood; Jones (C.), Roberts, John; Beasley, Jack, Dunne, Dougall, Bastin.
Derby County:	Kirby; Cooper, Collin; Nicholas, Barker, Keen; Crooks, Wileman, Bowers, Ramage, Duncan.
Scorer:	Jack
Attendance:	66,905

This was one of only 11 senior appearances Syd Wileman made in just over seven years with the Rams before moving to Port Vale in June 1938. Coalville-born, he was signed from Gresley Rovers in April 1931. He scored one goal for the first team, in a 1–1 home draw with Newcastle United in January 1934. David Jack's goal was hotly disputed for offside, but in the last 10 minutes Cliff Bastin had what appeared to be a perfectly legitimate goal disallowed, and Arsenal were good value for their win.

January 25th, 1936   *Fourth round: Derby County 2, Nottingham Forest 0*

Derby County:	Kirby; Udall, Jessop; Nicholas, Barker, Keen; Crooks, Napier, Bowers, Ramage, Halford.
Nottingham Forest:	Ashton; Edgar, Barrington; McKinlay, Smith, Pugh; Stubbs, Gardiner, Dent, Peacock, Simpson.
Scorers:	Halford, Bowers.
Attendance:	37,830 (record).

FOOTBALL LEAGUE Division One

October 24th, 1925   *Derby County 7, Stoke City 3*

Derby County: Olney; Wightman, Crilly; McIntyre, Thoms, Plackett; Thornewell, Whitehouse, Bedford, Storer, Murphy.

Stoke City: Dixon; McGrory, Milne; Walker, Bestwick, Maxwell (J.E.); Ralphs, Davies, Paterson, Eyres, Archibald.

Scorers: Bedford 3, Storer 2, Whitehouse, Murphy (Derby); Davies 2, Archibald (Stoke).

Attendance: 16,874

December 14th, 1929   *Derby County 5, Grimsby Town 4*

Derby County: Wilkes; Carr, Collin; McIntyre, Barker, Scott; Crooks, Stephenson, Bedford, Ramage, Mee.

Grimsby Town: Read; Wilson, Jacobson; Priestley, Swaby, Wrack; Barley, Bestall, Robson, Coleman, Wright.

Scorers: Stephenson 4, Bedford (Derby); Bestall, Carr (og), Wright, Robson (Grimsby).

Attendance: 13,880

Grimsby were denied a fifth equaliser when Harry Wilkes saved a penalty taken by Joe Robson in the last minute.

February 21st, 1931   *Derby County 1, Newcastle United 5*

Derby County: Kirby; Cooper, Collin; Keen, Barker, Malloch; Crooks, Barclay, Bowers, Ramage, Mee.

Newcastle Utd: Burns; Nelson, Fairhurst; McKenzie, Davidson, Weaver; Boyd, Bedford, Hutchison, Starling, Wilkinson.

Scorers: Barker (Derby); Bedford, Hutchison, Wilkinson 3 (Newcastle).

Attendance: 17,547

Harry Bedford's return to the Baseball Ground in his 11th game for Newcastle.

December 8th, 1934　　　*Derby County 9, West Bromwich Albion 3*

Derby County:	Blore; Udall, Collin; Nicholas, Barker, Hann; Crooks, Stockill, Gallacher, Ramage, Duncan.
West Bromwich:	Pearson; Shaw, Trentham; Murphy, Richardson (W.), Sankey; Glidden, Carter, Richardson (W.G.), Sandford, Boyes.
Scorers:	Crooks 3, Stockill 3, Gallacher 2, Nicholas (Derby); Richardson (W.G.), Sandford (pen), Glidden (Albion).
Attendance:	14,782

December 15th, 1934　　　*Blackburn Rovers 2, Derby County 5*

Blackburn Rovers:	Binns; Gorman, Whyte; Whiteside, Carver, Pryde; Bruton, McLean, Thompson, Brennan, Turner.
Derby County:	Blore; Udall, Collin; Nicholas, Barker, Hann; Crooks, Stockill, Gallacher, Ramage, Duncan.
Scorers:	Bruton (pen), Thompson (Blackburn); Gallacher 5 (Derby).
Attendance:	12,543

September 5th, 1936　　　*Derby County 5, Manchester United 4*

Derby County:	Kirby; Udall, Howe; Nicholas, Hann, Keen; Crooks, Stockill, Bowers, Napier, Duncan.
Manchester Utd:	John; Redwood, McLenahan; Brown, Vose, McKay; Bryant, Wassall, Bamford, Ferrier, Manley.
Scorers:	Crooks, Bowers 4 (Derby); Wassall, Bamford 3 (Manchester Utd).
Attendance:	21,194

Jack Bowers transformed the match with four goals in 15 minutes after United had led 4–1 with 26 minutes to go. United had also conceded four goals to Bowers on their last visit to Derby on April 18th, 1931.

February 3rd, 1937   *Derby County 5, Arsenal 4*

Derby County: Scattergood (K.); Bell, Howe; Nicholas, Barker, Keen; Jeffries, Stockill, Astley, Ramage, Duncan.

Arsenal: Boulton; Male, Compton (L.); Bastin, Roberts, Copping; Kirchen, Bowden, Drake, Davidson, Milne.

Scorers: Astley 3, Stockill 2 (Derby); Drake, Bastin (pen), Kirchen, Howe (og) (Arsenal).

Attendance: 22,064

January 29th, 1938   *Derby County 1, Manchester City 7*

Derby County: Wright; Bell, Howe; Keen, Nicholas, Ward; Crooks, Dix, Astley, Napier, Duncan.

Manchester City: Swift; Dale, Barkas; Percival, Marshall, Rogers; Toseland, Emptage, Heale, Doherty, Brook.

Scorers: Astley (Derby); Heale 3, Doherty 2, Brook, Toseland (Manchester City).

Attendance: 13,625

The Rams also lost heavily to City at Maine Road, by 6–1, the previous September, yet the Manchester club, then the champions, went down to the Second Division at the end of the season. They had won 5–0 at the Baseball Ground on February 24th, 1937, on their way to the title.

October 22nd, 1938   *Derby County 5, Manchester United 1*

Derby County: Boulton; Nicholas, Howe; Hann, Barker, Ward; Crooks, Stockill, McCulloch, Dix, Duncan.

Manchester Utd: Breedon; Griffiths, Roughton; Gladwin, Vose, Manley; Wrigglesworth, Wassall, Smith, Carey, Rowley.

Scorers: McCulloch 2, Dix, Crooks, Vose (og) (Derby); Smith (Manchester Utd).

Attendance: 26,612

Dave McCulloch's first game for Derby, after he had become their costliest player with his £9,500 move from Brentford.

Appendix Six

DERBY'S FIRST AND LAST LEAGUE MATCHES UNDER THE MANAGEMENT OF GEORGE JOBEY

August 19th, 1925   *Hull City 0, Derby County 0*

Hull City: Maddison; Gibson, Bell; Johnson, O'Brien, Bleakley; Richardson, Swan, Mills, Martin, Thom.

Derby County: Olney; Tootle, Crilly; McIntyre, Thoms, Plackett; Thornewell, Whitehouse, Fairclough, Storer, Murphy.

Attendance: 11,209

James Tootle, signed from Southport on Christmas Day 1924 as cover for either full-back position, made only seven League appearances for the Rams.

September 2nd, 1939   *Derby County 1, Aston Villa 0*

Derby County: Boulton; Wilcox, Howe; Nicholas, Barker, Ward; Walsh, Redfern, McCulloch, Stamps, Duncan.

Aston Villa: Rutherford; Callaghan, Cummings; Massie, Allen, Iverson; Edwards, Martin, O'Donnell (F.), Starling, Broome.

Scorer: Nicholas (pen).

Attendance: 8,039

DERBY COUNTY'S WIDEST WINNING MARGIN IN A MATCH
UNDER GEORGE JOBEY'S MANAGEMENT...

March 19th, 1927   *Derby County 8, The Wednesday 0*

Derby County: Olney; Carr, Crilly; McLaverty, Thoms, Storer; Thornewell, Gill, Bedford, Whitehouse, Murphy.

The Wednesday: Mellors; Walker, Felton; Leach, Kean, Marsden; Hooper, Kirkwood, Trotter, Strange, Wilkinson.

Scorers: Whitehouse 4, Bedford 3 (1 pen), Gill.

Attendance: 19,321

This was Derby's biggest win since their record away victory against Bristol City by the same margin on September 29th, 1923, in Cecil Potter's second season as manager. Wednesday, the Second Division champions of 1925–26 (with Derby also promoted as runners-up), followed a remarkable escape from relegation in 1928 by winning the First Division title in 1929 and 1930 (on the second occasion again with the Rams in second place), and in each of the next three seasons they finished third. Four-goal Jackie Whitehouse was transferred to the Wednesday early in 1929.

It was against the Wednesday that the Rams had equalled their biggest-ever League win in scoring nine goals without reply (six for Steve Bloomer) at the Baseball Ground on January 21st, 1899. They had beaten Wolves by the same score in a home match on January 10th, 1891 (five for winger Johnny McMillan) a week after losing 8–0 at Blackburn.

Derby's top goals tally in one game during George Jobey's time was also nine at home to West Bromwich Albion, who replied three times, on December 8th, 1934.

...AND THE BIGGEST SCORE AGAINST THEM WHILE HE WAS IN CHARGE:

September 11th, 1937   *Stoke City 8, Derby County 1*

Stoke City: Wilkinson; Brigham, Scrimshaw; Tutin, Turner, Soo; Matthews, Antonio, Steele, Westland (J.), Baker.

Derby County: Scattergood (K.); Bell, Howe; Nicholas, Barker, Keen; Crooks, Hagan, Astley, Dix, Duncan.

Scorers: Steele 5, Westland 3 (Stoke); Astley (Derby).

Attendance: 32,954

Derby avenged this defeat with a 4–1 win in the return game. Freddie Steele had also scored five goals in a 10–3 home victory against West Bromwich Albion the previous season. Westland, Stoke's other scorer in the big defeat of Derby at the Victoria Ground, guested for the Rams during the 1939–45 war. The Rams' highest-scoring match with Stoke while George Jobey was manager resulted in a 7–3 home win at the Baseball Ground in 1925, when Derby's scorers were Bedford 3, Storer 2, Whitehouse and Murphy.

The Rams also lost by a seven-goal margin when Everton defeated them 7–0 at Goodison Park in Ken Scattergood's first League game on Christmas Day, 1936. Their biggest home reverse during Jobey's time was suffered by a 7–1 margin on January 29th, 1938 against Manchester City, who had beaten them 6–1 at Maine Road earlier that season. Peter Doherty, a Cup winner with Derby in 1946, scored twice in both games.

Appendix Seven

⚽

MAJOR IMPROVEMENTS AT BASEBALL GROUND IN JOBEY ERA

- New £16,000 main stand, incorporating the club's offices and with seating for 3,300, came into big-match use for the first time on September 4th, 1926, when Liverpool were the visitors for the return of First Division football after promotion. Derby County won 2–1 with goals from Gill and Bedford, Edmed replying. Teams:

  Derby County: Olney; Cooper, Crilly; McIntyre, Thoms, Plackett; Thornewell, Gill, Bedford, Storer, Murphy.
  Liverpool: Riley; Lucas, McKinlay; Jackson, Cockburn, Bromilow; Edmed, Hodgson, Forshaw, Chambers, Hopkin.

- During the 1932 close season £750 was spent on increased cover on the popular side opposite the main stand.

- A double-decker stand was erected at the Osmaston end in time for the 1933–34 season. The first League match in front of this new stand resulted in a 1–1 draw with Everton on August 30th, 1933, Bowers and Dean scoring. Teams:

  Derby County: Kirby; Cooper, Collin; Nicholas, Barker, Keen; Crooks, Hutchison, Bowers, Groves, Duncan.
  Everton: Sagar; Cook, Cresswell; Britton, White, Thomson; Geldard, Dunn, Dean, Johnson, Stein.

Jimmy Dunn, Everton's Scottish international inside-right, was the father of the player of the same name who was with Derby County during the 1950s.

- A similar double-decker stand at the Normanton end was officially opened on September 7th, 1935, when Derby County, having lost their two opening games away to Everton and Preston without scoring, gained a 4–0 win over Bolton Wanderers with goals from Gallacher (penalty), Ramage, Duncan and Groves. Teams:

  Derby County: Kirby; Udall, Collin; Nicholas, Barker, Keen; Crooks, Groves, Gallacher, Ramage, Duncan.

  Bolton Wanderers: Jones; Smith, Finney; Goslin, Atkinson, Taylor (G.); Taylor (T.), Eastham, Milsom, Westwood, Cook.

- Before the building of the new main stand alongside Shaftesbury Crescent in 1926, the dressing rooms were under the stand at the Normanton end of the ground which preceded the double-decker. Earlier still, the players entered the pitch at the opposite (Osmaston) end, from a hut situated near what was known, from the baseball days, as Catcher's Corner.

- The improvements at the Baseball Ground, which Derby County had bought from Sir Francis Ley for £10,000 in July, 1924, after plans to move to the Municipal Sports Ground off Osmaston Park Road had been dropped, led to a crowd of 37,830, the Rams' biggest at home while George Jobey was manager, attending a fourth-round FA Cup-tie in which Nottingham Forest were beaten by 2–0 on January 25th, 1936. Halford and Bowers scored.

- Following repairs to the bomb damage done to the Osmaston stand during the 1939–45 War, the record was broken on February 11th, 1950, when there was a crowd of 38,063 for a fifth-round Cup-tie against Northampton Town, who lost 4–2.

- After another new stand, originally known as the Ley Stand, had been built at a cost of £150,000 on the popular side in time to greet another return of First Division football in 1969, the record was raised to the final one of 41,826 for a League match with Tottenham Hotspur, who were defeated 5–0, on September 20th, 1969.

- Derby County moved into their new stadium at Pride Park in 1997. The Baseball Ground had been their headquarters since 1895, following their switch from the County Ground they had shared with the county cricket club and horse racing.